BTS BY ARMY: 2020

BTS BY ARMY: 2020

EDITED BY
WALLEA EAGLEHAWK

BULLETPROOF

Copyright © 2021 selection and editorial matter, Wallea Eaglehawk; individual chapters, the contributors.

All rights reserved. No part of this book may be reprinted or reproduced or utilised in any form or by any electronic, mechanical, or other means, now known or hereafter invented, including photocopying and recording, or in any information storage or retrieval system, without permission in writing from the publisher.

ISBN 978-0-6450486-6-7 (paperback)
ISBN 978-0-6450486-7-4 (eBook)

Cover and interior artwork by Cecilia González
Cover design by Paula Pomer

First published in 2021

Bulletproof
Meanjin, Australia
www.bulletproof.revolutionaries.com.au

CONTENTS

Related Titles..7
Contributors 9

Intro: Dear BTS 13
    Wallea Eaglehawk
BTS: Expect the unexpected...17
    Wallea Eaglehawk, Manilyn Gumapas, and Aurora Delle
Jung Kook: The golden maknae, a born singer 43
    Naazneen Samsodien
V: Both art and artist...73
    Demie Tuzara and Manilyn Gumapas
Jimin: A kaleidoscope of filters 105
    Kate Koncilja and Jasmine Proctor
j-hope: Crossing lines when it comes to music 139
    Nikola Champlin
Suga: Setting into motion the journey towards the authentic self......165
    Rajitha Sanaka and Kate Koncilja
Jin: It's definitely the forehead, but it's more than that too................195
    Padya Paramita
RM: Only human 221
    Wallea Eaglehawk
Outro: Love, ARMY 261
    Wallea Eaglehawk

Credits 263

RELATED TITLES

Related titles from Bulletproof

I Am ARMY: It's Time to Begin edited by Wallea Eaglehawk and Courtney Lazore

Love Yourself: Essays on self-love, care and healing inspired by BTS edited by Wallea Eaglehawk and Keryn Ibrahim

Related titles from Revolutionaries

Idol Limerence: The Art of Loving BTS as Phenomena by Wallea Eaglehawk

Related titles from Moonrise

Through the darkness, I will love myself edited by Wallea Eaglehawk, Nikola Champlin and Padya Paramita

CONTRIBUTORS

Editor

Wallea Eaglehawk is a social theorist, author of *Idol Limerence: The Art of Loving BTS as Phenomena,* and co-editor of *I Am ARMY: It's Time to Begin, Through the darkness, I will love myself* and *Love Yourself: Essays on self-love, care and healing inspired by BTS.* Alongside her creative practice, Wallea is the CEO and Editor-in-Chief of Revolutionaries, and imprints Bulletproof and Moonrise. A scholar of limerence, identity, love, and BTS, Wallea identifies as a practising revolutionary. Find her on Twitter, Instagram, and Medium @walleaeaglehawk.

Contributors

Manilyn Gumapas is a Filipino American sociologist, writer, travel enthusiast, and artist based in the suburbs of Chicago. Her happy places include driving with the windows down and volume up on BTS' discography, playing with her hamster, and relaxing among her ever-growing collection of Squishmallows. Manilyn's recent work can be found in *I Am ARMY: It's Time to Begin.* A people person at heart, she loves connecting with others through shared interests and her values of love, community, inclusion, cultural diversity, and equity. Find Manilyn on Twitter @ManilynGumapas and Instagram @manilyngabrielle.

Aurora Delle is a passionate believer in the transformative power of the written word. With a background in English Literature and Education, Aurora's purpose is to share her experience with others, encouraging them to find and develop their own voice. As Revolutionaries' Editorial Director, her intent is to shape words into powerful tools of change. When she is not reading, writing or editing, Aurora can be found giving in to her wanderlust and exploring the world around her. Find her on Twitter and Medium @auroradelle, and Instagram @helloitsaurora.

Naazneen Samsodien is a writer, BTS fanbase administrator, and the Head of Human Capital in corporate South Africa. She has a keen interest in fandom, particularly ARMY, and has spent many years participating in fandom-related activities. She has written for various online blogs and her most recent work can be found within the pages of *I Am ARMY: It's Time to Begin*. Naazneen is wildly curious, always uses too many words, laughs a lot and considers herself a citizen of the world. Connect with her on Twitter @sweetrupturedl8 or Instagram @miss_naazneen.

Demie Tuzara is a British-Filipino writer based in London, England. She is the founder and editor of Poetically Magazine, an online literary and visual arts publication for wordsmiths, storytellers and the poetically inclined. With education and training in multimedia journalism, she also freelances for online publications as a feature writer specialising in fashion, art and culture. Find her on Instagram @yours.demetria and Twitter @yours_demetria.

Kate Koncilja is a writer and researcher from the Chicago suburbs who aspires to enter the scholarly world and study the psychology and sociology of fandom. A lifelong artist who expresses herself through many forms – most prominently dance, fiction, poetry, and video editing – she will do anything possible to avoid those creative first deaths. Her other passions include BTS, personality typing, and hot chocolate. You can find her on Twitter @Kate_Kon7 and Instagram @perpetual_kibou7.

Jasmine Proctor is a writer, researcher, amateur astrologer, and a lifelong fangirl. Within the realm of academics, her interests lie at the intersection of fan studies and political economic theory, an area she is currently

CONTRIBUTORS

pursuing in her graduate research. Her work is published in *Love Yourself: Essays on self-love, care and healing inspired by BTS*. Outside of scholarship, Jasmine is an ARMY, an avid supporter of all forms of fan content, and a plant mum. Find her on Twitter, Instagram, and Medium @iamjazzrae.

Nikola Champlin received her M.F.A. in Poetry from the Iowa Writers' Workshop and her B.A. from Yale University. She is one half of the Editors-in-Chief at Dream Glow Magazine, a literary journal for BTS ARMY. For Moonrise, she co-edited the recent creative collection *Through the darkness, I will love myself*. Her writing focuses on "ecopoetics," which captures the environment in crisis, and she's inspired by BTS' social and political commentary shared through art. Her poetry has appeared in the Denver Quarterly, the Spoon River Poetry Review, the Alexandria Quarterly, and the Cimarron Review, among other publications. You can find her on Twitter @nikola_champlin.

Rajitha Sanaka is a writer, teacher, and formerly an award-winning journalist from the city of Hyderabad, India. Her work centres around feminism and mental health. She loves reading, dancing, and 'joyscrolling' BTS' content on the internet. She enjoys learning about people, cultures, and places through books and travel. She also spends a lot of time exploring the million-dollar question: "Who Am I?" BTS are her guiding lights, whom she loves and respects unconditionally. Find her on Instagram @rasthas.

Padya Paramita is a Bangladeshi-born, Brooklyn-based writer, editor, and pop culture enthusiast. She is currently an MFA candidate in creative writing at Columbia University where she uses creative nonfiction to explore intersectional representation in pop culture. Her work has been published in them, ColorBloq, Xeno Zine, and Moonrise's *Through the darkness, I will love myself*, for which she was also a co-editor. Padya is the Co-Editor in Chief of Dream Glow Mag, a literary journal inspired by the work of BTS. You can find her on Twitter @padyatheleo.

DEAR BTS
Wallea Eaglehawk

It was early 2021, late one Wednesday night, when I had the overwhelming desire to give BTS a gift. 2020 in many respects was not a good year, yet as a fan of the group, otherwise known as an ARMY, who had lived through every song, album, performance, interview, variety show, and VLive with BTS, I was still processing the enormity of their achievements. How is it that I can best celebrate a year that saw BTS missing ARMY more than ever, and honour the path that they have been walking all this time? That was the question that plagued me for all of five seconds before the answer appeared before my eyes: Write a book, of course.

You see, BTS' most well known message is "love yourself", which is often followed by "speak yourself". This message is what underpins my work within the fandom when publishing articles and books, working with other ARMY, and is a consistent thread throughout my professional and personal lives. This was the message that first gave me a clear direction to funnel my passion and purpose, which has seen a number of book projects that focus on ARMY telling their own stories, and the opportunity to tell my own. But what I had not yet traversed, and had not yet truly considered, was telling the story of BTS.

In one sense, it's obvious that ARMY should be the first place to look when wanting to learn about BTS. After all, it is the fandom that lives through every moment with the group, knows every lyric, sees and hears all in the Twitterverse. Yet my hesitation has been that we are unable to speak with BTS, to ask them questions face to face, to build our story of them. What if we say something wrong? What if we misinterpret what they intended with a lyric or a message? Being a historian of BTS without working with them directly has never been an interest of mine, for it errs on the side of exploitation and would be near-impossible to get right.

So here I was, minding my own business when the thought came to me. Instead of trying to encapsulate all of who BTS are and tell every micro-detail of their existence, why not seek to build an analysis of each member in the year of 2020 from interviews, lyrics, and shared moments with ARMY? Instead of trying to say it all, why not frame it as a gift from ARMY to BTS that says "We see you, we hear you, we understand you, and this is what we interpreted from you in 2020"? Through this, I can continue on with my ethos of "speak yourself", where ARMY are able to speak their own interpretations of BTS, instead of claiming them to be the be-all and end-all of representations. And, just as BTS have urged us to love ourselves, we can now turn our attention to showing BTS all the reasons why they should love themselves, for our relationship is symbiotic and reciprocal, after all.

Just like that, a special project was born called *BTS in our words*, which was the original title of this book and also encompassed a digital archive of fan artefacts, both to be released on June 13, 2021, BTS' 8th birthday. I put a call out for chapters, asking for bold and dynamic interpretations of each member in the context of 2020. Through this process I was able to reconnect with writers I had published previously, and meet some new faces, too. The task before us was quite simple on the surface, but daunting and complex to complete. Each author had to conduct their own research, compile relevant sources, and ensure their analysis was true to the discernable facts. The utmost care was taken in using BTS' words and work to illustrate an image of who we saw them as in 2020, and it was no easy task; though it was incredibly worthwhile.

These are just eight stories, eight interpretations, encompassing BTS, Jung Kook, V, Jimin, j-hope, Suga, Jin, and RM (reverse fan chant

INTRO: DEAR BTS

order, for your information), of many. The intention is to show each member through a collection of their moments in a way that comes close to how each author perceived them to be. Through this, we are able to give BTS a gift on their birthday that shows them what we loved most about each of them in 2020. We were there, witnessing every moment that they shared, we saw it all, and this is who we believe them to be: Seven incredible human beings who we are lucky enough to walk this path with.

Dear BTS,

Happy 8th birthday. This book was written by ten ARMY from around the world and published by an all-ARMY publishing company. Though we cannot speak with you directly, nor write a book that shares new stories or truths, what we can do is reflect who you showed yourselves to be in 2020 back to you.

While this book is firstly a gift to you, it is a gift to our fellow ARMY who wish to celebrate you on this day, and every other day for that matter. Further, we hope that anyone interested in learning more about who you are and connecting with you on a human level will find this book and find joy, solace, and understanding amongst these pages. We know and trust that the right people will find this book at the right time.

Thank you for all that you do, and all that you are. We know 2020 was a difficult year for you, but we appreciate you for including us in your journey as you always have done. Just as you have seen and heard us, we see you, we hear you, we love you, too.

Love,
ARMY

EXPECT THE UNEXPECTED
Wallea Eaglehawk, Manilyn Gumapas, and Aurora Delle

BTS, 방탄소년단 — Bangtan Sonyeondan, in English, Bulletproof Boy Scouts — at the end of 2019 were seemingly on top of the world. The septet reigning from Seoul, South Korea, were wrapping up their biggest year to date with a series of music award show performances that saw them embodying Greek gods on the world's stage and looking back at some of their most memorable releases since their debut in 2013 with a sense of pride and accomplishment. 111 awards and 21 music show wins later,[1] this chapter joins BTS as they travel to New York for the New Year's Eve ball drop.

It is here that we see members 김남준, Kim Namjoon, RM; 김석진, Kim Seokjin, Jin; 민윤기, Min Yoongi, Suga; 정호석, Jung Hoseok, j-hope; 박지민, Park Jimin, Jimin; 김태형, Kim Taehyung, V; and, 전정국, Jeon Jungkook; Jung Kook on the precipice of something big in 2020. Little did they know what was to come next, yet with the clarity of hindsight this book affords us, we are now able to look back on what was BTS' most astounding year yet.

Despite setbacks and restrictions, they ended 2020 on a high, with more accolades and achievements than ever before. This chapter gives an overview of what was BTS' breakthrough year to not only reminisce and celebrate all they have done in the face of adversity, but to provide context for the chapters to come. Chapters that show a deeper, more nuanced understanding of the seven individuals who together as BTS reached all new heights throughout an unprecedented global pandemic.

When it comes to BTS, it's safe to say that we can expect the unexpected. But this time around it was something that was outside of their control which was unexpected, and it felt like all hope was lost. This provided an opportunity for BTS to do what they do best: face adversity and setbacks head-on, and do something completely unexpected.

In 2020 BTS once again wowed their global audiences, this time with performances, stages, events, and initiatives that focussed on connection, healing, and community that acted as a beacon of hope to millions of people around the world. This is just a glimpse into their success story in the context of 2020.

If this is your first time with Bangtan, then welcome, we hope this chapter acts as a gateway and propels you on to learn more about the group. If you've been here for a while now, thank you, it's good to see you again. We hope you enjoy this overview and relive the highs that 2020 provided. No matter who you are: welcome to BTS, it's so good to have you here. Now, it's time to begin. Let us go now to New Year's Eve 2019... before it all began.

As the Time's Square Ball descended in celebration over New York City, BTS welcomed the beginning of a new decade like many others — full of hope and anticipation, looking forward with excitement to the possibilities that the new year held. Having appeared as guests on *Dick Clark's New Year's Rockin' Eve* two years prior, the rising international popularity of the septet saw them invited back to the celebration, however this time as headliners. This performance marked the beginning of a significant year for the group, a year that saw them achieve unparalleled success in the midst of global change.

Murmurs of a pneumonia-type virus gaining traction in China were starting to be heard as early as December 2019, with the World Health Organization (WHO) becoming officially involved in the search for answers on the same day as BTS' year-ending performance — December

31, 2019.[2] However, life continued on as normal for the vast majority, with these murmurs remaining part of the background noise, not quite loud enough to cause a disturbance. Early into the new year, on January 7, Big Hit Entertainment announced the highly anticipated comeback of BTS — *Map of the Soul: 7*.[3] With the release of a four-phase comeback map that promised multiple music videos, concept photos, a full tracklist, and the announcement of the global art project *Connect, BTS*, it's no wonder that album pre-sales surpassed the four million mark in less than one month.[4]

Several days after this announcement, the comeback schedule commenced with the release of the first of two official comeback trailers for the album, *Interlude: Shadow*, performed by Suga. The second official comeback trailer performed by j-hope, *Outro: Ego*, dropped one month later. With this last release, and taking into account the *Persona* comeback trailer performed by RM and released one year earlier, BTS' rap line had completed their exploration of the Jungian concepts that gave their name to each track.

A week after the premiere of *Interlude: Shadow*, the first title track from the album, *Black Swan*, was released accompanied by an art film version of the music video performed by the Slovenian-based MN Dance Company. The official music video was to be released over one month later in early March, delighting ARMY and taking them by surprise with no prior announcement of its release. Debuting at number 57 on the US Billboard Hot 100,[5] reaching number 7 on the Gaon Digital Chart,[6] and achieving number 2 on the US Digital Songs Sales chart,[7] *Black Swan* provided a glimpse into the depths that BTS had traversed with the creation of their latest album.

With the first three tracks released discussing abstract ideas such as the Jungian concept of the shadow self and the challenges of reconciling with this darker part of the psyche, the ego, and ultimate acceptance of oneself, as well as expressing the haunting fear of the "first death" or the loss of a life-giving passion, it was established early on that *Map of the Soul: 7* was to be an album of significance. As BTS' seventh studio album, *Map of the Soul: 7* was set to display a deeply personal side of the group, presenting their latest work as an introspective confessional, reflecting on BTS' seven years of growth as individuals and as a group.[8] It came as no real surprise then that multiple sources, including Billboard[9] and Rolling Stone,[10] declared BTS' early 2020 comeback as one of the most highly anticipated albums of the new year.

A unique component of the group's comeback was the launch of the global art project, *Connect, BTS*. Taking place in five cities across the world from January 14 to March 27, the project brought together 22 global artists who resonated with BTS' philosophy and were willing to add their own unique interpretation and imagination to this, ultimately redefining the relationship between art, music, and people.[11] With installations created in London, Berlin, Buenos Aires, Seoul, and New York, as well as the ability to view parts of the project online, *Connect, BTS* provided an opportunity for ARMY and non-ARMY alike to connect with both art and each other on an introspective level. Based on the belief of the power of art to change the world, *Connect, BTS* allowed BTS to successfully showcase a new side of the group, establishing themselves as much more than K-pop idols.

During the middle of BTS' comeback schedule, Big Hit Entertainment announced *Map of the Soul Tour* dates, with the worldwide tour originally set to showcase 37 performances slated for 17 cities.[12] Keeping true to their 2019 record of being the highest grossing touring group,[13] BTS sold out stadiums within a matter of days.[14] BTS maintained an intense promotional schedule during this time, solidifying their hold on the international, and in particular, U.S. music scene.

January saw RM featured on Younha's track *Winter Flower* which saw great success around the world, as well as BTS sharing the performance stage with Lil Nas X at the 2020 Grammy Awards for his *Old Town Road* collaboration with RM. Shortly after this groundbreaking stage, the equally momentous first live performance of *Black Swan* took place on *The Late Late Show with James Corden*. February provided another performance of an epic scale, with BTS taking over Grand Central Terminal for their first live performance of the title track *ON*, taking place alongside a series of light-hearted interviews on *The Tonight Show Starring Jimmy Fallon*. The series of US TV-based promotions ended with the now infamous *Carpool Karaoke* episode featured as a part of *The Late Late Show with James Corden*. Each appearance brought further recognition to the group, providing BTS with the opportunity to share their individuality with a growing audience, engaging fans with their endearing nature. And this couldn't have come at a better time.

As the new year progressed and talk of an atypical virus steadily became louder, global fears regarding the coronavirus were pulled from the background noise and into the spotlight. With the number of confirmed cases growing daily and spreading across continents, uncertainty and unease slowly began to take hold. WHO declared the viral outbreak a Public Health Emergency of International Concern on January 30.[15] Collectively, we sat on the cusp of a global shift, unaware of what was to come.

While the sense of fear and uncertainty spread steadily across the globe, it did nothing to diminish the excitement that ARMY held for the official release of *Map of the Soul: 7*. The worldwide release saw both the *Map of the Soul: 7* album and a dance-focused music video, *Kinetic Manifesto Film: Come Prima*, for the album's lead single *ON*, drop on the same day, February 21. The official music video for *ON* was released one week later, with both versions breaking records. *Kinetic Manifesto Film: Come Prima* became the fifth-largest debut in YouTube history,[16] with the official music video claiming the title for the biggest YouTube premiere[17] and becoming the fastest Korean video to reach 10 million views.[18] Receiving critical acclaim, the title track debuted at number 5 on the US Billboard Hot 100, becoming the groups most successful debut at the time.[19]

Exactly one week after achieving these successful highs, South Korean ARMY were hit with a devastating blow — the cancellation of the Korean leg of the *Map of the Soul Tour* due to increasing concerns regarding the spread of Coronavirus.[20] Despite the disappointment, ARMY turned this into an opportunity to bring positivity into the world, with a large number of fans donating their refunded tickets to charity to assist with coronavirus relief and prevention efforts.[21] WHO officially declared the outbreak as a pandemic a short time later on March 11, and from then onwards the global landscape began to change dramatically.[22] Amidst the growing chaos and concern caused by the pandemic, Jimin and Jung Kook featured on Lauv's single *Who*, perhaps returning the favour from 2019 when Lauv appeared on a remix of BTS' *Make It Right*. Adding to BTS growing list of features and solo works for the year also came V and his song *Sweet Night* which featured on the soundtrack for the popular Korean show *Itaewon Class*.

With the first travel bans, quarantine orders, and intensified hygiene and social distancing practices being put into place, the way we lived our lives rapidly began to change. It came as no real surprise then to hear of the postponement and then cancellation of some of the worldwide *Map of the Soul Tour* in March and April respectively.[23] With feelings of isolation increasing, we began seeking alternate ways to find human connections and comfort. And we weren't alone.

The physical disconnect that resulted from the pandemic did in fact provide opportunities for growth. Spending more time alone and clouded in fear and uncertainty, many turned online for support, searching for content, connections, and solace. Recognising this need in both themselves and ARMY, BTS joined their fans in the online space when both BTS and ARMY required it the most. While the group had always been active in engaging with their fans on a variety of online platforms, the pandemic saw this connection grow further. From an increase in the number of live broadcasts hosted by the members, to a focus on sharing a more personal experience with ARMY, BTS responded to the changing global landscape in a way that provided solace for both their fans and themselves. New content milestones were reached and shared with ARMY, including the iconic 100th episode of BTS' dynamic variety show, *Run BTS!* With their increase in online activity culminating in the very first at-home concert streaming series, *Bang Bang Con*, which shared a variety of previously held concerts and musters over a two-day period, BTS made the pandemic bearable for many fans.[24] With over 50 million

ARMY tuning in to their first online concert, there is no denying that BTS was able to adapt and fill a need that was created by the pandemic.[25]

Following their massively successful *Bang Bang Con* weekend in April, May of 2020 brought no shortage of BTS content despite the continuation of the unprecedented and unpredictable pandemic. At the *Kids' Choice Awards* on May 2, 2020, BTS took home the Favorite Music Group award, offering a short but sweet encouragement to ARMY to stay safe and connected.

On May 6, South Korean singer-songwriter IU released the nostalgic pop rock song *eight*, on which Suga featured, wrote, and produced. Debuting at number one on South Korea's Gaon Digital Chart,[26] *eight* would later go on to receive several accolades during year-end ceremonies, including a nomination for Song of the Year at the *2020 Melon Music Awards*[27] and winning Best Collaboration at the *2020 Mnet Asian Music Awards*.[28]

eight was not all Suga had in store for the month of May, though. Not long after the release of his collaboration with IU came cryptic images tweeted from the BTS Twitter account, sending ARMY into a frenzied anticipation. Fans scrutinised activity coming from all platforms and carefully inspected the blurred images counting down from D-7, to D-6, to D-5, and so on. On May 22, the day the D-2 image was expected to drop, fans were treated to not another blurred teaser image but an entire full-length, solo mixtape under his Agust D alter ego, *D-2*. In addition to original tracks exploring complex themes of self-reflection and critiques on society, *D-2* featured collaborations with none other than fellow BTS member RM, American artist MAX, NiiHWA, and Kim Jong Wan of South Korean alternative rock band Nell. *D-2* would later earn ranks among Genius' 50 Best Albums of 2020[29] and SCMP's best K-pop solo albums of 2020.[30]

At this point, however, COVID-19 was not the only crisis facing the world. Ongoing racial tensions in the United States continued to escalate when police murdered George Floyd, a 46-year-old Black American, in Minneapolis, Minnesota. Still reeling from the March 2020 police murder of Breonna Taylor, a 26-year-old Black American in Louisville, Kentucky, daily protests by citizens against police brutality emerged not just across the United States but also globally.[31] The music industry did not remain silent either, with several music artists calling for action from their fellow artists and pledging donations in support of Black Lives Matter. On June 4, BTS released a statement:

> "우리는 인종차별에 반대합니다.
> 우리는 폭력에 반대합니다.
> 나, 당신, 우리 모두는 존중받을 권리가 있습니다.
> 함께 하겠습니다.
> We stand against racial discrimination.
> We condemn violence.
> You, I and we all have the right to be respected. We will stand together."[32]

Following this statement, BTS and Big Hit Entertainment donated $1 million USD to Black Lives Matter.[33]

K-pop has had a long history of actively staying out of social and political issues,[34] a point of tension for international fans when incidents of cultural appropriation or other macro- or micro-aggressive occurrences arise. However, BTS' statement and donation sat atop an already ongoing awareness of their music's roots in Black music and culture; in a 2017 press conference for BTS' *Wings* tour, Big Hit Entertainment CEO Bang Sihyuk publicly accredited BTS' sound as having "Black music [as] the base."[35]

That BTS so publicly joined efforts for equality for a culture both they and the K-pop industry at large have benefited from spoke volumes for both ARMY and non-ARMY alike. Moved by the group's generosity, ARMY were quick to mobilise in response, and, in 24 hours, matched it in a "#MatchAMillion" endeavour spearheaded by charity fan collective One In An ARMY.[36] Later in the year, BTS would share their thoughts on this historic moment with *Variety*: "it's very simple really. It's about us being against racism and violence. Most people would be against these things. We have experienced prejudice as well ourselves. We just want to voice the fact that we feel it's the right of everyone to not be subject to racism or violence."[37]

At the same time as ARMY strove to "#MatchAMillion", YouTube's *Dear Class of 2020* occurred on June 7. BTS appeared as both performers and commencement speakers alongside Beyoncé, Michelle and Barack Obama, Lady Gaga, Malala Yousafzai, and more in an online event celebrating graduating students of all levels whose ceremonies were cancelled due to the COVID-19 pandemic.

During their commencement speech, each member took turns sharing anecdotes of their own memories of graduation, as well as personal words of encouragement both specific to the pandemic and for life in general. Each member's comments promoted a humble reminder of moving at one's own pace, acknowledging the reality and humanity of the pace of life, accessible rather than promoting the more commonplace toxic positivity or romanticisation of hustle culture. Such remarks joined their existing repertoire of these themes across the band's music, such as the countercultural lyrics found in tracks such as *Paradise* and *Tomorrow*, and in to-be-released *Dis-ease*.

BTS' *Dear Class of 2020* performance consisted of their recent tracks *Boy With Luv* and *Mikrokosmos* and also offered an unexpected surprise: The septet performed their 2017 track *Spring Day* for the first time in years. This sudden reappearance of the widely beloved ballad — and longest-charting song of all time on popular South Korean streaming service Melon[38] — packed an emotional punch for any listener familiar with the sentimental longing woven throughout its lyrics. While the *Dear Class of 2020* performance of *Spring Day* was the first reappearance of the track in 2020, it would certainly not be the last, a recurring illustration of the winter felt by BTS and ARMY as the pandemic continued to separate both while also offering the hopeful reminder that no winter lasts forever.

Simultaneously occurring during this first half of June was the 2020 BTS Festa, a series of events and releases celebrating BTS' seventh anniversary since their debut. Beginning with the endearingly chaotic *Airplane pt. 2 (Summer ver.)*, the 2020 BTS Festa had a number of surprises in store for ARMY, including family portraits, choreography videos, birthday party videos, Jung Kook's solo track *Still With You*, and a touching animated music video to *We Are Bulletproof : The Eternal*. The festivities wrapped on June 14 with *Bang Bang Con: The Live*, a live iteration of April's *Bang Bang Con*.

Bang Bang Con: The Live set a sky-high precedent for music artists seeking to connect with their audiences digitally during the COVID-19 pandemic. During the set, BTS performed songs both old and new, including some of what they had in store for the postponed *Map of the Soul* world tour. Approximately 756,000 paid viewers from 107 countries concurrently tuned in to watch the hour-and-a-half-long program, earning Big Hit Entertainment just under $20 million from ticket sales.[39] Equivalent to 15 shows at a 50,000 seat stadium, these metrics earned BTS the record for biggest audience for a paid virtual concert in history.[40]

BTS continued to ride their momentum of success and released their fourth Japanese studio album, *Map of the Soul: 7 ~ The Journey ~* on July 15. Containing Japanese versions of songs from *Love Yourself: Answer* (2018), *Map of the Soul: Persona* (2019), and *Map of the Soul: 7* (2020), as well as previously released 2019 single *Lights*, the album also introduced four new tracks: two instrumentals, *Intro: Calling* and *Outro: The Journey*, and two original songs, *Stay Gold* and *Your Eyes Tell*. The former became the theme song for the Japanese drama *Rasen no Meikyū (Helical Labyrinth)*; the latter, written and composed by Jung Kook, became the theme song for a Japanese film of the same name, released later in 2020.

The end of July brought another exciting announcement: The group's next digital single, a fun and upbeat summer track recorded entirely in English, would be released on August 21. Apart from the unprecedented all-English lyrics, ARMY were quick to point out another notable difference about this announcement. While official news regarding upcoming releases were typically disseminated first through official platforms such as the official BTS or Big Hit Entertainment accounts on

Twitter and Weverse, the news about this particular new single was first dropped on a personal livestream featuring all seven members.[41] Though their official account would indeed share this news later on,[42] the initial members-centered announcement marked the beginning of what would be a self-directed era of music and production in *BE*.

Though the first half of the year proved to be a busy and exciting time — amidst the uncertainty and suffering of the world — for BTS and ARMY, nothing came close to the new heights reached between August and December 2020. To follow in the wake of *Map of the Soul: 7*, BTS announced that they would be working on a new album slated for release at the end of the year. What was different about this project, however, was that it was going to be entirely managed and produced by the group themselves.

As the months progressed, BTS shared new details about the production of what would later be announced as *BE*. Each member got a unique role, such as production manager or producer, and the group regularly shared videos of meetings and other behind-the-scenes looks into the process. What stood out the most, and what BTS themselves seemed excited about, was that each member was going to contribute towards songwriting in a way that their busy schedule hadn't allowed for previously. They were able to bring their songs, some of which had been earmarked for mixtape releases, or put on the 'not now' pile for years, to the proverbial — or perhaps literal — table and make an album that was unlike any other.

The self-made album progress continued to tease and enthral fans in the lead up to the first single release in August. But just days before, BTS released another gift unto the world, this time in the form of their annual holiday show. Typically, BTS travel to another country on vacation to film for *Bon Voyage*, with 2019 seeing them traverse the rugged New Zealand countryside, camp under the stars, and be flung off a tall structure on a bungee rope.

Of course, due to the restrictions COVID-19 imposed, 2020 saw a different kind of vacation show called *In the Soop* (In the Forest), where

BTS travelled to a countryside property a few hours away from Seoul. It was here, next to a lake and against the backdrop of forested hills, that BTS sought solace and retreat. Spending their days on the water, playing games and cooking food — BTS were able to unwind and spend downtime together while the world (though a few months after filming in May/June) watched on. Juxtaposed against the quiet and wholesome adventures of *In the Soop* that was released in weekly instalments from August 19, was the release of BTS' highly anticipated single, *Dynamite*, on August 21.

Dynamite undoubtedly showcased BTS' ability to deliver something unexpected, this time the theme was disco, seemingly a light year away from early 2020 releases of *ON* and *Black Swan*. Filmed in a studio, the music video provided Americanised disco-era visuals from the Korean perspective of the group, with a BTS-twist, of course. Merging nostalgia and English with the charm, aesthetics, and raw talent of BTS created an unstoppable force to be reckoned with. There were no gimmicks, no hidden meanings, *Dynamite* provided a moment of relief from the pain and suffering of the world, an opportunity to smile and dance, a chance to be transported for all those who watched on. It's no wonder then, that the music video broke the record for most viewed YouTube video in 24 hours with 101.1 million views.[43]

Off the back of the immediate success of *Dynamite* came a rise in radio plays across the US, a market which was notoriously difficult for BTS to crack with their predominantly Korean language songs. This time, however, with *Dynamite* being all English, teamed with persistent campaigning from ARMY, clever strategy from Big Hit Entertainment and of course, the culmination of BTS' hard work over the past seven-odd years, the song was getting noticed... BTS were getting noticed around the world in a way they hadn't been before. At the end of August, *Dynamite* debuted at #1 on the Billboard Hot 100 chart, a first for BTS and the first for a South Korean group.[44] When *Dynamite* held on to its #1 position for a second week, BTS took to Twitter to share a chaotic, 14-second video where they yelled and rejoiced with great excitement.[45] After a difficult year, it was beginning to feel like things were shifting rapidly, and *Dynamite* provided fuel to the fire of hope for both BTS and ARMY alike.

September was a meaningful month for BTS who continued to promote *Dynamite* alongside preparing for their highly anticipated live concert *Map of the Soul ON:E* in early October. Their documentary, *Break the Silence*, was released in cinemas on September 10 which provided further insight into the group during their 2018-2019 Love Yourself world tour. On September 21 NPR Music released BTS' *Tiny Desk Concert* which saw the group in burnt orange and denim outfits reminiscent of *Dynamite*'s nod to disco. The performance garnered BTS attention from new audiences who had previously written them off as being fake, auto-tuned, and talentless. *Tiny Desk* asserted BTS' raw talent and ability to perform even on the smallest of stages.

On September 19, BTS attended the inaugural Korea's Youth Day at President Moon Jae-in's Blue House as honorary youth leaders. It was here that they gave a moving speech on their experiences of youth, the trials, and tribulations they have faced together, and their hopes for future generations to come. "I hope you can change the world with the power of your thought, and in turn, become the beacon of light to guide the youth of the future," says Jin, "We will always cheer you so you can help and support each other. Like yesterday's youth, like today's youth, just as we've always done until now, I hope you continue on that road without stopping."[46]

A few days later on September 23, BTS spoke at the United Nations General Assembly for the second time after their first address in 2018. During their speech they reflected on life through the pandemic, shared their concerns and experiences, and looked to the future with a glimmer of hope. Their message was earnest, clear, and straight from the heart. Though they were invited as global superstars, they spoke as peers of all young people facing uncertainty and suffering during 2020. "Life goes on, let's live on,"[47] was their parting message which rippled throughout the Twitterverse and beyond as a beacon of hope, just as *Dynamite* had been.

Speaking at both Korea's Youth Day and the United Nations General Assembly, amidst the release of laid-back *In the Soop* and the rise of *Dynamite*, cemented BTS as global leaders. Leaders in not only the realm of music, but culture, as their influence on their generation, and the generation of tomorrow, was being recognised by institutions at home in Korea and around the world.

At the end of September, BTS appeared on *The Tonight Show with Jimmy Fallon* for a week-long residency; something which had not been seen before. Over five nights BTS performed *Dynamite* twice alongside *Black Swan*, *Home*, *Idol*, and *Mikrokosmos*, all shot in different settings ranging from the overgrown interior of a chapel to Gyeongbokgung Palace. The group also joined Fallon to play games such as Zoom Olympics and Dance Your Feelings, all filmed remotely from Seoul, and shared insights about their time in school and what to expect from *BE*. During BTS week, *The Tonight Show* saw a 1300% increase in social media activity,[48] undoubtedly showing the unrivalled enthusiasm and outpouring of joy from ARMY both in the U.S. and overseas for the week-long celebration and recognition of BTS from such a significant Western show.

October started with the release of *Savage Love (Laxed – Siren Beat)*, a remix by Jawsh 685 and Jason Derulo featuring Jung Kook, Suga, and j-hope. Ten days later on October 12, the track reached #1 on the Billboard Hot 100 chart, becoming the second #1 for BTS, and the first of their songs with Korean lyrics.[49] *Dynamite* came in at #2, and history was made once again with BTS occupying the top two spots of the Hot 100.[49]

BTS received the Van Fleet Award on October 7, "in recognition of the group's promotion of cultural ties between the U.S. and South Korea."[50] The Korea Society board chair, Kathleen Stephens, acknowledged the positive influence of BTS in her introductory remarks: "BTS set the world alight, not just by setting records for number one songs and albums, but also by inspiring audiences of all backgrounds and cultures with their universal messages of hope, humanity, and love."[50] This award once again solidified BTS as leaders both within the music industry, and beyond to meaningfully influence diplomatic relations between Korea and other nations.

The highlight for October came with the highly anticipated two-day concert, *Map of the Soul ON:E*, which was originally going to host a live audience as well as stream online.[51] However, due to COVID-19 concerns, the format changed to online only, and pulled in 993,000 paying viewers from 191 regions around the world.[51] It was here that BTS delivered their first full stadium-esque concert for the year and wowed their global audience with what was to be their global tour for *Map of the Soul: 7*. ARMY were given a look into their high-concept VCRs — narrative clips played during costume and set changes — as well as never-before-seen live solos from *Map of the Soul: 7*, unrivalled unit stages, and, of course, powerful group performances with new choreography to boot. Not only did *ON:E* set a new standard within the fandom, but it undoubtedly made waves throughout the entertainment industry, surely setting the standard for pandemic performances.

To round out the monthly recognitions, on October 14, BTS won Top Social Artist at the *Billboard Music Awards* for the fourth year in a row.

A little over a week before the release of *BE* on November 11, BTS were announced as *WSJ Magazine*'s Music Innovators of the Year.[52] This award recognised their global influence and contribution to the changing face of music, another honour to add to the list for 2020; the group's recognition in the West was continuing to grow in leaps and bounds.

On November 20, *BE* finally made its way into the world which marked an important moment for BTS. This self-made, self-directed mini album was hailed as the most cohesive and BTS-esque album to date and shot up the charts. Providing an insight into how the group felt throughout the pandemic, *BE* offered comfort and hope for listeners both new and old. The title track *Life Goes On* echoed the sentiments shared in BTS' UN address from September — "life goes on, let's live on"[47] — and showed an authentic glimpse into the everyday lives of the group during 2020. The music video, directed by Jung Kook, was genuine, humble, and wholesome, with the same essence of *In the Soop*. It was clearly showing the same group who had not long ago released *Dynamite*, but this time in a different light, one which provided messages of resilience and connection to millions around the world.

Five days later, members V, Jung Kook, RM, and Jimin sat in their house in the early hours of the morning, watching as Grammy nominations were announced on a livestream. To win a Grammy has been an explicit wish of BTS' for many years now, with speculation heightening throughout 2020 due to the positive reception and astounding success of *Map of the Soul: 7* and *Dynamite*. They watch the nominees for Best Pop Duo/Group Performance being read out, eyes wide as they wait. Before the announcement can be verbalised they are jumping from the couch yelling with excitement — RM throwing his phone — they saw three letters on the screen: BTS. *Dynamite* netted the group their first Grammy nomination, such a recognition swiftly moved the fandom to an outpouring of love and celebration for BTS in a moment of shared euphoria.

On November 30, *Life Goes On* debuted at #1 on the Billboard Hot 100 chart, giving BTS their third #1; and a meaningful one at that. On December 5 *BE* peaked at #1, too, giving cause for yet another celebration of all BTS had achieved, and the long-awaited recognition ARMY felt they very much deserved.

December marked the beginning of awards season in Korea and around Asia, which has always been BTS' time to shine. Typically, these awards shows are an opportunity for the group to showcase multiple stages, with the most spectacular performances taking place at the *Melon Music Awards* which often feels more like a BTS concert than an awards ceremony. Despite there being no live audience, 2020 was no exception for the group as they performed *Black Swan*, *ON*, *Life Goes On*, and *Dynamite*.

The two hands-down highlights of the night were the opening to *Black Swan* which saw Jimin and Jung Kook gracefully flying through the air and embodying the swan, and the dance break in *Dynamite* which saw an undeniable nod to the late Michael Jackson. To top it off, BTS won six awards including Best Artist, Best Album (*Map of the Soul: 7*), and Best Song (*Dynamite*), a success which was echoed in awards ceremonies throughout December.

On the 9th, BTS were announced as *TIME*'s Entertainer of the Year in an article which described them as "a case study in music-industry dominance through human connection."[53] For the last time in 2020, BTS were recognised by a Western cultural institution and honoured for their talent, dedication, and authenticity.

December was a time of recognition, celebration for BTS, and... solos. Jin released *Abyss*, Jimin released *Christmas Love*, and V released *Snow Flower*— all three members wanted to give a gift to ARMY, straight from the heart. On New Year's Eve, the group finished up the year with a live performance as part of a concert hosted by Weverse, a fitting full circle moment.

Though they may have ended the year onstage performing, the place where BTS stood was vastly different to New Year's Eve 2020. Most noticeably, they were at home in Seoul, sharing the stage with other performers from their company, Big Hit Entertainment. Yet the biggest difference, perhaps, is how far they had travelled throughout the pandemic, despite all the cancellations and restrictions; a distance they could ironically only travel while remaining at home. In 2020, the world was an unexpected place more than ever while everyone grappled with unprecedented and harrowing circumstances. Yet, what was most warming, and most unsurprising for all those who were familiar with BTS, was that the group rose to the occasion, and delivered the unexpected. In a time that could have drastic consequences for BTS and their company, they pushed forward and continued to value connection and community above all else. Though the year was trying for BTS in many ways, which you will soon see, they persevered.

How is it that 2020 was the year that BTS reached unparalleled success, when so many others did not? The answer here is quite simple: Because the foundations on which they were built, on which their connections with ARMY existed, were solid and transcendent. When times got tough, BTS turned to VLive to speak with ARMY, to share mundane moments and craft bracelets and make food, to share the news of *BE* and celebrate nominations, #1 songs, and birthdays. Livestreaming concerts, making television shows out of holidays, spreading joy through playing games… these weren't new endeavours for BTS. This was the norm, as they have always sought to include their global fanbase and connect with them in a variety of ways to create meaning and share love.

Perhaps the pandemic provided the time and space for more people to connect with BTS on a human level, to find joy in their music and their content. Perhaps that is why BTS' year shone so brightly. But above all else, they most definitely shone so bright because they remained authentically themselves, shared their experiences genuinely and continued to hone their craft — all while continuing to walk alongside ARMY through times both happy, sad, and everywhere in between. This is where BTS and ARMY ended 2020: Together.

Now let us turn to each member to see how they spent their year. You might learn something new, you might feel as if you are meeting an old friend. These are the stories of seven young men that aim to compile moments, interviews, lyrics, performances, and more to build a profile of who they were in 2020. These nuanced interpretations by ARMY are intended to be juxtaposed against this chapter — with the sheer enormity of awards, honours, and achievements, with the flashing lights of success — to give what each author hopes is an accurate reflection of who each member was as they navigated the uncertainty of a pandemic and the ever-rising star of BTS. If you ever wondered what makes BTS so good, or what on earth the big deal is: Your answers might lie here. But most of all, what you will find are a collection of stories and experiences that are inherently human. For as we walk this path together with BTS we do not do so as fan and idol; we do so as humans, together.

References

[1] Fernandez, C. (2019). *BTS won so many awards in 2019, even ARMYs are shocked.* https://www.koreaboo.com/news/bts-won-so-many-awards-2019-even-armys-shocked/

[2] World Health Organization. (2020). *Listings of WHO's response to COVID-19.* https://www.who.int/news/item/29-06-2020-covidtimeline

[3] BIGHIT MUSIC [@BIGHIT_MUSIC]. (2020). #BTS #방탄소년단 map of the soul : 7 comeback map #MAP_OF_THE_SOUL_7 [Tweet]. https://twitter.com/BIGHIT_MUSIC/status/1214957638623973376

[4] McIntyre, H. (2020). *Presales of BTS's new album have now reportedly passed 4 million.* https://www.forbes.com/sites/hughmcintyre/2020/02/06/presales-of-btss-new-album-have-now-reportedly-passed-4-million/?sh=6e75bdac4373

[5] Billboard. (2020). *The Hot 100 chart.* https://www.billboard.com/charts/hot-100/2020-02-01

[6] Gaon Music Chart. (2020). *2020 Week 04 Digital Chart.* http://gaonchart.co.kr/main/section/chart/online.gaon?nationGbn=T&serviceGbn=ALL&targetTime=04&hitYear=2020&termGbn=week

[7] McIntyre, H. (2020). *BTS's 'Black swan' debuts as the second-bestselling song in the U.S.* https://www.forbes.com/sites/hughmcintyre/2020/01/27/btss-black-swan-debuts-as-the-second-bestselling-song-in-the-us/?sh=1efb839d6a30

[8] Benjamin, J. (2020). *BTS opens up about the past, creativity and inspiration for 'Map of the soul: 7.'* https://variety.com/2020/music/news/bts-interview-new-album-map-of-the-soul-7-video-1203511131/

[9] Billboard. (2020). *The 30 most anticipated albums of early 2020.* https://www.billboard.com/articles/columns/pop/8548159/most-anticipated-albums-early-2020

[10] Bernstein, J., Blistein, J., Browne, D., Ehrlich, B., Freeman, J., Greene, A., ... Vozick-Levinson, S. (2020). *70 most anticipated*

albums of 2020. https://www.rollingstone.com/music/music-lists/2020-album-preview-drake-bieber-springsteen-adele-931360/

11. Hollingsworth, J. (2020). *K-pop band BTS launches global art project.* https://edition.cnn.com/style/article/connect-bts-artist-projects-intl-hnk-scli/index.html

12. BIGHIT MUSIC [@BIGHIT MUSIC]. (2020). BTS map of the soul tour 일정 안내 #BTS #방탄소년단 #Mapofthesoultour [Tweet]. https://twitter.com/BIGHIT_MUSIC/status/1219771684904792064

13. Rolli, B. (2019). *BTS were the top-grossing touring group of 2019.* https://www.forbes.com/sites/bryanrolli/2019/12/06/bts-were-the-top-grossing-touring-group-of-2019/?sh=52a7b76b6199

14. Rolli, B. (2020). *BTS's 2020 North American stadium tour produces several sellouts in first weekend.* https://www.forbes.com/sites/bryanrolli/2020/02/10/btss-2020-north-american-stadium-tour-produces-several-sellouts-in-first-weekend/?sh=7bc88dd948d8

15. World Health Organization. (2020). *Statement on the second meeting of the International Health Regulations (2005) Emergency Committee regarding the outbreak of novel coronavirus (2019-nCoV).* https://www.who.int/news/item/30-01-2020-statement-on-the-second-meeting-of-the-international-health-regulations-(2005)-emergency-committee-regarding-the-outbreak-of-novel-coronavirus-(2019-ncov)

16. McIntyre, H. (2020). *BTS scores the fifth-largest debut in YouTube history with their latest video.* https://www.forbes.com/sites/hughmcintyre/2020/02/25/bts-scores-the-fifth-largest-debut-in-youtube-history-with-kinetic-manifesto-film--come-prima/?sh=46553702495d

17. Rolli, B. (2020). *BTS's 'On' video had the biggest premiere in YouTube history.* https://www.forbes.com/sites/bryanrolli/2020/02/27/btss-on-video-had-the-biggest-premiere-in-youtube-history/?sh=12d55e2e77ae

18. Baek, J. (2020). *[Official] BTS "On" 2nd MV, exceeded 10 million views in an hour. . . Korea's shortest record.* https://entertain.naver.com/read?oid=076&aid=0003536419

19. Billboard. (2020). *The Hot 100 chart.* https://www.billboard.com/charts/hot-100/2020-03-07
20. Eggertsen, C. (2020). *BTS cancels Korean tour dates over coronavirus outbreak.* https://www.billboard.com/articles/business/touring/9325071/bts-cancels-korean-tour-dates-over-coronavirus-outbreak
21. Benjamin, J. (2020). *BTS fans inspired to donate concert ticket refunds to Coronavirus relief.* https://www.billboard.com/articles/news/international/9324851/bts-army-donate-tickets-refunds-coronavirus-relief-suga/
22. World Health Organization. (2020). *WHO Director-General's opening remarks at the media briefing on COVID-19 - 11 March 2020.* https://www.who.int/director-general/speeches/detail/who-director-general-s-opening-remarks-at-the-media-briefing-on-covid-19---11-march-2020
23. Yglesias, A. (2020). *BTS cancel 2020 Map of the soul world tour dates due to COVID-19 restrictions.* https://www.grammy.com/grammys/news/bts-cancel-2020-map-soul-world-tour-dates-due-covid-19-restrictions
24. BTS_official [@bts_bighit]. (2020). 방에서 즐기는 방탄소년단 콘서트 □방.방.콘□ *Coming soon!* #방방콘 #방에서즐기는방탄소년단콘서트 [Tweet]. Twitter. https://twitter.com/bts_bighit/status/1248264411510263809
25. McIntyre, H. (2020). *BTS's online concert event was a massive success.* https://www.forbes.com/sites/hughmcintyre/2020/04/20/btss-online-concert-event-was-a-massive-success/?sh=98f26f5e94a9
26. Gaon Chart. (2021). *gaon chart.* http://gaonchart.co.kr/main/section/chart/online.gaon?nationGbn=T&serviceGbn=ALL&targetTime=19&hitYear=2020&termGbn=week
27. Melon Music Awards. (2021). *Melon music awards.* https://www.melon.com/mma/vote2.htm
28. Kim, H. (2020). 2020 MAMA, nominations revealed… IU 'Song of the year' 3 → Cockpit 'Aloha', etc. http://www.newsinside.kr/news/articleView.html?idxno=1093153

29 Genius. (2020, December 21). *The Genius community's 50 best albums of 2020*. https://genius.com/a/the-genius-community-s-50-best-albums-of-2020

30 Herman, T. (2020). *The best K-pop solo albums of 2020: BoA, Kai, Hwa Sa, Baekhyun and Taeyeon leave fans begging for more*. https://www.scmp.com/lifestyle/k-pop/artists-celebrities/article/3114302/best-k-pop-solo-albums-2020-boa-kai-hwa-sa

31 Cave, D., Albeck-Ripka, L., & Magra, I. (2020). *Huge crowds around the globe march in solidarity against police brutality*. https://www.nytimes.com/2020/06/06/world/george-floyd-global-protests.html

32 방탄소년단 [@BTS_twt]. (2020). 우리는 인종차별에 반대합니다. 우리는 폭력에 반대합니다. 나, 당신, 우리 모두는 존중받을 권리가 있습니다. 함께 하겠습니다. We stand against racial discrimination. We condemn violence. You, I and we all have the right to be respected. We will stand together. #BlackLivesMatter. [Tweet.] https://twitter.com/BTS_twt/status/1268422690336935943

33 Benjamin, J. (2020). *BTS and Big Hit Entertainment donate $1 million to Black Lives Matter (EXCLUSIVE)*. https://variety.com/2020/music/news/bts-big-hit-1-million-black-lives-matter-donation-1234627049/

34 Lee, J. (2020). *Rethinking the K-pop industry's silence during the Black Lives Matter movement*. https://theconversation.com/rethinking-the-k-pop-industrys-silence-during-the-black-lives-matter-movement-141025

35 Do, K. (2017). *Bang Shi Hyuk talks about why BTS hasn't created English songs*. https://www.soompi.com/article/1092547wpp/bang-shi-hyuk-talks-bts-sings-korean

36 Rearick, L. (2020). *BTS donated $1 million to Black Lives Matter. Fans matched it.* https://www.teenvogue.com/story/bts-million-donation-black-lives-matter-fans-match

37 Davis, R. (2020). *BTS on the decision to donate to Black Lives Matter: 'Prejudice should not be*

tolerated.' https://variety.com/2020/music/news/bts-black-lives-matter-donation-1234789434/

38 KStarLive. (2020). *In-depth look on why 'Spring Day' is actually the dark horse of BTS when it comes to music charts in South Korea.* https://www.kstarlive.com/news/2020/09/18/in-depth-look-on-why-spring-day-is-actually-the-dark-horse-of-bts-when-it-comes-to-music-charts-in-south-korea-381550

39 McIntyre, H. (2020). *BTS's virtual concert 'Bang Bang Con: The Live' was a massive moneymaker.* https://www.forbes.com/sites/hughmcintyre/2020/06/16/btss-virtual-concert-bang-bang-con-the-live-was-a-massive-moneymaker/?sh=4d24348f59c5

40 Frater, P. (2020). *BTS' 'Bang Bang Con: The Live' claims record viewership for online concert.* https://variety.com/2020/digital/asia/bts-big-bang-con-the-live-record-online-concert-1234635003/

41 BTS. (2020). *HoneyFM <JiJinJung's R.A.D.I.O #Bigannouncement.* [Video]. https://www.vlive.tv/video/204818

42 BTS_official [@bts_bighit]. (2020). *[공지] #BTS 디지털 싱글 발매 안내 (+ENG/JPN/CHN) [Link attached].* [Tweet]. https://twitter.com/bts_bighit/status/1287414626930450432

43 Spangler, T. (2020). *BTS 'Dynamite' breaks YouTube record for most-viewed video in first 24 hours, with 101 million views.* https://variety.com/2020/digital/news/bts-dynamite-youtube-record-most-viewed-24-hour-1234743960/

44 Dinges, G. (2020). *BTS earns first No. 1 debut with 'Dynamite' on Billboard's hot 100 chart.* https://www.usatoday.com/story/entertainment/music/2020/08/31/bts-dynamite-k-pop-stars-get-first-no-1-debut-billboard-hot-100/5656594002/

45 방탄소년단 [@BTS_twt]. (2020). *This is just… #우리아미상받았네* [Tweet]. https://twitter.com/BTS_twt/status/1303343927676731392

46 Pinkvilla Desk. (2020). *BTS deliver inspiring speech for National Youth Day at Blue House; Hand over time capsule to be opened in 2039.* https://www.pinkvilla.com/entertainment/hollywood/bts-deliver-inspiring-speech-national-youth-day-blue-house-hand-over-time-capsule-be-opened-2039-563696

47. BANGTANTV. (2020). *BTS (방탄소년단) speech at the 75th UN general assembly* [Video]. https://www.youtube.com/watch?v=5aPe9Uy10n4
48. Cantor, B. (2020). *"The tonight show starring Jimmy Fallon" has best social media performance ever, sets multi-week ratings & viewership highs during BTS week*. https://headlineplanet.com/home/2020/10/06/the-tonight-show-starring-jimmy-fallon-breaks-social-media-record-sets-multi-week-ratings-viewership-highs-during-bts-week/
49. Curto, J. (2020). *Jason Derulo, thirst king, returns to no. 1 after 11-year drought with 'Savage love'*. https://www.vulture.com/2020/10/jason-derulo-bts-jawsh-685-savage-love-number-one.html
50. The Korea Society. (2020). *2020 annual gala - BTS - Van Fleet award* [Video]. https://www.youtube.com/watch?v=7EhFU5flJk4
51. BTS Wiki. (2020). *Map of the soul ON:E*. https://bts.fandom.com/wiki/Map_of_the_Soul_ON:E
52. WSJ. (2020). *BTS: Music innovator* [Video]. https://www.wsj.com/video/series/innovators-2020/bts-2020-music-innovator/B0BCE257-BDCA-4AAB-A04C-C619B069DE1E
53. Buner, R. (2020). *TIME entertainer of the year: BTS*. https://time.com/entertainer-of-the-year-2020-bts/

Jung Kook

THE GOLDEN MAKNAE, A BORN SINGER
Naazneen Samsodien

Introduction: Here, hold my hand, let's fly to that future[1]

It's a sunny afternoon on Hollywood Boulevard in 2014. Jung Kook, Jimin and V, armed with nothing but 200 flyers and their natural charisma, are inviting people to attend BTS' free concert. Jung Kook, with large expressive doe-eyes and cherry-coloured hair exclaims, "oh my goddd" into his fist when confronted with hoards of people on the street.[2] I get a thrill every time I think about how Jung Kook was on the precipice of superstardom and he had no idea how his life was about to change.

Fast forward to 2020 and once again, Jung Kook is on an American street. This time, he is not asking strangers to attend a BTS concert. Instead, BTS are a headlining act at *Dick Clark's New Year's Rockin' Eve with Ryan Seacrest*. Jung Kook is one-seventh of BTS, the world's most popular band. Six years after handing out flyers to strangers, Jung Kook displays the same wide-eyed wonder when he recognises his face on billboards in Times Square and exclaims, "This is so awesome!"[3]

Jeon Jungkook, known by his stage name Jung Kook, was born on September 1, 1997, in Busan, South Korea. While not much is known about his childhood, in 2020 Jung Kook shared with the *Wall Street*

Journal that he was raised in a happy, creative household[4] — no doubt a fertile place to foster his numerous creative abilities. Jung Kook is beloved for his creativity, his angelic vocals, his mischievous sense of humour, and his unending list of talents as BTS' Golden Maknae (maknae meaning youngest in Korean). Mostly, however, ARMY loves Jung Kook because of how much *he* loves *us*.[5] At debut, a 15-year-old Jung Kook was not only the main vocalist for BTS, but also one of the lead dancers, a sub rapper, and the centre of group choreography — all quite astonishing when you consider he temporarily lost interest in being a singer, wanted to pursue dance instead, and had no rapping experience at all.[6]

In 2020, Jung Kook composed and produced some of his finest work. In fact, I believe his vocals and writing outshine his pre-2020 efforts, showing his growth as an artist. *My Time, Still With You, Your Eyes Tell*, and *Stay* are amongst his 2020 releases as solo and group tracks. They are a mixture of autobiographical works — telling the story of his struggles feeling separated from ARMY during the year — as well as his growth and maturation journey into adulthood. *My Time* in particular, his solo track from BTS' *Map of the Soul: 7*, sits alongside his first solo song, *Begin*, as a deeply personal insight into the exciting but also overwhelming experiences Jung Kook has been through in order to reach for his dreams.

As the youngest member of BTS, Jung Kook has always had the older members as the de facto spokespersons. Therefore, it's often hard to fully detail Jung Kook's life and thoughts, as he is innately private and shy. That said, as with most artists, his music speaks eloquently of his triumphs and challenges. For Jung Kook, BTS, ARMY, and music comprise, in my opinion, the map of his soul. In Jung Kook's chapter, I will endeavour to use his words to build a coherent narrative illustrating his beginning, his euphoric middle, and the journey into his time, the now.

Begin: The world was so big, and I was so small[7]

Jung Kook's map of the soul

In a *Bangtan Bomb* posted at the start of 2020, Jung Kook talks sincerely of his goals, aspirations, and hopes for the year. Like all of us, he had no idea how much 2020 would change his life, and so he is hopeful and earnest in his wishes for himself and ARMY. "Watch how I change,"[8] he pledges, giving us insight into his resolution to show ARMY his growth and development as an artist and human being.

2020 for Jung Kook began with BTS' release of *Map of the Soul: 7*, a self-referential album inspired by Jungian psychology which expands on the themes of individuality and personal growth. Using the concept of Jung's 'map of the soul',[9] BTS explores their 'persona', 'shadow', and 'ego', contrasting their seven-year journey with the social mask they wear as idols, their feelings of self-alienation, and their true sense of identity.[10] *Map of the Soul: 7* is described by BTS as "deeply personal"[11] and Jung Kook uses his solo track, *My Time*, to vividly create a storytelling mechanism to illustrate the disconnect he feels in relation to those around him. *My Time* conveys a sense of movement, an urgency of time and space moving too fast as Jung Kook explores how his growing fame has alienated him from his peers. It's quite ironic, I find, that 2020 brought the world to a standstill and potentially gave Jung Kook the opportunity to find his time, set a new pace, and reconnect with the world.

In order to understand Jung Kook in 2020 however, it's important to juxtapose his now with what came before — his beginning. *Begin*, Jung Kook's first solo song from the BTS album *Wings*, explores his life as a young boy leaving home to move to Seoul to follow his dreams. The song is, of course, not his literal beginning, but his *new* beginning with BTS — the framework on which his most recent solo, *My Time*, is built:

> The fifteen-year-old me who had nothing
> The world was so big, and I was so small
> Now I can't even imagine
> Myself who had no scent, who was completely empty[7]

In *Begin*, Jung Kook chronicles his journey into a new city, overwhelmed by the pace, sights, and sounds. He describes himself as being "empty" and credits the BTS members, his *hyungs* (Korean for older brother), as giving him his unique colour and piecing the tapestry of his life together.

The long hours, the workload, the difficult schedule isn't what he found the hardest to bear; with *Begin*, Jung Kook shares how it's their collective pain that's his biggest burden. "When my brother is in pain, it hurts more than when I'm in pain",[7] he heart-rendingly admits. Years later, the wellbeing of his hyungs remains what's most important to him, showing how the strength of their bond has only deepened over time.[12] The BTS members filled Jung Kook with new life through their belief in his talents, their support, guidance, and their love. The wide-eyed Jung Kook in *Begin* is therefore different from the wiser Jung Kook in *My Time*, something he acknowledges. "Did that child really grow up to become me?" he muses to the graduating class of 2020 when referencing his teenage years. "I feel like I've come a very long way."[13]

If *Begin* was the start of Jung Kook's life with BTS, then *My Time* is the progression of living in the world and graduating into adulthood more rapidly than anyone else. *My Time* fits into *Map of the Soul: 7*'s 'shadow' concept, exploring the most unconscious part of Jung Kook's personality — his dark side. Like the autobiographical *Begin*, in *My Time,* Jung Kook pens his life story and uses the analogy of time zones to express his feelings on his growth and development.

> 24, I feel as though I've become an adult faster than anyone
> My life has been a movie all the time
> I raced to where the sun rises every single night
> It even feels like I've been to someone's tomorrow,
> a world too big for that boy[14]

My Time opens with a reference to 24 — both I believe a nod to his Korean age, as well as to literal time — as Jung Kook starts to unpack his progression from the innocence of his childhood into adulthood, drawing into focus how he's missed the sometimes complex, sometimes tumultuous adolescence in between. In the pursuit of his dreams, Jung Kook lost his childhood and parallels *Begin* by acknowledging how small he felt in relation to the big world he was inhabiting. Jung Kook expands on the theme he started in *Begin*, and explores his feelings of growing up too fast and losing common ground — or time — with those his age. His life experiences as a celebrity are vastly different to the experiences of the average 24-year-old. As he rapidly enunciates, "Friends ridin' subway, I'll be in the airplane mode",[14] he's acknowledging that while his friends were experiencing normal things like taking the train to school or work, he was on an aeroplane en route to performing to millions of fans in different countries or preparing to face cameras and questions from virtual strangers. This disconnect has left him feeling out of sync with others his age, as if he is operating in a different time and space. Furthermore, the rapid start to the song also underscores the feeling of speed and mimics time moving quickly in concert with the beat.

BTS' second virtual concert for 2020, *Map of the Soul: ON:E*,[15] introduced Jung Kook's highly anticipated performance of *My Time*. In black leather on Day One, and a sultry red suit and matching leopard print shirt on Day Two, Jung Kook was primed to showcase a darker, more sensual, side to his personality, echoing Jung's 'shadow' concept. "I wanted to let our fans know the real story about me," Jung Kook tells Spotify.[16] The real story he alludes to is the misalignment between his ego — who *he* is — and his persona — who the world perceives him to be. On stage, Jung Kook starts his performance alone, cloaked in darkness. Around him are multiple projections of his person, all moving in sync, highlighting his loneliness and isolation from everyone but himself. While Jung Kook's *Wings* tour stage for *Begin* is highly impressive, I'm excited by the growth evident in his performance of *My Time*. *My Time* showcases Jung Kook with a heightened self-awareness — evident not only in his facial expressions, but in his overall physicality — as he emotes with more than just his voice. His entire body is telling the story. His onstage charisma, sex appeal, confidence, and swagger is mind-numbing to watch. While *Begin* is an energetic, rousing triumph, *My Time* delivers a moving, riveting performance in which he incorporates his vocals, his dance, and his stage presence to enable the story he is trying to tell.

I find the development from *Begin* to *My Time* fascinating, heartbreaking, yet hopeful at the same time. Jung Kook's solo songs display a natural progression from boyhood to adulthood, and paint vivid pictures of how difficult life in the fast lane can be. Yet despite that, *Begin* and *My Time* also displays a consistent view of Jung Kook's resilience and hopefulness. "Fly with me",[7] he invites the BTS members at the end of *Begin*, asking them to soar beside him, always together. While *Begin* is about BTS, it's fitting to note that ARMY are BTS' wings. In essence, Jung Kook calls BTS *and* ARMY to soar beside him. Similarly, with *My Time,* he ends the song on a hopeful note. In the final verse, he declares his intention to call, to hold, to touch, to reach out to someone. His earlier "I can't" becomes "I will"[14] in Jung Kook's quest to bridge the gap and connect. Dancers flit onto the stage, continuing to mirror him in his attempt to find time with them, but they disappear again, proving time elusive. "Happy that we met each other", he declares, "now til' the very end".[14] Despite being on a different plane than others, Jung Kook remains hopeful and happy as he searches to find his time. As *My Time* comes to an end, on stage Jung Kook remains standing on a clock, the dancers now surrounding him, finally in the same space and time.

I'm a born singer[17]

In the immediate aftermath of Jung Kook's performance of *My Time*, social media exploded with acclaim for his smooth dance moves, powerful stage charisma, and astounding vocals.[18] 'Jungkook' and 'MY TIME' shot to the top of worldwide Twitter trends as ARMY processed his performance via amusing hyperbole like 'vocal king' to enthusiastically hail his talents. Jung Kook's vocals are most commonly praised by critics for his emotive tone and ability to sing in any style and genre[19] — or described as honey, flexible, and pure.[20] These descriptors are not meant to detract from its beauty, but rather I believe, to underscore the comfort inducing, smooth, bright and warm tones of his vocal colours. It's surprising, however, to realise that at the beginning of his journey, singing was not initially a passion for Jung Kook, it's something he has come to love intensely over time. During a 2020 interview with *BTS Japan Official Fanclub Magazine*, Jung Kook speaks candidly about his relationship with singing and how it became a passion. "You might think that I had a dream of becoming a singer ever since I was a child. To be honest, even when I went to audition on the show, I still wasn't clearly aware I had this dream to become a singer."[21] It was observing RM's work ethic, however, that inspired Jung Kook to want to succeed.

It's not unusual to hear Jung Kook lament how he could have improved a performance, or how he will work harder to show ARMY a better or different side to his capabilities. In fact, I would argue that it's something he mentions religiously at most opportunities. In 2020, Jung Kook starts to exhibit other elements to his vocal style, incorporating a boldness I have not seen before — more soul, a huskiness even — indicating his experimentation with his technique. He effortlessly incorporates more runs, harmonies, and hits higher notes more consistently. During BTS' appearance on *James Cordon's Carpool Karaoke*, I was stunned at the seemingly effortless execution of his high note during *ON*'s bridge.[22] Furthermore, while Jung Kook has always participated in producing additional vocals on BTS tracks, his background harmonies — in particular during live performances of *Life Goes On*,[23] and BTS' *Tiny Desk (Home) Concert*[24] — show impressive growth and vocal stability. I found that Jung Kook's vocals evolved in 2020 to include new bursts of colour, also evidenced in the demo version of his bridge in *Dis-ease*[25] or his ad libs in the final version of the same song. His harmony during *Who* is goosebump inducing, rivalled only by *Your Eyes Tell* and *My Time*, underscoring his unique ability to adapt his vocals to suit different styles. While the members of BTS have always been strong advocates of Jung Kook's vocals — j-hope praising his ability to make the listener feel relaxed,[26] Jin referring to his "luxury brand vocals"[27] — various producers,[19] including *Euphoria*'s DJ Swivel[28] and *My Time*'s SleepDeez, have also praised Jung Kook's vocal abilities, calling *ON*'s bridge "a flat out flex". [29]

His elocution when singing in English has also shown improvement. 2020 saw Jung Kook featured on three tracks where his contribution was in English only. *Who*, *Savage Love*, and *Dynamite*. His pronunciation has reached the point where it's almost impossible to tell he is not a native English speaker. Another example is his cover of Lauv's *Never Not*,[30] which he shared on Twitter in May. Compare this to his earlier Justin Bieber covers and his improvement in pronunciation is marked, along with his breath control and tone.

"I wanted to be a singer," Jung Kook says during *Burn the Stage*. "But I don't think I knew at all that I needed to work hard to become one."[6] Despite Jung Kook's initial lack of interest in singing, I believe that his hard work to improve his vocals is evident. I find he's the golden thread around which all the other beautiful voices also shine, harmonising to create a symphony. He remains, however, hyper aware of his never-ending learning curve. "I am well aware that I am not good enough," he tells j-hope.[26] While I believe Jung Kook is too hard on himself, it's this self-awareness that drives his determination to be a singer ARMY can be proud of. It fuels his passion and enables his growth. "I want to become a singer that can touch people with his voice," Jung Kook vowed in 2013,[31] something that he continues to echo in 2020. During *You Quiz on the Block*, Jung Kook talks about how his improvement is constant. "There were no absolute rules for me. I worked and practiced my vocal whenever I can. 24 hours."[32] As I watch *In the Soop* or any recent episode of *Run BTS!*, I see his ambition in practice as I observe how much Jung Kook casually sings. He is a songbird — constantly humming, ad libbing, or singing karaoke in the background — a technique he also uses to improve his vocals.[33]

During 2020 I posit that Jung Kook became BTS' ad lib king — as evidenced most epically by the *In the Soop* theme song.[34] He demonstrates a keen ability to listen and interpret what the producer wants — in this case, Suga — and expresses that want intuitively. His playful runs in the studio are so impressive, the members insist that he record them. Jung Kook's improvisation is what makes the final version of the track so fun. His comfort with singing is incredible to witness when one considers that he almost did not debut because he was too shy to sing in front of anyone.[35] His continued hard work and humility is why ARMY show so much love and appreciation via Twitter tags like 'JUNGKOOK BEST MAIN VOCALIST' — or in 2020, the hashtag '#9YearsWithJungkook'

JUNG KOOK: THE GOLDEN MAKNAE, A BORN SINGER

crowned him a born singer by praising his passion for singing, his work ethic and his dedication.

> I'm a born singer, a bit belated confession (I swear)
> A mirage that used to be ever so far away is in front of my eyes (It's here)
> I'm a born singer, perhaps a bit early confession
> But, I'm so happy, I'm good[17]

Above is the first verse Jung Kook sings of *Born Singer*, a song BTS performed standing on a rotating, circular disk at the end of the *Wings Tour Final Trilogy III*. The song is a dedication to them fulfilling their dreams of being on stage, despite the obstacles they faced. It strikes me that Jung Kook parallels *Born Singer* at the start of his solo live performance of *Begin*, by rotating on the same circular disk, except this time, he is alone.

Euphoria: When I'm with you I'm in utopia[36]

The hyungs put my puzzle pieces together[37]

If *Begin* narrates Jung Kook's confusing and overwhelming start with BTS, *Born Singer* highlights the achievement of his dream to be on stage beside his hyungs. There's a moment during 2020's *Bang Bang Con: The Live* when Jung Kook is caught on camera watching the members lose themselves on stage. RM floats by in the foreground and Jung Kook's smile broadens involuntarily, his large eyes sparkling as he watches his bandmates with adoration.[38] What I love about this moment is that the level of trust, love, and goofy affection Jung Kook shows for the members comes from spending years together. "All the things I can say, the thoughts that I have, the singing — I have grown together with the members by my side and it is all thanks to the members that all this was possible," he tells *Esquire*.[39] The stage, ARMY and BTS are his euphoria, his happy place. And to quote his solo song of the same name, "when I'm with you, I'm in utopia".[36]

In 2020, BTS went into lockdown together. It's well documented that the members have lived together since before their debut. For a 13-year-old Jung Kook, the other members were older and played a huge influence in his development. In fact, one could argue that many of his habits, likes, dislikes, his views, and opinions were shaped by those around him. It's the 'colour'[7] they gave him that he refers to in *Begin*, and it's the acknowledgement that "I feel as though I've become an adult faster than anyone"[14] in *My Time*.

Social learning theory[40] posits that learning is a cognitive process that takes place in a social context and can occur through observation, direct instruction, or through the observation of rewards and punishments. Therefore when a particular behaviour is rewarded regularly, it will most likely persist. The converse is also true. During *Burn the Stage*, Jung Kook expands on social learning theory by referencing how at a young age, he most likely learnt social cues, how to speak, behave, and govern himself by watching the members around him.[37] These are usually behaviours learnt from parental figures in home environments. "The guys filled me in one by one. And I think maybe that's how I became what I am now. I could be a manifestation of all their characters coming together."[37] What Jung Kook articulates as being a composite personality, is most likely adopting the social queues, norms, and values of the group. Older members are often seen giving Jung Kook advice and mentoring him through personal and professional challenges. The advice and food for thought, however, is always paired with encouragement and praise. "When has Jung Kook ever done a bad job?" remarks RM during *Break the Silence*.[41]

Both *Begin* and *My Time* are anchored in this trusting relationship because the members aided his growth and development. In 2020, this familial bond was never more apparent to me than when watching *In the Soop*, where the mundane work of cooking, cleaning, and teamwork is a requirement. All BTS members are happy to help play their part because as Jung Kook says, they are "a real family".[42] This familial bond is indicative of various social queues inherent in their household. "I don't know why they always look for me, but I think it's a good thing. That means I'm helpful. It feels quite good and I felt proud."[43] For Jung

Kook, being helpful and feeling useful to the members also fills him with immense happiness and pride, underscoring the fact that his utopia is always amongst — and in the service of — his hyungs.

As *My Time* proves, Jung Kook was trying to find his place in the world and his ability to sync his current context with those around him. While watching *In the Soop*, I was struck by Jung Kook reconnecting with the members themselves, taking turns to spend time with each individually. This bonding however, is done in his unique way. Jung Kook is able to engage with each member in a way that is meaningful and displays an awareness of their needs, as well as his own. He is content to paint quietly beside RM and j-hope, carouse with Jimin, cook beside Jin and Suga, or share a drink and conversation with V. *In the Soop* gifted Jung Kook with an opportunity to disengage from the world, in order to reconcile with those closest to him. It's also worth noting the development of the theme song for *In the Soop* is another example of connection. His line, "a space we are in together"[44] also alludes to their uniting by being in the same time and space and parallels his intent in *My Time*.

Jung Kook has often spoken about the hard work of the BTS members, and how inspired he becomes by watching them work. "We made our debut and I was a big frog in a small pond," Jung Kook reflects during *Burn the Stage*.[6] What Jung Kook expressed here was his belief that BTS was amazing — that *he* was amazing — until they debuted and he saw how talented their peers were. Jung Kook wanted to be a singer, a dancer, an entertainer. But it was his debut that made him realise how hard he needed to work to achieve his dreams. Inspired by the members around him, Jung Kook wanted to learn to compose music and write lyrics, so that he too might be able to contribute to the creation of a BTS album with more than only his voice.[45]

In 2007, a team of researchers defined 'grit' as "perseverance and passion for long-term goals."[46] This orientation includes working hard to overcome challenges and investing consistent effort over time, despite adversity or plateaus. It's my belief that Jung Kook shows characteristics of a gritty individual. He approaches his professional achievement as a marathon and stays the course for the long term. The research asserts, in fact, that grit is essential to high achievement. However, examining the definition, it seems to apply to all BTS members. And if we assume that Jung Kook has steadily been observing and learning, acquiring knowledge and skill from the members around him, it might be safe to presume that BTS as a whole is a high-performing team composed of gritty individuals. Prolonged exposure to their grit has in turn increased his own. Achievement is not always only about intellect— it's as important as having drive and staying power.[46] Jung Kook has admitted that he did not always work as hard as he should, nor does he consider himself an intellectual. But in surrounding himself with a team of high-performing individuals, his own motivation levels rose. Of his goals, Jung Kook says, "It's like a foggy mountain top."[42] His destination is not clear, but he will keep climbing higher in an attempt to improve and do better.

During *In the Soop*, Jung Kook tells us that he spent the enforced lockdown honing his craft. "If you really love to receive love, then show those who love you how much you've improved yourself."[47] Jung Kook loves his hyungs and he loves ARMY. By observing BTS, he has developed a passion for music and by wanting to connect with ARMY, he works to develop himself.

thankyouarmy2020[48]

In 2020, alongside the release of BTS' album *Map of the Soul: 7*, *Connect, BTS* was also launched — an ambitious global art project that highlighted artists from around the world, across different mediums. *Connect, BTS*, for someone who has a talent for creating art, must have been very exciting for Jung Kook. "I think it means that everything is connected," he says with insight during a visit to the New York installation.[49] The connection he alludes to, I surmise, is his connection with the outside world, his peers, with his hyungs and, ultimately, his connection with himself and ARMY. "If there's something I can do, if our voices can give strength to people, then that's what we want and that's what we'll keep on doing," he vows during his UNICEF address,[50] offering his voice to comfort ARMY. Jung Kook's way of remaining connected to ARMY during 2020, was through his music.

JUNG KOOK: THE GOLDEN MAKNAE, A BORN SINGER

Following in *My Time's* footsteps, *Still With You*, Jung Kook's ethereal, jazzy solo track was released in June during BTS' annual Festa celebrations. In an exchange with *Variety*, Jung Kook shares that the song was written to work through his emotion during the COVID-19 outbreak.[51] It's not hard to imagine that being unable to perform, being unable to connect with fans and feel the energy and love from ARMY was one of the many difficulties Jung Kook faced. "It (the song) means that if the rain is a coronavirus, I will go to our fans even if the rain pours down," he tells *Weverse Magazine*.[42] Using his words and his voice, Jung Kook is offering to be a shelter for ARMY from the rain — a metaphor for the hurt, pain, and loneliness the pandemic has brought — which might be why *Still With You* opens with the sound of rain, drawing you into a comforting embrace as the ballad unfolds:

> Your faint voice that brushes past me
> Please call my name just one more time[52]

Still With You paints a vivid picture of Jung Kook alone in his room yearning for the attachment he's lost and continues the theme of disconnect he began with *My Time*. While the air conditioner is noisy, without the sound to fill the space, he would be swallowed by the silence. Alone with his thoughts, he longs to hear his name called — perhaps while he is on stage amidst ARMY who love him — to provide him with comfort. Across the world, people have been forced to remain isolated from loved ones. And while Jung Kook might live with the other members, he is separated from ARMY, his greatest source of love. Like so many of us have come to realise, there is no substitute for human touch — a call Jung Kook also makes in *My Time,* when he laments being unable to touch, to call, or to hold.

Jung Kook's bond with ARMY comes primarily from the euphoria of the stage. As he articulates during the *Grammy Mini Masterclass*, "Our ARMY and performing. I can live happily with those two."[53] ARMY forms an integral part of Jung Kook's identity and working hard to please ARMY, receiving love, appreciation, and affection from ARMY is something that brings him immense joy, satisfaction, and is in fact, his main motivator. After *Bang Bang Con: The Live*, Jung Kook writes ARMY a postcard and admits, "I realised once again during our concert that singing and dancing in front of ARMY is the reason I exist."[54] The connectedness to his purpose and goals becomes clear when he is amongst ARMY on stage, doing what he loves best. In the absence of physical connection, Jung Kook uses his songs as stories to describe his feelings. *Still With You* is therefore a love letter to fans after the cancellation of the *Map of the Soul World Tour*.

"When I meet you again, I'll look into your eyes and tell you I've missed you."[52] He chooses the word "when" and not "if", indicating that he is hopeful he will meet ARMY again, that our time together will return. The song is especially touching when he sings, "If I had known it would be like this, I would've kept more of them in my memories."[52] These lines are incredibly relatable as Jung Kook talks about the human experience of regret. Hindsight — especially in the midst of a pandemic where people are suffering unimaginable losses — affords all of us the opportunity to wonder about what we could have done differently, what we should have done — taken another look, paid more attention, said something more, or less.

Following *Still With You*, *Your Eyes Tell*, Jung Kook's second writing credit for 2020, tells the story of how love has transformative powers and can bring colour into the darkness of someone's existence. It also explores longing for, as well as seeking comfort from your loved one. While the song was most likely adapted to also reference the theme of the film soundtrack (OST) it features on, there are parallels to Jung Kook and his relationship with ARMY as well. Like *Still With You*, Jungkook's writing efforts in 2020 reference the distance he feels from ARMY and how the love that flows between himself and ARMY is a part of his identity. As *Your Eyes Tell* progresses, fear and doubt begin to colour the narrative as the subjects of the song begin to worry that they might be separated and left to face the world alone. "A future without you would be a world without colour, monochrome and cold".[55] The song laments the desperation of being separated from the person you love. However, there is also the promise of something wondrous and beautiful because it's only in the darkness that colour can really shine. Like in *Mikrokosmos*, when Jung Kook sings, "Starlight that shines more in the deepest night",[56] with *Your Eyes Tell* he is reminding us that the darkness — this difficult time we're all living through — holds beauty too. Jung Kook's eventual reunion with ARMY is the promise of a colourful tomorrow.

During *Bang Bang Con: The Live's* ending ment (the time during a concert when BTS share their thoughts with ARMY) Jung Kook admitted that by watching fan videos of their concerts, he was able to simulate the fervour of being on stage.[57] *Still With You* was born from this yearning to experience vivid flashbacks of emotion. Despite their melancholy notes, *Still With You* and *Your Eyes Tell* do feel hopeful and uplifting too, turning the focus to the promise of the future. Much like Jung Kook's current reality, where there is no definitive ending to the pandemic, so too *Your Eyes Tell* ends without a concrete resolution. However, despite an uncertain future, like Jung Kook and ARMY, the song's protagonists remain hopeful that they will find a way back to each other. *Still With You* ends with Jung Kook lamenting that "even if our steps might be in different frequencies, I'd like to walk on this path with you".[52] As Jc points out in her blog for *Bulletproof*,[58] this sentiment harkens back to Jung Kook's words in a conversation with *Dispatch*. "I will always be here. You can come any time you want to see me, and when you need to leave, you can leave at any time."[59] He's saying even if you've left him, even if your steps are not aligned or in sync, whenever you're ready to come back, he will be waiting to walk beside you. I'm reminded of *My Time* too, where Jung Kook's steps are out of sync with the world around him. Yet despite that, he still offers to proverbially adjust his gait to stride beside ARMY.

Yeah we are not seven, with you[60]

In exploring Jung Kook's euphoria, I would be remiss to not mention his solo song of the same name. Unlike *Begin* and *My Time* which are autobiographical, *Euphoria* is not. The song is intricately tied into

BTS' alternative universe storyline where each member plays a different character in a complex storyline spanning multiple albums. *Euphoria* forms part of the *Love Yourself* series and is — from a storytelling perspective — a prelude to *Love Yourself: Her*, even though it was released after and only features on the final album in the series, *Love Yourself: Answer*. Whether a coincidence or not, *Euphoria* is also a beginning, just like Jung Kook's first solo track. As the trilogy is based on the concept of eventually learning to love yourself, *Euphoria* is the start of the journey towards self-love and self-acceptance.

In 2020, Jung Kook continued his journey towards loving himself. *My Time*, while not strictly speaking about the concept in linear terms, I do believe has elements of the intent. Jung Kook's vow to find his time and reconnect with others and his promise to himself to shed his isolation and loneliness, point towards prioritising his needs. Furthermore, *Map of the Soul: 7*, I would also argue, is a valentine to ARMY, as BTS' persona — the face they show to the world — *is* ARMY. The entire album is filled with references to their struggles, but also how through ARMY's love and support, they have found healing, contentment, and self-love.

> Throw stones at me
> We're not afraid anymore
> We are we are together bulletproof (Yeah we have you have you)
> Even if another winter comes,
> even if someone stops me, I walk forward
> We are we are forever bulletproof (Yeah we got to heaven)[60]

In the music video for *We Are Bulletproof: The Eternal*, BTS reference their *Wings Tour Final Trilogy III* performance of *Born Singer* where they face ARMY on stage. With a kaleidoscopic purple ocean of ARMY surrounding them like stars, their tears flow as they run towards us, their *Mikrokosmos*. Jung Kook and his hyungs began their journey as only seven, but became bulletproof through the love that ARMY bestowed upon them. They achieved heaven on earth. Relieved, Jung Kook softly whispers the final verse, "Yeah we are not seven, with you."[60]

My Time: My life has been a movie all the time[14]

The golden maknae

Like *We Are Bulletproof: The Eternal*, BTS' *Mikrokosmos* conjures fantastical images of star-studded galaxies, distant moons, and glittering dreams. Jung Kook's opening verse of *Mikrokosmos* is filled with references to celestial bodies, singing "we're all shining".[56] This imagery reminds me of the way RM once described Jung Kook. "He's changed from a boy to shining the most like a man."[61] Shining. Glittering. Like *gold*.

Jung Kook has been associated with gold — a metaphorical representation of being gifted, talented, successful, or prosperous — practically since debut. Due to his seemingly endless array of skills, RM nicknamed him the 'Golden Maknae' — as everything he touched seemed to turn to gold. Jung Kook's uncanny ability to excel at the ordinary — winning a game during an episode of *Run BTS!* — or the extraordinary — beautifully capturing BTS at their finest during one of his Golden Closet Films (G.C.F) — is legendary within the fandom. Jung Kook's talents span singing, dancing, rapping, sports, gaming, drawing and painting, cinematography, producing, and even cooking. Particularly noteworthy is Jung Kook's keen eye for light and colour, movement and texture, skills he highlights through his interest in filmmaking, as well as art. Neither RM, nor Jung Kook, could have imagined how the moniker would eventually evolve into a facet of Jung Kook's personal brand.

During an *Ask Anything* Q&A in October, Jung Kook was asked what talent he had cultivated during the pandemic. "(I found) That I have a talent for art," he replied.[62] Naturally gifted, his sketches, paintings, and doodles have long showcased his ability to capture moments and bring them to life on paper or canvas. His creations have been displayed at BTS exhibitions — most notably his painting of Suga from the *Wings* short film — which I believe is a staggering example of his raw talent. BTS members often comment on Jung Kook's golden capabilities by praising his limitless potential and sharing their admiration for his skills. "You're a genius!"[26] j-hope quips during their *BE-hind 'Full' Story* conversation when Jung Kook describes his ability to create music from scratch. In a 2020 *Bangtan Bomb, Jung Kook's Art Class*,[63] he effortlessly sketches on a whiteboard, much to j-hope's astonishment. "It's crazy good!"[47] he exclaims, echoing his disbelief during *In the Soop* when Jung Kook painted two vistas on canvas with the same ease. These feats have earned him additional titles like "Bob Ross"[47] or "Jung Kook Picasso"[62] in deference to his artistic flair.

His golden nickname, however, would also come to carry with it the weighty expectation of perfection. While it is quite clear that Jung Kook is naturally competitive and challenges himself to do better and be better, his strive for improvement does bring with it dangers for his emotional and physical wellbeing — as evidenced by his offstage collapse during *Burn the Stage,* when knowing his body was not in peak condition, he pushed himself nonetheless to ensure ARMY had the best possible experience.[37] Despite the perception that Jung Kook is good at everything he tries, he admits that this is not always the case. In fact, it's the expectation others have of him that fuels his compulsion to live up to being the Golden Maknae. In 2020's *Break the Silence*, Jung Kook shares, "People call me the Golden Maknae, but that's not how I feel, so I have to try harder to make myself appear that way."[64] For someone who was given the nickname in his early teens, it cannot be easy to constantly be under scrutiny. In a candid conversation with *Paper Magazine*, Jung Kook admits to feeling the "pressure" of fame.[65] When asked about the greatest challenge they face as a group, Jung Kook points to his fear of disappointing anyone due to his actions. "I realised that I should think twice before I do anything, and not forget where I am," he says.[65] Jung Kook has learnt that with fame comes unimaginable public examination, compounded by the expectation that he governs himself according to an impossible golden standard.

In 2018, Jung Kook shared a poem he wrote called, 'Gold', where he explores what being golden means to him, and shows that in spite of the burden of perfection, he is immensely grateful, humble, and proud to be celebrated for his talent.

> When my mother had me
> She dreamed about golden rain
> Wherever the rain goes, things turn golden
> I could not do anything
> I met you in the golden time
> I find myself starting to shine
> At first I was gold
> I looked around after a while
> Everything around me
> Turned into gold
> I don't want to lose
> This priceless light[66]

Moreover, Jung Kook's pride at being called the Golden Maknae is further evidenced by the fact that he named his music studio the Golden Closet, and his short films all carry the Golden Closet Film (G.C.F) title. "Stay gold", Jung Kook sings in BTS' music video of the same name, literally bathed in luminous golden light. "Until the end of time. Forever gold".[67]

I just paint my feelings onto the song[26]

In 2020, BTS tried their best to remain gold, but ultimately used their experience of life in isolation — their anger, their pain, their yearning for an existence that was gone, and their acceptance of a different future — and poured it into their album, *BE*. The entire album was completely autobiographical and exists in fact, *because* of the pandemic, once again proving that from devastation, something beautiful can emerge and flourish. Along with cultivating his cinematography skills as the director for the *Life Goes On* music video, *BE* also gifted Jung Kook with two writing credits for *Telepathy* and *Stay*. In Jung Kook's *BE-hind 'Full' Story* sit down, he talks about his growing capabilities to write music. "I feel quite comfortable about participating in composing now [...] I get to take part and my opinions are reflected in the work."[26] This admission is a far cry from the 2017 *Wings* concept book interview when he admitted knowing very little about composing and producing.[45]

During Jung Kook's *BE-hind 'Full Story'* reel, when j-hope asks him about his songwriting process, Jung Kook articulates his philosophy quite beautifully. "I don't try to force myself onto a song. I will break it,"[26] he says, gesturing with his hands, his ARMY tattoo shifting in the light. "Instead I just paint my feelings onto the song as if I'm colouring."[26] The metaphor is beautiful and runs parallel to both the literal use of colour he references in *Your Eyes Tell*, as well as his artistic talent with paint on canvas. Like his approach to music, instead of squeezing something into a predetermined mound, he has the ability to reshape it and create whatever he wants.

In 2020, two tracks Jung Kook wrote for his mixtape were included in BTS albums instead. *Your Eyes Tell* for *Map of the Soul:7 - The Journey* and *Stay* for *BE*. While *Your Eyes Tell* was a song Jung Kook admits suits his overall aesthetic very well, and *My Time* was a very personal, vulnerable self-portrait, *Stay* has a different energy altogether. Jung Kook tends to gravitate towards sad, melancholy ballads, but mentor Bang Si-hyuk advised him to consider songs from multiple perspectives.[26] Jung Kook is not only a vocalist, but he is also a dancer. Therefore writing songs is not only about personal preference. The entire experience of the song is enhanced when considering it from various perspectives — lyrics, the emotion, inflection, and tone when singing, as well as the performance it might birth on stage. In 2020, Jung Kook proved again that he was stepping outside of his comfort zone and creating something that could appeal to different types of people. Ultimately, Jung Kook's goal is to be able to tell any story, in any genre, to any audience, and have it be an experience anyone can relate to.[26] *Stay* was conceived from his effort to step away from ballads and create something different.

At the *BTS Global Press Conference for BE*, Jung Kook expands on the message behind *Stay*, particularly since it was partly inspired by the pandemic. "I think we are far apart physically, but we always stay together," he says.[68] Again, Jung Kook circles back to connection, emphasising once more how important connecting to others is to him. *Stay* exudes festival vibes and while it inspires you to move, the song strikes a surprisingly tender chord — another reminder of the time in which it was created. While *Stay* is fun and uplifting, Jung Kook created a song that is also deliberately sentimental.

As a storytelling technique, Jung Kook is using his music to share his loneliness and isolation from his fans, but also to use it as a bridge in which to reach out. The song opens with Jin and Jung Kook questioning whether their memories of being on stage with ARMY is nothing more than a dream. Jung Kook continues the second verse with, "I quietly cast a spell",[69] reminding me of another magical reference in BTS' discography, *Magic Shop*. Like *Stay*, *Magic Shop* coincidentally is another song co-written by Jung Kook about ARMY. Inside the *Magic Shop*, BTS and ARMY seek comfort within one another.

"Together, wherever"[70] the passage ends, indicating that time and distance no longer matter because between BTS and ARMY there is an unspoken and unbroken bond that endures even during this forced separation. *Stay* opens with Jung Kook and Jin waking and wondering whether their memories of ARMY are a dream. By contrast, the song ends with Jung Kook closing his eyes and realising that it wasn't a dream and that he is forever with ARMY. *Stay* is a reminder that although BTS and ARMY can't meet in person right now, they are, and will always, be together, connected.

I'm reminded of a small moment during BTS' *Life Goes On* performance at the 2020 *Melon Music Awards*.[23] The stage design is all dark blues and indigos, with hundreds of little lights twinkling to simulate the night sky. The stars are ARMY, suspended in and around the members — connected despite space and time. "I remember",[1] V and Jimin harmonise, while incandescent, purple confetti joins the twinkling lights to heighten the poignant, dream-like atmosphere. On stage, Jung Kook looks up at the simulated sky, his gaze transfixed on the images of the hundreds of ARMY projected above. Like the stars, ARMY are Jung Kook's light, and the awareness that *Life Goes On* will sustain us until we can be together once more.

Conclusion: Life goes on, let's live on[50]

BTS' Golden Maknae embodies love — love for the hyungs who raised him, cared for him, and treated him so well. Love for the stage, the home that welcomes him, energises him, and inspires him. And love for his ARMY, whose consistent efforts have gifted him his beginning, continue to inspire his euphoria, and who will help him reconnect and find his time.

"Until my arms, my feet, my lungs are worn out, until my voice is exhausted, I want to keep singing," Jung Kook vows during a *You Quiz on the Block* appearance.[32] I'm filled with goosebumps every time I read his oath, in awe of his fervent devotion. Singing, something once so foreign to him, has become his life's passion. "A born singer!" the host of *Let's BTS* exclaims after Suga extolled Jung Kook's talents.[71] Yes, a born singer with a golden heart.

In early 2020, Jung Kook was asked to deliver a message to his future self. His response stuck with me. "Please be happy," he says with a smile.[72] Despite it all — the wealth, the fame, the notoriety, the ups and downs — Jung Kook is just like you and I. He longs for happiness, for better days, for love, and for affiliation. It's the same sentiment he echoed in October during the final day of their virtual *Map of the Soul ON:E* concert. "To hear your voices after so long is really moving," he confesses.[73] Sweating and tired, Jung Kook veritably beams from his happy place — on stage with BTS and ARMY — his energy restored, his heart full. "I'm really happy."[73]

References

[1] BTS. (2020) Life goes on [Song]. On *BE*. Big Hit Entertainment; Doyoubangtan. (2020). *Life goes on* [Translation]. https://doyoubangtan.wordpress.com/2020/11/20/life-goes-on/

[2] Kpop Channel TV. (2020). *BTS American hustle life episode 8* [Video]. https://www.dailymotion.com/video/x7xjdrq

[3] BANGTANTV. (2020). [EPISODE] BTS (방탄소년단) @ Dick Clark's New Year's Rockin' Eve 2020 [Video]. https://youtu.be/Mxu7et015mo

[4] Jeong, E. (2020). *Why BTS runs the world*. https://www.wsj.com/articles/bts-cover-story-interview-be-new-album-dynamite-11605114374

[5] @GirlWithLuv24. (2020). *Jungkook's love for ARMY : "I felt like I was just thinking about ARMY" "the volume of ARMY* [Tweet]. https://twitter.com/GirlWithLuv24/status/1280885282879893505?s=20

[6] Park, J. (Director). (2018). I can't stop (Season 1, Episode 5) [TV series episode]. In "Hitman" Bang (Executive producer), *Burn the stage*. https://youtu.be/j6zWwAoEi_w

[7] BTS. (2016) Begin [Song]. On *Wings*. Big Hit Entertainment; Doolset. (2018). *Begin* [Translation]. https://doolsetbangtan.wordpress.com/2018/06/14/begin/

[8] Bangtan Subs. (2020). [ENG] 200101 [BANGTAN BOMB] Happy New Year 2020! - BTS (방탄소년단) [Video]. https://youtu.be/xmuhphr5gbQ

[9] Stein, M. (1998). *Jung's map of the soul: An introduction* (Illustrated ed., Vol. 5). Open Court.

[10] Bookish Theories. (2020). *BTS Jungkook my time explained: Lyrics and map of the soul: One performance breakdown and analysis* [Video]. https://youtu.be/CInvQefYMS0

[11] BANGTANTV. (2020). *BTS global press conference "Map of the soul : 7"* [Video]. https://youtu.be/akn5Uemr4Wc

12. *BTS' My biography: Jungkook (Japan FC)*. (2020). https://jungkooktimes.com/2020/10/03/bts-my-biography-jungkook-japan-fc/
13. YouTube Originals. (2020). *Full replay: Dear class of 2020* [Video]. https://youtu.be/rxpTjcouaeQ
14. BTS. (2020) My time [Song]. On *Map of the Soul:7*. Big Hit Entertainment; Doyoubangtan. (2020). *My time* [Translation]. https://doyoubangtan.wordpress.com/2020/02/21/my-time/
15. BTS. (2020). *Map of the soul ON:E*. Seoul, South Korea: Olympic Gymnastics Arena.
16. BTS universe. (2020). BTS (방탄소년단) Full interview with Spotify | Meaning of their solo songs, MOTS: 7 and old playlists [Video]. https://youtu.be/DnmO9o7W1JE
17. BTS. (2013) Born singer [Song]. On *SoundCloud*. Big Hit Entertainment; Doolset. (2018). *Born singer* [Translation]. https://doolsetbangtan.wordpress.com/2018/06/01/born-singer/
18. *BTS' Jungkook trended at #1 worldwide and in the US after his My Time performance on MOTS ON:E online concert*. (2020). https://www.allkpop.com/article/2020/10/bts-jungkook-trended-at-1-worldwide-and-in-the-us-after-his-my-time-performance-on-mots-one-online-concert
19. @jeonfolders. (2020). *Jungkook — Praises and appreciation for his vocals from producers, critics, singers, vocal coaches/trainers, etc*. [Tweet]. https://twitter.com/jeonfolders/status/1340669221093605376?s=20
20. @jeonglitters. (2021). *a long thread of BTS' main vocalist, Jeon Jungkook getting recognised & praised for his outstanding, unique and skilful vocals* [Tweet]. https://twitter.com/jeonglitters/status/1354823047220346880?s=20
21. @BtsJapanese. (2020). *(trans) japan fc magazine vol 8. Jungkook Biography* [Tweet]. https://twitter.com/BtsJapanese/status/1313471421125808128?s=20
22. The Late Late Show with James Corden. (2020). *BTS carpool karaoke* [Video]. https://youtu.be/T4x7sDevVTY

23. BANGTANTV. (2020). BTS (방탄소년단) Black Swan Perf. + ON + Life Goes On + Dynamite @ 2020 MMA [Video]. https://youtu.be/PtaP4UkZKyc
24. NPR Music. (2020). *BTS: Tiny desk (Home) concert* [Video]. https://youtu.be/gFYAXsa7pe8
25. Vaeyung. (2021). *[Bridge] Jungkook (BTS) "Dis-ease" demo ver.* [Video]. https://youtu.be/6DkaXgKookE
26. BANGTANTV. (2021). BTS (방탄소년단) Jung Kook's BE-hind "full" story [Video]. https://youtu.be/ZOwcwjC4D7A
27. BANGTANTV. (2020). [2020 FESTA] BTS (방탄소년단) Answer : BTS 3 units "Jamais Vu" Song by Jin & j-hope & Jung Kook [Video]. https://youtu.be/4XnDtD6uTgo
28. Full Sail University. (2019). *The making of "BTS - Euphoria" | Full sail university* [Video]. https://youtu.be/NqM1shar6O4
29. @SleepDeez. (2020). *He can sing in full voice better than a lot of singers I've ever heard without his voice breaking* [Tweet]. https://twitter.com/SleepDeez/status/1235031132271300608?s=20
30. @bts_twt. (2020). *Never not* [Tweet]. https://twitter.com/BTS_twt/status/1256648835272605697?s=20
31. Bangtan Subs. (2014). *[Eng] 131019 [Episode] BTS letter to ARMY in birthday party* [Video]. https://youtu.be/0Btb2esy5qU
32. *BTS' Jungkook reminisces his first days in Seoul, his fears & realizations on BTS' "You quiz on the block" show.* (2021). Swahili Seven. https://kenyabtsarmy.com/2021/03/24/bts-jungkook-reminisces-his-first-days-in-seoul-his-fears-realizations-on-bts-you-quiz-on-the-block-show/
33. BTS. (2018). *[V Live] BTS live : JK* [Video]. https://www.vlive.tv/video/94185
34. Bang S. & Lenzo Y (Executive Producers). (2020). *BTS In the soop* [TV Show]. Big Hit Entertainment.
35. @ktaebwi. (2017). *[TRANS] OSEN interview w/ Bang Shi Hyuk PD (3/3)* [Blog Post]. https://ktaebwi.tumblr.com/post/159953723607

36 BTS. (2018) Euphoria [Song]. On *Love Yourself: Answer*. Big Hit Entertainment; Doolset. (2018). *Euphoria* [Translation]. https://doolsetbangtan.wordpress.com/2018/06/01/euphoria/

37 Park, J. (Director). (2018). Just give me a smile (Season 1, Episode 3) [TV series episode]. In "Hitman" Bang (Executive producer), *Burn the stage*. https://dai.ly/x7u8o9j

38 @modooborahae. (2020). *"my first and last role model" "my eternal leader" "my rapmon hyung"* [Tweet]. https://twitter.com/modooborahae/status/1272899400604569603?s=20

39 Holmes, D. (2020,). *The boundless optimism of BTS.* https://www.esquire.com/entertainment/music/a34654383/bts-members-be-album-interview-2020/

40 Bandura, A. (1976). *Social learning theory* (1st ed.). Prentice-Hall.

41 Park, J. (2020). You can call me idol (Season 1, Episode 2) [TV series episode]. In "Hitman" Bang (Executive producer), *Break the silence*. https://www.weverse.io/bts/media/2090

42 Kang, M. (2020). *Jung Kook "I hope this feeling never fades."* https://magazine.weverse.io/bridge/en/61

43 Bang S. & Lenzo Y (2020). BTS cooking challenge (Season 1, Episode 7) [TV series episode] In "Hitman" Bang (Executive producer), *In the soop*. https://www.weverse.io/bts/media/3495

44 KPOP vine. (2020). BTS (방탄소년단) - "In the soop" (Full ver.) LYRICS [Video]. https://youtu.be/uSg1oahT3ic

45 @_puriiizu_. (2017). *BTS wings concept book [Eng]* [Interview Translation]. https://www.wattpad.com/445024335-bts-wings-concept-book-eng-%E2%9D%9D-interview-jungkook-%E2%9D%9E

46 Duckworth, A. L., Peterson, C., Matthews, M. D., & Kelly, D. R. (2007). Grit: Perseverance and passion for long-term goals. *Journal of Personality and Social Psychology*, 92(6), 1087–1101. https://doi.org/10.1037/0022-3514.92.6.1087

47 Bang S. & Lenzo Y (2020). Together, and on their own (Season 1, Episode 6) [TV series episode] In "Hitman" Bang (Executive producer), *In the soop*. https://www.weverse.io/bts/media/3438

JUNG KOOK: THE GOLDEN MAKNAE, A BORN SINGER

48 @jeonggukupdates. (2020). *Still With You - an original song produced by Jungkook, sung by Jungkook. File name: thankyouarmy2020* [Tweet]. Twitter. https://twitter.com/jeonggukupdates/status/1268564626989445120?s=20

49 BANGTANTV. (2020). [BANGTAN BOMB] BTS at the CONNECT, BTS exhibition in New York - BTS (방탄소년단) [Video]. https://youtu.be/fXXl_ENR4Ak

50 UNICEF. (2020). *BTS return to the United Nations | UNICEF* [Video]. https://youtu.be/lVbod1-Nx7A

51 Davis, R. (2020). *BTS is what the world needs now: Band members talk going global, the responsibility of being role models.* https://variety.com/2020/music/news/bts-members-talk-going-global-1234791114/

52 BTS. (2020) Still with you [Song]. On *SoundCloud*. Big Hit Entertainment; Doolset. (2020). *Still with you (Jungkook)* [Translation]. https://doolsetbangtan.wordpress.com/2020/06/04/still-with-you-jungkook/

53 Prudential Center. (2020). BTS (방탄소년단) - Mini masterclass [Video]. https://youtu.be/GuZJWDX4pTQ

54 *Dear. ARMY Special Postcard from BTS Jungkook. (2020).* Swahili Seven. *https://kenyabtsarmy.com/2020/10/29/dear-army-special-postcard-from-bts-jung-kook/*

55 BTS. (2019) Your eyes tell [Song]. On *Map of the soul:7 - The journey*. Big Hit Entertainment; BTSTrans. (2020). *Your eyes tell* [Translation]. https://bts-trans.tumblr.com/post/623808534091644928/jpneng-lyrics-your-eyes-tell-by-bts

56 BTS. (2019) Mikrokosmos [Song]. On *Map of the soul: persona*. Big Hit Entertainment; Doyoubangtan. (2020). *Mikrokosmos* [Translation]. https://doolsetbangtan.wordpress.com/2019/04/13/mikrokosmos/

57 *BTS shares heartfelt messages and future worries at the end of Bang bang con: The live.* (2020). https://btsbomb.com/bts-members-bang-bang-con-ending-speech/

58. *Still with you and your eyes tell: a glimpse of Jung Kook's heart.* (2020). https://link.medium.com/5cygvwfWMfb
59. Doyoubangtan, V. A. P. B. (2018). *"BTS, the road to the sea."* https://doyoubangtan.wordpress.com/2018/04/20/translation-of-dispatch-dicons-bts-interview-bts-the-road-to-the-sea/
60. BTS. (2020) We are bulletproof: the eternal [Song]. On *Map of the soul: 7*. Big Hit Entertainment; Doyoubangtan. (2020). *We are bulletproof: the eternal* [Translation]. https://doyoubangtan.wordpress.com/2020/03/09/we-are-bulletproof-the-eternal/
61. K Things. (2018). *[ENG SUB][180729] We love BTS -how members think about jk- charms of Jungkook* [Video]. https://youtu.be/wH8hn-neExQ
62. AskAnythingChat. (2020). *BTS 2 minutes of pure chaos bonus footage* [Video]. https://youtu.be/MKVc4hUtpwY
63. BANGTANTV. (2020). [Bangtan bomb] Jung Kook's art class - BTS (방탄소년단) [Video]. https://youtu.be/zbSYc62O-pg
64. Park, J. (2020). The opposite side (Season 1, Episode 5) [TV series episode]. In "Hitman" Bang (Executive producer), *Break the silence*. https://www.weverse.io/bts/media/2120
65. Russell, E. (2019). *Break the internet: BTS*. https://www.papermag.com/break-the-internet-bts-2641354203.html
66. BTS. (2018). *Run BTS! 2018 - EP.56* [Video]. https://www.vlive.tv/video/81492
67. BTS. (2020) Stay gold [Song]. On *Map of the soul: 7 - The journey*. Big Hit Entertainment; BTS-TRANS. (2020). *Stay gold* [Translation]. https://bts-trans.tumblr.com/post/621375036365881344/jpneng-lyrics-still-gold-by-bts
68. HYBE LABELS. (2020). BTS (방탄소년단) global press conference "BE" (+ENG) [Video]. https://youtu.be/T31mfmw8bS8
69. BTS. (2018) Magic shop [Song]. On *Love yourself: Tear*. Big Hit Entertainment; Doyoubangtan. (2018). *Magic shop* [Translation]. https://doyoubangtan.wordpress.com/2018/05/24/love-yourself-tear-track-07-magic-shop/

JUNG KOOK: THE GOLDEN MAKNAE, A BORN SINGER

70. BTS. (2020) Stay [Song]. On *BE*. Big Hit Entertainment; Doyoubangtan. (2020). *Stay* [Translation]. https://doyoubangtan.wordpress.com/2020/11/20/stay/
71. KBS WORLD TV. (2021). *ARMY lights the way for us (Let's BTS!) l Eng l KBS World TV 210330* [Video]. https://youtu.be/YDLBTN5sHlc
72. MTV News. (2020). *BTS deliver heartfelt messages to their future selves for "Map of the soul: 7" | MTV News* [Video]. https://youtu.be/e57S-6RCDIY
73. Youth Lover. (2021). *BTS - full online concert- BTS map of the soul ONE (with eng sub) "watch till end"* [Video].https://youtu.be/Wgvx7PtmEec

V

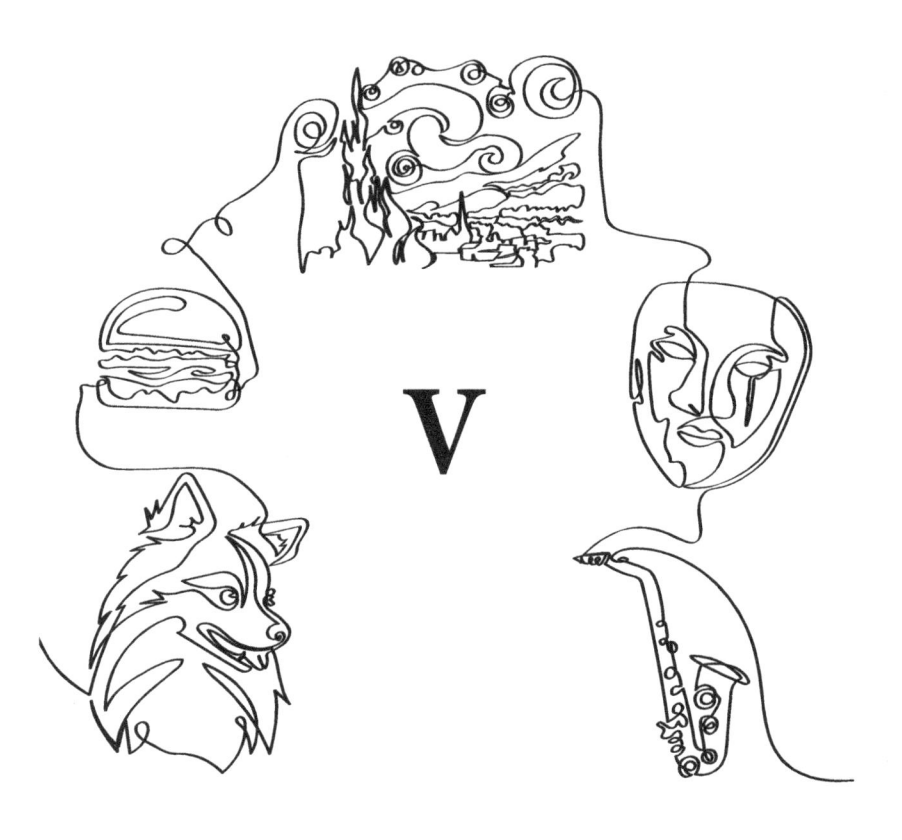

BOTH ART AND ARTIST
Demie Tuzara and Manilyn Gumapas

> "ARMY... You are all part of my story, memory, and scenery."
> — V, Love Yourself Tour in Singapore, 19 January 2019[1]

It's December 30th, 2020. V of BTS, birth name Kim Taehyung, is celebrating his 26th birthday with a livestream on VLive.[2] On Twitter, 'HAPPY V DAY' and other hashtags and greetings have been trending before his actual birthday, occupying the top four of the worldwide trends. '#HAPPYVDAY' amassed five million tweets on his actual birthday, the most tweeted birthday tag for an idol.[3]

In the livestream, V's favourite strawberry cake is in front of him as he thanks ARMY for all the birthday wishes, as well as charity donations made in his name and birthday billboards that even trended in South Korea. He proposes the viewers of the livestream sing *Happy Birthday*, and he claps along with ARMY virtually singing his birthday greeting. From the American Eagle billboards in New York's Time Square to the Burj Khalifa in Dubai, ARMY from all over the world are doing their bit to show their appreciation for V on his birthday.[4]

It's mere hours until the end of 2020. V connects with ARMY the way he does best, communicating with them through social media and making his presence online known. From his VLives and YouTube streams to his posts on Twitter and Weverse, V's interactions with ARMY were a constant throughout 2020 despite the roadblocks and the physical restrictions that COVID-19 imposed on the world. This is one of the many aspects about V that make him who he is: a comfort to ARMY through the good and the bad, offering unconditional love no matter the circumstance. It was he who coined the famous phrase "I purple you", after all, declaring his love for ARMY as solid, reliable, and everlasting as the last colour of the rainbow.[5]

V's unconditional love made all the difference for ARMY in 2020. Although 2020 was a challenging year, it did nothing to deter the members of BTS and their drive to produce more content in an effort to stay connected with ARMY more than ever amid the pandemic. V in particular had a very fruitful year, with the most viewed fancam in 2020,[6] the most viewed solo VLive in real time,[7] the most streamed Korean soloist on Soundcloud with his songs *Scenery* and *Winter Bear*,[8] and being the only artist worldwide to achieve the most #1s on iTunes with the single *Sweet Night*.[9] V's 2020 is a portrait of works he shared with the world from the bottom of his heart, painted with a brush that has been in evolution since his debuts as both music and visual artist. In examining this portrait closely, we can begin to understand V's own *story, memory, and scenery*. Through each of these, we see V's unmatched skill to transform the most powerful force in the world — love — into an art form of its own through his music and his art. V is love personified, from his love for his fellow members of BTS to his love of ARMY, from his love of nature and art to his love of the world around him.

Story: I still wonder, wonder, beautiful story[10]

> "I want to open not our stories, but other people's stories through our music. People have happy, sad, and painful stories. We want to take those stories and make them into music."
>
> — V (2016)[11]

V: BOTH ART AND ARTIST

It is January 17th, and BTS' first release of the year, *Black Swan,* has just dropped. With a narrative of self-doubt and insecurities superimposed with the anxiety of dying a 'first death' when it comes to one's passion, the song is a confession of the fear of losing one's drive and no longer feeling connected to what one loves to do. V's own lyrics within the song — the penultimate line of which is sung by Jimin — illustrates the beginning sensations of this first death: "A slow heartbeat in my ears / Bump, bump, bump / Trying to escape with no avail / Jump, jump, jump / No tune affects me anymore / Weeping a silent cry".[12] The interpretation of such a haunting concept is visceral, the anecdote hitting close to home for V himself who opened up about his own personal struggles and his experience of burnout that we subsequently discovered towards the latter part of 2020. This relatable illustration would only be the beginning of many more that V would offer ARMY in 2020.

There is an eerie quality and dark imagery to *Black Swan* that brings a sense of familiarity from songs in their previous albums, and specifically in earlier song releases that prominently featured V. Similar to *Black Swan,* this concept of inconsolability is consistent throughout the lyrics of *Stigma,* V's first solo release from the group's fourth studio album *Wings*. In *Stigma,* V sings, "Deeper, deeper, the wound just gets deeper / Like pieces of broken glass that I can't reverse / Deeper, it's just the heart that hurts every day";[13] this cutting and dispirited energy mirrors that of *Black Swan*. *Stigma* had seen V debut his own original sound and begin cultivating his musical self-expression and style. It sets the foundation to V's sound that is unique to his own, and delves into the layers of his blooming artistry. A unique song that blended staccato vocals, intense falsettos, and spoken dialogue, V's self-described neo-soul track established itself as the beginning of his explored musical style, a stylistic expression of intentional storytelling that is still evident in his song releases today.

That same dark and intense lyrical and sound production followed in V's song *Singularity* from *Love Yourself: Tear,* the second instalment of BTS' *Love Yourself* trilogy. An R&B slow jam featuring a languid bass and hypnotising melody, *Singularity* is a song about self-identity, battling between one's true self and their persona. The lyrics in *Singularity's* pre-choruses intimates the same ominous melancholy established in both *Black Swan* and *Stigma*: "The pain in my throat gets worse / Try to cover it / I don't have a voice" and "Have I lost myself / Or have I gained you".[14] As V's second official solo track in the group's collective musical endeavours, this introduction to the *Love Yourself: Tear* album showcased another side to V's artistry that ARMY hadn't yet been exposed to: a sense of mystery, angst, and sensuality.

Dark, brooding and mysterious, the narratives of both *Stigma* and *Singularity* are analogous to *Black Swan*. Through the lyricism and its conceptual delivery, they all reflect the same intense imagery and enigmatic sound that V embodies extremely well. A vivid storyteller through his unique soundscape and musical craftsmanship, V has the ability to make his listeners feel what he is feeling, and also reflect further on their own feelings. Adept in his multidisciplinary approach to his work, V possesses a deep emotional understanding of his art that he consistently showcases to ARMY and the rest of the world.

Storytelling as an art and inspiration through the stories in curated art is a concept that V is quite familiar with. As an admirer of art himself and an enthusiast of contemporary painters such as Vincent Van Gogh, Gustav Klimt, and Jean-Michel Basquiat, it's fitting for V to understand the processes of sharing art with the world. In the *Bangtan Bomb: Preparing for Connect, BTS*, V encouraged the audience to view art through their own lens, "Rather than thinking art is too difficult, view the exhibition and focus on your own experiences and emotions. Then, I'm sure it will be a valuable experience."[15] This is what makes V's own art inimitable and unique to his own style: As seen in *Stigma*, *Singularity*, and his subsequent releases, V creates art in a way that tells not only his story, but allows others to relate with their own stories.

V himself demonstrated relating to artwork in a video that focused on one of the exhibitions titled *Catharsis* by Danish artist Jakob Steensen. V commented on the immersive installation of the forest and related it to a trip to New Zealand with the members, featured in the fourth season of their reality travel show *Bon Voyage*. He recalled the clear blue sky and the white snow mountains of New Zealand and how the views reminded him of the digital reimagined forest simulation, sharing that, "I still haven't forgotten the preciousness of Mother Nature and the happiness I felt from it."[16]

V using nature as inspiration for storytelling in his work is something that is consistent throughout his artistry. One year prior to the launch of *Connect, BTS*, V had released *Scenery*, his first musical solo venture outside of BTS' collective discography. A musical release unlike anything we had yet to hear from V's previous work, *Scenery* ventured towards a more personal soundscape. Self-produced and self-written, the track carried a more nostalgic and intimate feel than what we have been previously exposed to. A pop ballad dedicated as a gift to ARMY, the song is more personal to V as Kim Taehyung. With V's natural, baritone vocals over a melodic piano instrumental, the song is a mixture of Korean and English and details a wistful experience of spectating moments. There is a sense of longing in the lyrics, telling a sentimental story of the narrator's wandering heart and the contemplation of both past and future.

Memory: *Yesterday's you, now it's all clear*[17]

> "It will be okay, because today's me is doing fine"
> — *Inner Child* (2020)[17]

With the release of *Map of the Soul: 7*, the theme of contemplating both past and future continued. In addition to songs featuring all seven members of BTS, V appeared in subunit songs such as *Friends*, alongside Jimin, and *Zero O'Clock*, featuring all four members of BTS' vocal line: Jung Kook, Jimin, Jin, and V himself.

V's solo track *Inner Child* credited him as lyricist and composer in the official Korean Music and Copyright Association website,[18] his first songwriting credit of 2020 following his 2019 release *Winter Bear*. The fourteenth track of *Map of the Soul: 7*, *Inner Child*, is V's musical illustration of *inner child work*, a psychological practice explored by Carl Jung.

> "In every adult there lurks a child — an eternal child, something that is always becoming, is never completed and calls for unceasing care, attention and education. That is the part of the human personality which wants to develop and become whole."
>
> — Carl Jung, 1954[19]

A child archetype linked to past experiences and memories of innocence, creativity, and playfulness along with hope for the future, the inner child of our unconscious mind is a part of us that 'never grew up'. It is the subconscious capacity of the psyche that retained its wonder for life and curiosity for the world. A person's inner child is integral to their psychological well-being and can be identified as a source of strength as experiences in someone's early life can play a significant part in their development as an adult.

Applying this knowledge to V's solo track, it allows us to delve into his identity as a trainee idol and also his craftsmanship as a musician. A press release revealed that *Inner Child* is "a song to V's past self back when he was going through a rough time."[20] In comparing V's younger self — the seventeen-year-old Daegu native who auditioned and became a trainee for Big Hit — to the twenty-six-year-old, Grammy-nominated artist he is now, it is evident that such an evolution was not one without significant change and hardships.

> At that time, we had it tough
> While looking up at those stars in the sky, too far out of reach
> You at that time, didn't believe in galaxies
> But I saw it, a silver galaxy[17]

This opening verse immediately sets the scene, introducing V's past struggles as he recalls the experiences and memories from his trainee years. Assigned with the role of the "Secret Weapon"[21] in the group, V was not revealed to the public until they officially debuted. In his first vlog on

V: BOTH ART AND ARTIST

BANGTAN TV, V confessed how being the hidden member made him feel lonely. "When all of the members were shooting for their own logs, I was the only one who couldn't, so I was very sad," he shared.[22] The younger version of himself being unable to "believe in galaxies" alludes to the uncertainty he felt about such moments in his life: his intense training as an idol, his dream of debuting and making it in the cut-throat industry, all the while remaining anonymous in the eyes of the public.

> It must have hurt, it must have been so difficult
> I ran towards the endless light[17]

The pre-chorus illustrates his determination to keep going despite the hardships he was facing. As the hidden member, there were a lot of things from which V was restricted. He couldn't be included in photos and he also couldn't be shown in the pre-debut vlogs that BTS used to communicate with ARMY. But regardless of this, it did not deter V and he continued to run *towards an endless light*. Running towards said light may allude to BTS seeking ARMY in a sea of lights; in the *Preparing for CONNECT, BTS Bangtan Bomb,* V shared, "When we hold concerts, we see ARMY smile and that's healing for us."[15] ARMY have been, and are continuing to be, a source of strength and comfort for BTS — as BTS is to ARMY. This love is expressed tenfold, especially by V who coined the "I purple you" phrase to articulate the adoration he has for ARMY in his unique way.

> It tingles, that summer day's air
> The cold sounds of grey streets
> I draw in a breath and knock at your door
> We gon' change
> We gon' change
> We gon' change
> We gon' change
> We gon' change[17]

In continuation of the lyrics, V revisits his past in order to comfort his inner child, despite the pain attached to the very idea. To reflect upon his past struggles in the form of a globally accessible song is a vulnerable yet valiant move, one that was very much well-received both in and out of the fandom. It's a well-known discourse in ARMY that V is an out-of-the-box, forward thinker. He colours outside of the lines, painting a unique perspective on aspects of life that is entirely his own trademark.[23] The recollection of his memories and his attempt to confront them is the first step he's taking in order to overcome his personal burdens. In acknowledging this metaphorical 'childlike version' of himself, he recognises the parts of himself that make him a multi-dimensional human being and allows himself to fully accept all parts of him as a person.

> Now I wish we would smile more
> It will be okay, because today's me is doing fine
> Yesterday's you, now it's all clear
> I want to hug the many thorns in the budding rose[17]

The knowledge that his present self is doing well now makes him want to reassure the past version of him that was filled with doubts and insecurities. The lyrics in the second verse, "I want to hug the many thorns in the budding rose"[17], glimpses V practising reassurance to his inner child. For one to parent one's inner child is a restorative process to one's well-being. By acknowledging and catering to the needs of V's doubtful past self, it enables him to better understand the present version of himself and allows him to navigate his wants and needs in life with contentment.

> The smiling kid, the child who was always laughing brightly
> When I see you like that, I can't help smiling[17]

The second pre-chorus in juxtaposition to the first shows V's growth as his perspective towards the situation changes. There's a lighter nuance

V: BOTH ART AND ARTIST

with the "smiling kid" who was "always laughing brightly" which hints V's carefree and mischievous personality when he was younger, something that was quite apparent in their early days as BTS. In Episode 6 of *In the Soop*, Jung Kook recalls "being scolded together" with V when they were trainees but he also brings to light the character development on V's maturity: "He used to joke around all the time but he's more reserved now."[24] It is not to insinuate and paint the picture of V as immature, but rather, how he has always possessed the childlike wonder and excitable qualities of the younger version of himself. He expresses himself a lot more soft-spokenly now, but it is unmistakable that he is content in his own vocation.

> Tonight, if I reach my hand to yours
> Can you hold that hand?
> I'll become you
> You just have to look at my galaxies
> Be showered with all those stars
> I'll give you my world
> The lights illuminating your eyes
> They're the me of now
> You're my boy, my boy
> My boy, my boy, my boy[18]

Although V was kept a mystery during his trainee years, it's apparent that he had a lot of potential and the lyrics "You just have to look at my galaxies / Be showered with all those stars / I'll give you my world"[17] implies this. Bang PD, the CEO of Big Hit Entertainment (now HYBE Labels), revealed that he knew the impact that V would have on the general public and amongst entertainment companies who would potentially want to recruit him as a trainee,[25] especially because of his visuals, thus his reasoning for waiting to announce V as the last member of BTS right before their debut.

This possible reflection can be the optimistic assertion that V needed as he follows it with, "You're my boy",[17] the complete affirmation he needed to give himself, from himself, and the reassurance he provides that everything will work out in the end. As the saying goes, it's always darkest before dawn, and we all need to endure struggles in our personal experiences to fully appreciate the blessings that life bestows on us.

As V tells the story of his journey from adolescence to adulthood, we see the mental growth and emotional maturity in the lyrics as it chronicles his time as a trainee, facing hardships and uncertainties about the future. It's packed with emotions and a lot of self-reflection. The story is rooted in past insecurities, but the song itself blossoms into the acceptance of said past and the welcoming of the future. The line "We gon' change"[17] acts as an affirmation to consider when struggling with one's self, to embrace change by acknowledging the struggle, accepting the situation, and taking responsibility. By reconnecting with our past self in order to heal the present version of us, we ultimately nurture our future counterpart.

It is through *Inner Child* that we see V turn towards himself in painting this portrait of his 2020, a fitting act in the era immediately following their *Love Yourself* content. The brushstrokes he uses are loving and gentle, speaking kindly to his younger self — an example we as ARMY can all follow when considering how we paint our own self-portraits.

In less than a month following *Map of the Soul: 7*'s release, V made history after becoming the first solo male artist to hit Number #1 on iTunes with his song *Sweet Night*.[26] Part of the original soundtrack to critically acclaimed South Korean drama *Itaewon Class, Sweet Night* quickly became the highest charting song to debut on US Billboard Digital Song Sales Chart by a Korean soloist.[27]

Sweet Night sails its listeners through an emotional excursion, telling a story of navigating through waves of vulnerability in disquiet waters. The song is a confession: both heartfelt and heart-rending, detailing the liability in relationships, the longing for what-ifs and what could have beens, the potential of something more but realising it too late. From V's previous work, we have witnessed his stylistic approach in using the wide range of his voice as an instrument. In *Sweet Night*, we see how V further engages himself as a storyteller and an artist for his musical craftsmanship.

V: BOTH ART AND ARTIST

Sweet Night is written in all English, a first for V's official solo releases. An analysis of the song and V's use of literary devices and mechanisms allows us to take a look at V's evolution as a lyricist.

> On my pillow
> Can't get me tired
> Sharing my fragile truth
> That I still hope the door is open
> 'Cause the window
> Opened one time with you and me
> Now my forever's falling down
> Wondering if you'd want me now[28]

The first verse is enriched with lyrical devices that highlight the emotive and visceral nature of the song: sharing "fragile truths", facts, and beliefs of the matter that cannot be held but is seemingly breakable and the imagery of "forever", an untouchable concept of permanence, anthropomorphised into a downfall. Windows of opportunities, the idiom of doors closing, another one opening — already the track is embellished with literary mechanisms of the English language. This itself is a reflection on V's growing artistry. Dabbling with the systems of a language is not an easy feat, especially when not in one's own native language.

> How could I know
> One day, I'd wake up feeling more
> But I had already reached the shore
> Guess we were ships in the night, night, night
> Ah-ah-ah, ah-ah-ah
> Ah-ah-ah, ah-ah-ah
> We were ships in the night, night, night[28]

The metaphorical confessions of "reaching the shore"[28] and realisations of being "ships in the night"[28] alludes to the synecdoche of almost relationships or relationships that have already passed, a reflection of *Itaewon Class'* main storyline and character dynamics.

> I'm wondering, are you my best friend?
> Feels like a river's rushing through my mind
> I wanna ask you if this is all just in my head
> My heart is pounding tonight, I wonder
> If you are too good to be true
> And would it be alright if I
> Pulled you closer[27]

The river rush in his mind alludes to the human mind's stream of consciousness, the flow of thoughts intertwined with the surging matters of the heart amplifies the emotional integrity of the song. *Sweet Night* is V's ode to vulnerability, tenderly portraying love and longing in the most beautiful of ways.

It's through the comfort found in *Sweet Night* that V was able to reach his widest audience yet with his relatable words and touching vulnerability. He became the World Record Holder as the leading global artist to top the most iTunes song charts worldwide, accumulating #1s in over 100 countries,[9] a title which was previously held by English singer-songwriter Adele for her 2015 release *Hello*. At the time of writing, *Sweet Night* has achieved its 118th #1 on iTunes[29] and has surpassed 120 million streams[30] on Spotify. The song has broken the record of most number #1s in the music charts, making V the first and only artist in the world to achieve this.

By this point in 2020, the unprecedented and unpredictable COVID-19 pandemic was in full swing. As global communities at large descended further and further into isolation, BTS only sought more ways to stay connected with ARMY. V's online presence was one of the most active out of the seven members in 2020,[31] with over 200 interactions with ARMY on Weverse,[32] a total of seven solo livestreams, and five collaborative livestreams with other members across VLive and YouTube. These live broadcasts, ranging from half an hour to an hour in length,

V: BOTH ART AND ARTIST

were comforting and soothing in nature. V simply stayed on camera with ARMY, and often played his favorite songs in a few livestreams aptly titled *TaeTae FM 6.13*, a reference to one of his nicknames and BTS' debut date of June 13.

The comfort that V offered ARMY throughout the year was not limited to livestreams or Weverse interactions. Appearing alongside his fellow BTS members in YouTube's *Dear Class of 2020*, V shared the following:

> I'd like to congratulate all of you who are graduating on this very special day. When you look back on this day years from now, how will you remember it? Many of us are at war with reality right now. But I hope we can take bits of this moment with us, in a photograph or a memo, to look back and remember June of 2020, and how it compares to the new today you will be embracing. In all honesty, I wasn't born with the talents of singing or dancing and wasn't much the persevering type, either. I began later than my friends, and I was lacking in some aspects, but I soon developed a joy and passion for singing and dancing. This joy has motivated my persistent efforts, and has led me to where I stand today. If there is anyone out there who cannot see where they should go from here forth, I urge you to listen to your heart. Things may feel a little difficult right now, but somewhere out there, luck and opportunity is waiting for you. I believe that. On that note, I will remember this day. Today may not be my own graduation, but I will try to look back upon this day years from now and remember it as a memory to treasure. And I look forward to the day you will stand and tell us your own story.[33]

In these encouraging remarks to the graduating classes of 2020, V expertly wove a tapestry of many characteristics for which he is well-loved: his interests in the arts, his willingness to open up about his personal experiences, and his humble acknowledgment of what he felt were his own shortcomings. With the latter, such an act may at first seem counterproductive within the context of a motivational speech; however, it is exactly such confessions that contribute to what ARMY loves so much about BTS: their relatability and their capacity to meet ARMY where they are at, regardless of occupation, class, status, and more.

V continued to offer words of comfort to ARMY in many more spaces throughout the year. When BTS appeared at the 75th United Nations General Assembly in September 2020 to offer a message of encouragement regarding the COVID-19 crisis, V shared the following thoughts on his own experience of the pandemic:

> I was frustrated and depressed, but I took notes, wrote songs, and thought about who I was. I thought, "If I give up here, then I'm not the star of my life. This is what an awesome person would do."[34]

With this, V again provided an intimate look into his very real, very relatable emotions. His admission of his frustration and depression, joined by that of his fellow members, ran contrary to celebrities' endeavours of romanticised community and struggle amid the pandemic such as the infamous cover of John Lennon's *Imagine* released earlier in the year, which was touted by audiences across the world as unrelatable and "tone-deaf".[35]

Only a few weeks after their visit to the 75th United Nations General Assembly, BTS connected with ARMY again through *Map of the Soul ON:E*, a series of two streamed concerts promoting their *Map of the Soul* album series. Finally, in addition to their performances of *Jamais Vu, Respect,* and *Friends* during *Bang Bang Con: The Live*, ARMY were able to watch BTS perform many of the *Map of the Soul* stages that had otherwise been stolen from the stage thanks to the COVID-19 pandemic. One of these performances included V's solo stage for *Inner Child*, featuring himself and a young child cast in a remarkable semblance to a young V, providing a literal illustration of the inner child concept as he sang directly to the child. Unlike his last solo within BTS, *Singularity*, *Inner Child* did not have any choreography. Apart from interacting with the young child, V's movement onstage was minimal, allowing viewers to focus more on the vocal performance. The lucky ARMY who comprised the live audience broadcast into the *ON:E* venue joined in singing the chorus towards the end, echoing the hopeful "We gon' change"[18] affirmation as the song came to a close.

In his ending ment during the first night of *Map of the Soul ON:E*, V let ARMY into his feelings regarding the pandemic once again:

> "I lived thinking: "It'll probably end soon", "I'll probably be able to see ARMYs soon", but as time went on, I felt a lot of anxiety about when this [situation] would really end. [...] we really prepared a lot of *Dynamite* stages and several interviews for ARMYs, but there was really nothing fun about it other than: I hope ARMY sees this. There was just the mindset that ARMYs would quickly see it and that tired ARMYs would have strength."[36]

Little did ARMY know that the speech at the United Nations General Assembly, their words during the *Map of the Soul ON:E* concerts, and the continued theme of relatability and comfort during the pandemic were only precursors to BTS' next release: *BE*, their ninth studio album, created directly in response to the COVID-19 crisis.

Scenery: When the world turns beautifully white, I'll spread those fading colors with you[37]

> "You are the most beautiful flower, more than anyone else in this world."
>
> — V to ARMY, Fancafe 090915[38]

V remained true to his artist form and took on the role of Director of Visuals, responsible for curating the visual aesthetics for *BE*.[39] Under V's direction, the visual concepts of *BE* illustrated the life of an ordinary person in their twenties. The members of BTS took each other's photos and videos and were able to create a candid comfortableness to share with ARMY. Taking mirror selfies, chatting, and jesting in a friend gathering of sorts all offered the essence of a laid-back and fun atmosphere whilst shooting was at the forefront of the concept album. As an avid photographer himself, V's approach as Director of Visuals reflected his eye for capturing scenes as they are and not necessarily as they should be, demonstrating once more his ability to connect with both the subjects and viewers of his work in the most candid and natural of ways.

In the *BE-hind Story* video on *BANGTAN TV*, the rest of the members praised V for his active participation and meticulous attention to detail that they felt made it all a success.[40] V himself shared, "We communicated smoothly, and I listened to all of their concept ideas and I organised everything around that. If we tried something too natural, it wouldn't be conceptual enough, so we did our best to strike a balance."[41]

Fronting the visual aspect of the *BE* album as the Visual Director, V's concept photo was also the first one to be released out of the seven members. Through V's 'room',[42] an enclosed set up specially curated to reflect who he was during the pandemic, we were introduced to a side of V as an artist beyond just music and an artist of his own ambience. It was fascinating to see his everyday visuals augmented through the group's self-made album.

The layout of V's room is akin to that of an art gallery. With green-and-white pinstripe wallpaper, a woven rug, and a rustic, warm tone chandelier, the room is decorated to have a vintage feel. The outstanding feature of the enclosed space is its symmetrical structure. With a framed photo and a red velvet sofa in the centre as the focal point, the remaining decorations are arranged to mirror one another. From the grandiose doors and ornate vases on matching tables to the two violins hanging on each side of the photo framed on the wall, the room emanates a vintage European atmosphere, sophisticated, classy, and comforting all at the same time: words that describe V himself as easily as they do his *BE* room.

This aesthetic V has curated for himself has served as an inspiration to ARMY beyond the scene (pun not intended) of music. With the rise of aesthetically pleasing visuals and the curation of one's lifestyle artistically on the internet in 2020, V became the inspiration for 'vantecore',[43] a unique aesthetic that encompassed his appreciation for the visual arts as well as simple yet eclectic fashion.

An alias that V created for himself, Vante was an identity separately crafted from his musical persona but still channelled his creative expression and high regard for the arts. Taking inspiration from Australian photographer Ante Badzim, the pseudonym was introduced in 2017 and was initially posted with V's own photography.[44] Snapshots of architecture and nature were the primary focus of his, but it soon grew beyond photography. As V shared more of his appreciation for different mediums of the arts, Vante evolved to be a unique artistic self-expression that was a combination of both V and Kim Taehyung.

Vante became a multi-faceted aesthetic that embodied V's love for the visual arts, such as paintings and drawings, as well as his own fashion sense that reflected a vintage European fashion — in particular, Italian and Parisian style. An ARMY's analysis of 'vantecore' described it as a combination of V's admiration for all art forms as well as the incorporation of his own signature style, also commenting that, "One could say vantecore is akin to being an old soul, but it's much more than that. It tempers old elements with modern ones, crafting something creative, contemporary, and new."[43] If one thing is certain, V does not just create art — with his unique style, he *is* art himself, an unforgettable scenery in his own right.

In addition to serving as Visual Director for *BE*, V also contributed a song that captures his artistry in all its raw and vulnerable form: *Blue & Grey*. Originally written in all English, the third track of the group's self-produced album was initially intended for V's yet-to-be-released mixtape. However, the members thought that it was so fitting of the current climate that they added it to the album.

Raisa Bruner, staff writer at *Time*, reviewed the song as "the most poetic — and introspective — track" in the *BE* album.[45] The song itself is mellow with undertones of guitar, setting the mood for the sad and seemingly melancholic song. *Blue & Grey* perfectly encapsulates and resonates the worries, uncertainties, and doubts felt by many so many people during the pandemic.

But, we need to consider the first appearance of *Blue & Grey* in order to fully understand the impact of such a simple but beautifully curated track. Aired on September 16th, 2020, V's version of the song appears in Episode 5 of *BTS In the Soop*.[46] It's a scene that only lasts a few minutes out of the hour-long program, but it's an unforgettable image: V is by himself as we see him get on the canoe and paddles into the river. We hear guitar strums in the background and V, no longer paddling, just drifts atop the still water, and the music begins to play.

> Where's my angel?
> I'm sick and tired of everything
> Someone came and save myself
> Cause I can't take it anymore[47]

The opening lines of the song are honest and vulnerable confessions. It matches the mood of the scene as V spends time by himself, in his own headspace with no distractions, mulling over his thoughts as he dedicates the moment for just music and himself.

The lyrics of *Blue & Grey* reach out and look for comfort amidst the chaos, the act of opening up and admitting that one needs help. Voicing one's concern is the first step and having that acknowledgement is a feat that needs to be encouraged.

> Everywhere I go
> Everywhere I see
> Can you look at me cause I am blue and grey
> Every time I cry
> Every time I smile

V: BOTH ART AND ARTIST

> Can you look at me cause I am blue and grey[47]

The lines that follow are a continuation of the song's stylised stream of consciousness. The use of repetition is effective as it alludes to an ongoing, monotonous feeling of helplessness that lingers — an almost desperate plea for someone to see through to the feelings of sadness and depression.

> I just wanna be happier
> Baby don't you let me go
> I feel tired in the winter sky
> Wish I could be stronger[47]

The snippet is an internal monologue and the simplistic nature of the lyrics is what makes it that much more effective. The fact that V initially wrote the song in English, and not his native tongue, offers the implication that he wants the song to reach as many people as possible without the language barrier. Though he is also overwhelmed by the emotions he is feeling, he provides the listener with a sense of comfort by stripping the barrier of language. He could have easily written the song in Korean, but he chose to go above and beyond and express his feelings in a language that would be more universal for ARMY, just as he did with *Sweet Night*.

Beyond his touching lyrics, a heartbeat can subtly be heard throughout the song. This is not the first time V has drawn upon sound effects created by objects other than instruments, and woven them into his music: In *Scenery*, V incorporated the natural sounds of camera shutters and footsteps on snow (which would also be used in his later release *Snow Flower*); in *Inner Child*, the reverberation effects used throughout the song help evoke a sense of nostalgia for one's inner child; in *Sweet Night,* the solo whistling paints a picture of lonesome longing. Throughout all of these, V also makes unique use of musical space, offering instrumental-only moments for the listener to reflect on the vibrant lyricism and vocal talents provided throughout the rest of the songs. All of these combined create a holistic aural experience, transporting the listener beyond the music and into an entirely different environment with V himself — the mark of an effective artist indeed.

There was a lot of speculation about *Blue & Grey* and the story behind it after its reveal. It wasn't until V's individual comeback interview from *Weverse Magazine*, released at the end of November a few weeks after the BE comeback, that the bigger picture was painted:

> "I wrote *Blue & Grey* when I was at my lowest point, when I was actually asking whether I could keep going with my work or not. Even the fun parts of work became a chore, and my whole life felt aimless. 'Where do I go from here? I can't even see the end of the tunnel.' Those kinds of thoughts hit me hard."[41]

V opening up about his struggles and sharing them so willingly with us — a constant theme in everything he does — makes us appreciate him more as a person and not just an idol. It reassures listeners that idols are not perfect either and that they are human beings too. This, for many ARMY who have their own doubts and insecurities, encourages the conversations about mental health. Through *Blue & Grey*, V validates our feelings and tells us to reach out, to look after ourselves and take care of one another.

> "Rather than just some stranger telling them to cheer up, I think it's better to say something like, "You seem depressed lately," or, "Seems like these days it's tough for you to perk up." *Blue & Grey* is the same: "You're depressed lately? Me too. We're in the same boat. Wanna talk about how you're feeling? You wanna feel better, right? I know, but sometimes it feels like you're being washed away by a whirlpool of stress." I want the listeners to hear me saying that to them."[41]

Blue & Grey was not the last gift V gave ARMY in 2020. Announced at midnight KST on the 25th of December, just days before his birthday, V released *Snow Flower*. The jazz- and R&B-hybrid track was a collaboration

V: BOTH ART AND ARTIST

between himself and singer-songwriter, rapper, and producer, Peakboy. ARMY were delighted to see this collaboration between V and his close friend from their 'Wooga Squad', a star-studded group featuring K-drama heartthrobs Park Seo Joon and Park Hyung Sik, *Parasite* protagonist Choi Woo Shik, indie artist Peakboy, and V himself.

ARMY is already privy to the family V has with BTS, and the sense of family he has painted purple between himself and ARMY ourselves. The Wooga Squad is yet another look into V's unerring ability to find family wherever he is. V himself has explained that 'Wooga' stands for family, an abbreviation for the phrase "Woori-ga gajok-inga?" ("Are we family?")[48] V's love for ARMY, his fellow members of BTS, and his friends and family at large truly shines through in all he does, least of all the work he does with them. In fact, *Sweet Night* and its use in the drama *Itaewon Class* was another example of the Wooga Squad in action as Park Seo Joon starred in the show. In an interview, Peakboy shared his thoughts on working with V on *Snow Flower*: "V as a singer and Kim Taehyung as a person are not that different. In fact, he is full of emotions and is a great friend who has a lot to learn from as an artist."[49]

While the theme of nature returns from *Scenery* and *Winter Bear*, there is a livelier feel to *Snow Flower* that differs from V's earlier releases. The song is a lot more playful and uplifting, very fitting to the theme of Christmas and the holiday season. Although the lyrics have clear motifs of the cold, winter tide throughout, there is a sense of warmth to the song that can only be connected with V and his evolving artistry.

> Hey snow
> It's coming today
> What else should I prepare?
> I'm ready to greet you, ok (Ok)
> Grey is
> Fallin' on the canvas
> You can just cover it white
> I'll give you the world (I'll give it to you)
> In this cold season

> You are my special event
> Your warmth will melt
> My blue and grey away (o-o-oh)[37]

The first verse of the song is light-hearted, an upbeat, melodic composition as V starts off with a greeting towards the cold weather, "Hey snow / It's coming today / What else should I prepare? / I'm ready to greet you, ok"[37] a sense of closeness that enables the reader to feel connected with V and the song. The welcoming lyrics in the beginning mirror that of a cordial acquaintanceship between friends, the concept of meeting each other after a while which is appropriate given the context that V always does his best to communicate with ARMY.

In the lyrics "Your warmth will melt / My blue and grey away (o-o-oh)"[37], the analogy of 'blue and grey' makes a comeback, drawing a line of familiarity for the listeners and creating a link to the wintery concept of the song, a continuing factor in V's previous solo releases. His love for winter is apparent, the foundations of his songs containing such imagery. But despite these revisited motifs, V's words are anything but cold. In fact, they provide the listeners a sense of warmth, cosiness, and understanding — something that is a consistent signature style in all of V's songs, especially in 2020. Despite the variant in sound, the value of sentiments are still very much the same.

> When the world is full of white flowers
> May our times be more special (eh-e)
> When time is standing still
> May these flowers fall on your sad smile (e-e-eh)[37]

There is something poetic about the 'white flowers' mentioned in the chorus. Its symbolisms are layered and, as we have grown to know V and his artistic approach to his work, we know that it has multiple meanings. The synecdoche of snowflakes as white flowers alludes to the beauty of the snow in the winter season but in the form of buds during spring's growth and renewal stages. The usage of blossoms, a characteristically

V: BOTH ART AND ARTIST

spring feature of the same chromaticism as snow which is a distinct element of winter, is a juxtaposition that works. This application of the 'white flowers' is layered, dichotomised, and metaphorised, showcasing V's elevated aptitude to the art of lyricism.

In reference to time at a stand still, it relates back to the COVID-19 pandemic when the world found itself on pause. For the listeners of the song, there is the feeling of reassurance being provided by V. In Peakboy's verse that shortly followed V's, he mentions "white angels here and there this year",[37] alluding to the individuals working in the medical fields and the essential workers front lining the pandemic.

> Did you see the snow?
> Like your eyes
> Believe in Santa Claus?
> I'll take away
> A warm gift with you
> Every time this season comes, like the tip of your nose
> Fall in love
> I'm just feeling
> Stay by my side
> I'll match your footsteps
> I'll sing this song
> (You make me wanna be a better man)[37]

There is a childlike wonder in the lyrics that V sings with Peakboy during the bridge. The duet between the two musicians as they harmonise the exchange is high-spirited, a jovial tune that reflects a new sound yet familiar sentiment in V's adroitness to his style of music. The spoken dialogues such as "I love you"[37] in the pre-chorus and "You make me wanna be a better man"[37] at the end of the bridge are positive, affirming confessions which add such an intimately V nuance to the song.

> When the world is full of white flowers
> May our feelings grow deeper and deeper

> May the flowers land on your smile
> Below the streetlamp frozen in time (Yeah-e)[37]

Ending the track with a slightly different version of the chorus, the 'white flowers' as well as the suspension of time are still the subjects of the verse. An integral part of the song, V shares his thoughts and the significance of the song through a note attached in the official blog release:

"I think that this year would be felt like a period of paused time, and that there would be many people with increased anxiety and gloominess as the year-end approaches. For today at least, I wish the white flowers come down into your heart and you are able to feel warm comfort and happiness even for a bit."[50]

Drawing similar concepts from his previous songs but producing a fresh sound, *Snow Flower* is a highlight of V's progression as an artist — song lyrics, music composition. and sound production wise. The ownership that he has over his craft is entirely commendable; it's evident that V is very meticulous and multi-layered about his work. He considers every aspect of the song, from the big, canvassed picture to the little brush-stroke details. He puts his artistry at the forefront of the development and distribution of his songs, allowing us to witness V's versatility as an artist whilst still maintaining his signature style.

Conclusion: The world is V's canvas

After this chronological look at V in the year of 2020, we've come back to where we started: It's December 30th, and V is celebrating his 26th birthday with a livestream, just a few days after releasing *Snow Flower*. In not even twenty-four hours, he will be joining his fellow BTS members in the *New Year's Eve Live* special presented by Weverse to wrap up the year.

Over the years, we have seen V grow as an artist and we have seen the foundation of his own artistry built through the songs he has created as the lyricist, composer, and producer. In 2020, V further developed himself musically and became more in tune with his vocal sound after a

V: BOTH ART AND ARTIST

successful 2019 with *Winter Bear* and *Scenery*. And, not only did we see him continue as an artist in his own standing this year; in 2020, ARMY was also able to observe V step into the role of Director of Visuals for their self-produced album.

The first brushstrokes in V's portrait of 2020 were dark and shadowy with *Black Swan*. We saw an explosion of colour with *Inner Child* as he reached back through the years to his younger self. Perhaps it is here in the composition of the portrait that V traded, even if only for a moment, a paintbrush for finger painting, daubing galaxies onto the canvas with childlike wonder and an acceptance that these additions to the painting are just as beautiful and valid as the rest of it. *Sweet Night*, then, is the brush that added other people into the painting, depicting a longing vulnerability between them. These people may also be painted with shades of *Blue & Grey*, surrounded by *Snow Flower*s.

All in all, V's 2020 is an expertly composed masterpiece in which V himself captures so much of the human experience, both at large and within the context of the COVID-19 pandemic itself. This ability to both illustrate the human experience and offer it so much comfort through his art is rooted in the same love that brought us 'I purple you'; the same love that captured his fellow BTS members in the most beautiful and candid of ways in *BE*; the same love that he has shown both himself and the world around him. From the intentionality and comfort he masterfully delivers in his music to his own personally curated style, V is a beautiful story, an unforgettable memory, and a mesmerising scenery. V is both art and artist. And with his impact, it's reassuring to see that the world is his canvas.

References

[1] @sceneryfortae. [@sceneryfortae]. (2019, January 19). *Taehyung's ending ment in english:*
"Armys who have done so much for me, making memories & always showing love, thank u so much for these memories. You're part of my story, memory and scenery. Thank u, i love you!" He's so fluent, i'm so proud @BTS_twt [Tweet]. https://twitter.com/sceneryfortae/status/1086622877615640576

[2] BTS. (2020, December 30). *V DAY !*. [Video]. https://www.vlive.tv/video/230500

[3] TTP. [@thetaeprint]. (2020, December 30). *[INFO] With 5M tweets, #HAPPYVDAY becomes the Most Tweeted Birthday Hashtag for a Korean Artist! Happy Birthday Taehyung* [Image Attached]. [Tweet]. https://twitter.com/thetaeprint/status/1344313081531412480

[4] BTS UAE. [@bangtanUAE]. (2020, December 29). *[HD/FULL] @BTS_twt V Lights up the Dubai sky in the Tallest Building in the World, Burj Khalifa. You can even hear ARMYs across the whole area cheering! Happy Birthday Kim Taehyung! Big thanks to @KIMTAEHYUNGBAR_ for this amazing birthday project! #TaehyungOnBurjKhalifa #BTS* [Video attached]. [Tweet]. https://twitter.com/bangtanUAE/status/1343953317030981633

[5] Williams, J. (2019, August 9). *What does 'I purple you' mean? BTS fans celebrate 1,000 days of Kim Taehyung's phrase of love.* https://www.newsweek.com/bts-kim-taehyung-purple-meaning-1453501

[6] TTP. [@thetaeprint]. (2020, January 6). *[NAVER] V again proved himself as the "King of Fancams" as he owns the most viewed fancam title for two consecutive years. V's BWL 2019 fancam is the most viewed fancam in kpop history with 130M views and his ON fancam is the most viewed fancam of 2020* [Image attached]. [Tweet]. https://twitter.com/thetaeprint/status/1346701783083704320

V: BOTH ART AND ARTIST

7   방탄소년단뷔 Publicity™ (slow). [@btsVpublicity]. (2020, December 30). @BTS_twt V, Kim Taehyung's Solo V LIVE ended with 11.6M viewers with 378K hearts making it the most viewed realtime solo live on the platform! #HappyBirthdayTaehyung #HAPPYVDAY #HappyTaehyungDay [Image attached]. [Tweet]. https://twitter.com/btsVpublicity/status/1344160132842713088?s=20

8   championt. (2020, December 31). *BTS's V is the most-streamed Korean soloist on Soundcloud for a second consecutive year*. https://www.allkpop.com/article/2020/12/btss-v-is-the-most-streamed-korean-soloist-on-soundcloud-for-a-second-consecutive-year

9   Rolli, B. (2020, July 22). *BTS is the first artist to have two songs top the iTunes chart in 100 countries*. https://www.forbes.com/sites/bryanrolli/2020/07/22/bts-no-1-itunes-100-countries-black-swan-your-eyes-tell/?sh=14e0fce9fb9e

10 V. (2020). 풍경 (Scenery) [Song]. Big Hit Entertainment; Genius. (2020). V - 풍 경 (Scenery) (English translation) [Translation]. https://genius.com/Genius-english-translations-v-scenery-english-translation-lyrics

11 YTN news. (2016, October 27). '방탄소년단' 세계 속으로 훨훨..." 믿고 듣는 아이돌 될게요" / YTN (Yes! Top News) [Video]. https://youtu.be/TOpLFkypqfM

12 BTS. (2020). Black swan [Song]. On *Map of the soul: 7*. Big Hit Entertainment; Genius. (2020). *BTS - Black swan (English translation)* [Translation]. https://genius.com/Genius-english-translations-bts-black-swan-english-translation-lyrics

13 BTS. (2016). Stigma [Song]. On *Wings*. Big Hit Entertainment; Genius. (2016). *BTS - Stigma (English translation)* [Translation]. https://genius.com/Genius-english-translations-bts-stigma-english-translation-lyrics

14 BTS. (2018). Intro: Singularity [Song]. On *Love yourself: Tear*. Big Hit Entertainment; Genius. (2016). *BTS - Intro : Singularity (English translation)* [Translation]. https://genius.com/Genius-english-translations-bts-intro-singularity-english-translation-lyrics

15. BANGTANTV. (2020, February 29). *[BANGTAN BOMB] Preparing for CONNECT, BTS - BTS (방탄소년단)* [Video]. https://www.youtube.com/watch?v=FFDxZtdxZzE
16. BANGTANTV. (2020, May 7). *[CONNECT, BTS] Secret docents of 'catharsis' by V @ London* [Video]. https://www.youtube.com/watch?v=niKMDl67gSc
17. BTS. (2020). Inner child [Song]. On *Map of the soul: 7*. Big Hit Entertainment; Genius. (2020). *BTS - Inner child (English translation)* [Translation]. https://genius.com/Genius-english-translations-bts-inner-child-english-translation-lyrics
18. KOMCA. *INNER CHILD - 100002782341*. (2020, February 21). http://www.komca.or.kr/foreign2/eng/S01.jsp
19. Jung, C. (1954, September 21). The development of personality. *The collected works of C.G. Jung, 17*. Princeton University Press.
20. Cantor, B. (2020, February). *New BTS single "ON" reflects on group's "calling and mindset as artists," more new song details revealed*. https://headlineplanet.com/home/2020/02/20/new-bts-single-on-reflects-on-groups-calling-and-mindset-as-artists-more-new-song-details-revealed/
21. Koreaboo. (2019, January 14). *V's confession about being BTS's "hidden member" will break your heart*. https://www.koreaboo.com/stories/bts-v-hidden-member-confession/
22. BANGTANTV. (2013, July 13). *130710 V* [Video]. https://www.youtube.com/watch?v=4FNbyrt7Tg8
23. Kiss Closure. (2020, April 2). *V having a unique perspective on things (Taehyung run BTS funny moments)* [Video]. https://www.youtube.com/watch?v=vIfdWodeUyo
24. Bang, S. & Lenzo, Y (Executive Producers). (2020). *BTS In the soop* [TV Show]. Big Hit Entertainment.
25. Korea Crush. (2020, March 28). *Why Taehyung was the last member to be unveiled? Touching story of his debut!* [Video]. https://www.youtube.com/watch?v=MofakANOnRg
26. Blue1310. (2021, January 7). *BTS V's "Sweet night" is 2020's 'Most-streamed song released by a Korean male soloist' and the*

V: BOTH ART AND ARTIST

'most-streamed Korean OST' on Spotify. https://www.allkpop.com/article/2021/01/bts-vs-sweet-night-is-2020s-most-streamed-song-released-by-a-korean-male-soloist-and-the-most-streamed-korean-ost-on-spotify

27 McIntyre, H. (2020, March 23). *BTS member V scores the second-bestselling song in the U.S. with 'Sweet Night'.* https://www.forbes.com/sites/hughmcintyre/2020/03/23/bts-member-v-scores-the-second-bestselling-song-in-the-us-with/?sh=58c288bea6c9

28 V. (2020). Sweet Night [Song]. On *ITAEWON CLASS (Original Television Soundtrack) Pt. 12*. Vlending Co., Ltd.; Genius. (2020). *V (BTS) - Sweet night lyrics* [Translation]. https://genius.com/V-bts-sweet-night-lyrics

29 TTP. [@thetaeprint]. (2021, April 1). *[INFO] Sweet Night has achieves its 118th #1 on Itunes (Nepal) extending its record as the song with the most number 1s in the history, making Kim Taehyung the first and only artist in the world to achieve this feat Congratulations Taehyung! #SweetNight118개국1위 @ BTS_twt* [Image attached]. [Tweet]. https://twitter.com/thetaeprint/status/1377616661998661647

30 방탄소년단 Publicity™□□⁷. [@BTSPublicity]. [2021, April 21]. *'Sweet Night' by V has surpassed 120 MILLION streams on Spotify!* [Tweet]. https://twitter.com/BTSPublicity/status/1381608041397723140

31 Lyons, S. (2020, January 15). *BTS's V is blowing up everyone's Weverse notifications again.* https://www.koreaboo.com/news/bts-v-playing-battleground-weverse-game-posting

32 Admin. (2020, August 12). *BTS V received his long-awaited award with an official title and he's so happy.* https://btsbomb.com/bts-v-weverse-certificate-head-of-entertainment/

33 BANGTANTV. (2020, June 7). *BTS commencement speech | Dear class of 2020* [Video]. https://www.youtube.com/watch?v=AU6uF5sFtwA

34. BANGTANTV. (2020, September 23). *BTS (방탄소년단) Speech at the 75th UN general assembly* [Video]. https://www.youtube.com/watch?v=5aPe9Uy10n4
35. Carras, C. (2020, March 19). *Celebrities singing 'Imagine' amid coronavirus panic brings on the eye roll.* https://www.latimes.com/entertainment-arts/music/story/2020-03-19/coronavirus-imagine-video-gal-gadot-celebrities
36. 스튜디오. [@STUDIO_0613]. (2020, October 10). *201010 taehyung ending ment* [Image attached]. [Tweet]. https://twitter.com/STUDIO_0613/status/1314923385135267840
37. V. (2020). Snow flower [Song]. On *Soundcloud*. Big Hit Entertainment; Genius. (2020). *V (BTS) - Snow flower ft. Peakboy (English translation)* [Translation]. https://genius.com/Genius-english-translations-v-bts-snow-flower-ft-peakboy-english-translation-lyrics
38. BTS FANCAFE. [@btsfancafe__twt]. (2018, January 7). *[fancafe] TAEHYUNG 090915 "When things get hard, stop for awhile and look back and see how far you've come. Don't forget how rewarding it is. You are the most beautiful flower, more than anyone else in this world"* [Image attached]. [Tweet]. https://twitter.com/btsfancafe__twt/status/949831739400101889
39. HYBE Labels. (2020, November 21). *BTS (방탄소년단) Global press conference 'BE' (+ENG)* [Video]. https://www.youtube.com/watch?v=T31mfmw8bS8
40. BANGTANTV. (2020, December 13). *BTS (방탄소년단) BE-hind story* [Video]. https://www.youtube.com/watch?v=cYX88pxQuCo
41. Kang, M. (2020, November). V "I wish we were back with ARMY, laughing together". *BTS BE comeback interview.* https://magazine.weverse.io/article/view?lang=en&colca=1&num=58
42. HYBE Labels. (2020, November 1). *BE | BTS.* [Video]. https://ibighit.com/bts/video/be/RR9JRcgdys46B7K36eDzbvr1.php
43. Lopez, A. (2021, February 6). *Vantecore — A look at V's multi-medium artistic expression.* https://medium.com/bulletproof/

V: BOTH ART AND ARTIST

vantecore-a-look-at-vs-multi-medium-artistic-expression-28c485f17e71

44 방탄소년단. [@BTS_twt]. (2017, June 3*). Photo by vante* [Image attached]. [Tweet]. https://twitter.com/BTS_twt/status/870941822113112064

45 Bruner, R., & Moon, K. (2020, November 20). *Breaking down every track on BTS' new album be.* https://time.com/5914352/bts-be-analysis

46 Bang, S. & Lenzo, Y (Executive Producers). (2020). *BTS In the soop* [TV Show]. Big Hit Entertainment.

47 BTS. (2020). Blue & grey [Song]. On *BE*. Big Hit Entertainment; Genius. (2020). *BTS - Blue & grey (English translation)* [Translation]. https://genius.com/Genius-english-translations-bts-blue-and-grey-english-translation-lyrics

48 Domingo, J. (2020, September 6). *The wooga squad: The crossover we didn't think we needed.* https://metro.style/culture/spotlight/the-wooga-squad-the-crossover-we-didn-t-think-we-n/26967

49 SceneryForTae. [@sceneryfortae]. *Peakboy "Working with him was so fun & it was a warm song. V is a kind, cute, and pure younger brother to me. V as a singer and Kim Taehyung as a person are not that different. In fact, he is full of emotions and is a great friend who has a lot to learn from as an artist." (2)* [Tweet]. https://twitter.com/sceneryfortae/status/1384458432946733056

50 V. (2020). Snow flower [Song]. On *Soundcloud*. Big Hit Labels; Doolset. *Snow flower (V)*. https://doolsetbangtan.wordpress.com/2020/12/24/snow-flower-v/

Jimin

A KALEIDOSCOPE OF FILTERS
Kate Koncilja and Jasmine Proctor

Introduction: "Which me do you want?"[1]

When BTS' highly anticipated fourth album *Map of the Soul: 7* was released on February 21, 2020, with it came a song that would seem to define the year for a certain Park Jimin: his solo track, *Filter*. Led by a Latin-inspired, sharp, yet pondering guitar bass beat, the song showcased a sultrier, more alluring side of Jimin that was both captivating and addicting. Before the release of *Filter*, ARMY had seen different sides of Jimin through his previous solo works, ranging from the hauntingness of *Lie*, to the soft mysticality that was *Serendipity*, to a more acoustic flavour embodied in *Promise*. While all three songs seemed to work as a narrative, weaving together the different pieces of who Jimin has become over the years, there was something about *Filter* that seemed to embody exactly who Jimin is today. In an interview with SiriusXM,[2] Jimin talked about this exact idea, saying his desire with *Filter* was to show a different side of himself beyond what audiences had seen before.[2] Rather, he stressed that the concept of a filter offers a multitude of definitions, not only in terms of how we might change an image or a photo, but also in how we might shift our own internalised preconceptions of reality.[2]

Born in the mountainside Geumjeong-gu district of Busan, South Korea[3] on October 13, 1995, Jimin is the main dancer and lead vocalist of BTS,[4] known for his magnetic stage presence and immaculate vocal stability.[5] This comes as no surprise though, as Jimin trained throughout his high school career in contemporary dance, holding the spot of top student at Busan High School of Arts in the modern dance major before being accepted into Big Hit Entertainment as a trainee.[6] Since their debut in 2013, Jimin is known even among the members as being the cute, hard-working, considerate, and dependable one,[7] key traits that still remain just as present. The artist, the dancer, and the performer; the highly empathic, hard-working, and loving — this is who Jimin is.

Filter, then, seemed to not only represent Jimin's desire to show a different side of himself musically, but also to challenge preconceived notions of who he is as an artist, a team player, and an individual up until this time. It was not just a call to understand the world differently, a little piece of Jimin's own ability to see things from all perspectives that we can "apply… to [our] hearts",[1] but also a declaration of how Jimin himself cannot be fit into one single understanding of his performance or personality. He, like the song relays, will always surpass any "preferences or criteria".[1] And this year truly revealed that, in spite of the setbacks and challenges that were put in his way. In particular, the different 'filters' of Jimin manifested in his ability to expand commonly perceived notions of him as either 'cutie,' 'sexy,' or 'lovely,' terms he too has previously imparted upon himself.[8,9] *Filter* seemed to be a response to this, that our universal definitions of each term need to expand alongside our understanding of who Jimin is today.

He has, of course, done this before. His career up until this point has been an evolution of the self, both onstage and off. Over the last seven years leading up to 2020, Jimin has amassed a wildly successful career, receiving praise for not only his performance as an artist, but in particular one of the defining features of his craft: his dance. The early years of his career saw him embracing hip-hop styles, taking on a more hyper-masculine appearance that translated into his performance. As time went on, Jimin was able to show more of his innate dance talent and background, with elegant stages for *The Most Beautiful Moment in Life: Part 2*'s *Butterfly* and later at the *2016 SBS Gayo Daejeon* awards performance. From there, we saw him incorporate more of his previous

JIMIN: A KALEIDOSCOPE OF FILTERS

training in contemporary, shifting our perspective on how 'sexy' can be redefined through an understanding of 'lovely'. Even in his vocal talents, we've seen Jimin blossom into someone who is comfortable in his abilities, showing off his colourful range in different styles and genres, from hip-hop to ballads to even disco. In all areas of performance, Jimin has excelled and been recognised for it, even receiving the recognition from the Kim Baek Bong Korean Fan Dance Conservation Society for his traditional fan dance (*buchaechum*) at the *2018 Melon Music Awards*.[10]

Offstage, ARMY have watched as Jimin changed styles, expressions, and, of course, hair colours, all the while remaining steadfast in his caring and genuine nature. What shifted most significantly, though, was his confidence. It was a process of growth and becoming comfortable in his skin. It was a process that, combined with his journey in musicality and dance, allowed him to grow into the Jimin we saw in 2020. And though that journey still continued into the last year, getting to where he is now in his career and his personal life has revealed a Jimin who feels comfortable in who he is, displaying his kaleidoscope of filters in 2020. It is that exact journey that seemed to be perfectly embodied within *Filter* as a song of expression, as a song that encapsulates Jimin's position within the multiplicity of his own identity.

Jimin has shown multiple facets of his identity in 2020 through the art form of dance. Like Jimin, dance is versatile and endlessly expressive. By creating shapes and movements to music, a skilled dancer can show a range of emotions and stories that differ, yet emerge from the same source — showing filters. For Jimin, then, each style of dance acts as another filter to express more. Allowing his "emotions and movements [to] flow with the overall feel of the music",[11] he offers versions of himself while dancing that are both elastic and genuine. Jimin, as filtered through turns, leaps, isolations, extensions, and moments of breath, appears reflected through a prism — a rainbow bursting with colour, showing the infinite beauty found within a single, shining light. These details of dance take time to appreciate, but like Jimin himself, their loveliness is undeniable at first glance. His performances throughout 2020 are perfect allegories demonstrating how he bloomed during the year, showing ARMY filters of himself both on and offstage.

Exploring expression has always been a goal for Jimin. Even pre-debut, he voiced explicit interest in it: "I'm really anticipating for that moment, for when we are out performing, what kind of sides to us will be shone upon."[12] This notion of giving better performance and showcasing different sides of himself is something Jimin constantly vocalises and is enabled by his determination. In 2020, Jimin's intention to explore expression came out clearly in BTS' vibrant summer single, *Dynamite*, a goal which he summarised for *Weverse Magazine*:

> "I tried out expressions I'd never tried before. […] I tried to be sentimental […] I even tried to look suave (laughs) and funny, too. I ended up focusing on painting a single picture rather than on each of the individual elements."[13]

"Sentimental," "suave," "funny"[13] — Jimin conveyed each of these emotions spectacularly in the music video, creating a collage in himself to represent all simultaneously. He continued experimenting with motion and emotion throughout the thirty stages of *Dynamite* he performed in 2020, freestyling, showing different poses, and varying facials wherever possible. One song allowed so much room for expression. Yet, to understand Jimin fully, we cannot stop here.

In Jimin's concept photos for *BE*, he sits on a couch, draped in silky black and surrounded by chaotic greenery — flowers in shades of pink, white, yellow, orange, and lilac. Instructed to curate a room with objects that best symbolised himself, Jimin noted, "I think the overall balance of colors in this room instead of any particular object best shows who I am."[14] Rather than honing in on any specific part, all facets must be appreciated in whole to define who 'Jimin' is. Through similarly studying Jimin's utilisation of expression through his dance and performances alongside his other accomplishments in 2020, we can appreciate the individual filters that layer together to become Jimin — the sweet 'cutie', charmingly 'sexy', and embodiment of 'lovely'.

Cutie: "Sometimes you get to know, broken is beautiful"[15]

If there's one word that is often associated with Jimin, it's 'cutie'. While the idea of cute can be attributed to his softer sides, his sweetness, or even the occasional falling-off-the-chair-laughing incident, 2020 saw Jimin embody his innate 'cutie' characteristics via the act of self-compassion and understanding, both through performance and presence. With the release of *Map of the Soul: 7* not only came *Filter*, but also the soulmate anthem of V and Jimin, *Friends*, a direct display of this empathetic melding. In this three-minutes-and-nineteen-seconds song, the pair reminisce about their high school days, giving ARMY a look into how their friendship shaped and shifted over the years.[16] The lyrics themselves talk about childish fights, growing up, and staying by each other's side through it all. They talk of inside jokes like the dumpling incident, Jimin's small pinky, and even their school uniforms, all the while reflecting on how much they have grown together. It's adorable and heartfelt, intimate and relatable, but also immensely nostalgic. Reflecting on the production of the track, Jimin commented that even the process of creating it brought back so many memories for both him and V.[17] ARMY have witnessed the growth of Jimin alongside V since their debut in 2013, but somehow *Friends* represented a more personal look at how their connection has grown over the years as well.

With the singularity of Jimin and V's friendship, it is appropriate there was only one performance of the song in 2020. At *BangBangCon: The Live*, the two 'soulmates' went back in time to emulate their middle-school selves, wearing dark uniforms and bright smiles on a set reminiscent of the past.[18] With minimal choreography and the usage of props, the performance's style was akin to musical theatre, and this was a perfect way to portray their relationship. The minimal staging allowed Jimin and V to have freedom in movement, and even in planned gestures, such as when the pair joined hands, it felt genuine. Here, there is an utter authenticity of Jimin and V existing in their natural states as performers and best friends — fitting, since it is *their* song. Thus, there is an undeniable honesty conveyed in the two members as each other's "soulmate"[16] which they use to be 'cuties' in their own way: by being themselves. For Jimin, *Friends* showed a filter of him as a born performer, travelling the stage, flashing different facials, and using his body to organically feel the music. ARMY have seen this Jimin frequently before, yet in this song he focused not only on entertaining an audience, but also on creating a cohesive stage with V. Through his movements and performance, this revealed his cute side centred on connectivity and truth, perfectly mirroring Jimin offstage.

But it was also through this song that ARMY were able to witness a side of Jimin that hadn't emerged before: his inner child. ARMY were swept along for the ride as Jimin and V retold their past history, walking down memory lane together, holding hands with their fans. The lyrics discuss his coming to Seoul, a story we've heard before through the other members, but this time it was in Jimin's words. While the song itself showed the 'cutie' we all know and love, learning how much his friendship with V and the experiences they went through means to him revealed a warmer, more vulnerable side. This connection to his past self, a topic he rarely delves into, alongside the best friend who he has grown up with over the past nine years helped elucidate the rediscovery of how being a 'cutie' meant a revisiting of Jimin's childhood self through music.

Friends, through its narrative of a soulmate friendship, reflected a means of self-empathy for Jimin. It was a form of *healing*. It is no exaggeration to say that Jimin defines the very understanding of empathy, possessing a magical skill of knowing how to be there for others and understand them on their own terms. He *exudes* external empathy. He *embodies* it. But this time around, Jimin took that empathy and directed it inwards in a radical act of not only self-love, but self-compassion. The creation of *Friends* was a means of healing inwards through connecting to not only his best friend, but the stories of his inner child that have led him to where he is today. These are the stories that have helped shape him exactly into that empathic and understanding human, the one that is there for everyone, and the one who cares *so much*. Being empathetic towards his past through storytelling enabled Jimin to define the idea of cute not just as an external manifestation of sweetness, but an internal process of warmth and self-love.

This idea was continued later in the year with December's release of his self-composed *Christmas Love*. In his note to ARMY that accompanied the track's release, Jimin stated that this was a gift to them in a time that was so difficult, saying he hoped it would help brighten the dark situation we were all facing.[19] While this was an act of external empathy towards ARMY, he continued the note by again going back to reflecting on his childhood. In it, Jimin disclosed that for him, snow had a lot of meaning as a child, something he would anticipate with wonder each winter season. This song was meant to embody that, being an escape back to the emotions of childhood in order to heal. As the note reflects, Jimin felt that "as we grow up, it seems we come to long a lot for our childhood experiences. With or without the current situation, I really want to reminisce and go back to the time and memory of when we were childish, pure, and spotless."[19] There is an innate desire to return to the past here, to find solace in childhood pleasures like the falling of snow (which Jimin discussed through his explanation of the Korean onomatopoeia, *"sobok-sobok"*[19]). Jimin continues to state that he hopes this song allows ARMY, like him, to reconnect to a brighter time in our childhood when responsibilities and the weight of adult reality didn't define who we are.[19]

Though *Christmas Love* is an explicit example, both it and *Friends* showcased how 2020 saw Jimin redefining his 'cutie' side to align with his practice of both external and internal empathy. Both acts informed the other, as his ability to express compassion externally to ARMY or his group members came from a place of self-empathy by extension. *Christmas Love* stemmed from Jimin's desire to return to his inner child as a form of healing from the weight of the year. *Friends*, while different in its origin, still embodied the same practice but in reverse — an external projection of empathy he shares with his best friend that transformed into a means through which Jimin explored his past self.

The compassion Jimin illustrated in his art was also given to ARMY throughout his response to COVID-19. A true 'cutie,' he utilised his high emotional intelligence to cover the distance and comfort fans in a difficult time for all. Early in quarantine, Jimin made visible efforts to spend quality time with ARMY through a number of livestreams. At first, these efforts were solo, more intimate VLives,[17,20,21] but Jimin later invited other members to join him in activities that ARMY could also do from their homes, such as whipping dalgona coffee[22] and making gimbap.[23,24] The effect of this heightened online presence was that ARMY still felt connected to Jimin and could have moments of happiness among the hardships caused by the pandemic. By reaching out to ARMY through a screen when he couldn't do so on stage, Jimin showed a filter always in the spotlight — his kind heart. However, his efforts hardly stopped there.

In addressing the class of 2020 at YouTube's virtual commencement, Jimin, part of the class himself, spoke about his worries for his classmates. He noted, "if things are not okay even in the slightest, we send you our most sincere consolation with all our hearts."[25] But further than just offering condolences, Jimin said something many ARMY have depended on since: "Remember there is a person here in Korea, in the city of Seoul, who understands you."[25] Knowing his propensity for empathy, it truly seems he does. Jimin recognises that having someone to share a struggle can make all the difference, and so he ended his speech by wishing "we can all give each other a warm pat on the back and say: 'it's okay.'"[25]

"'It's okay'"[25] — two words brimming with reassurance. In the *Break the Silence* documentary series filmed in 2019, Jimin expressed his gratitude for that phrase: "the fact that I have people who can tell me it's okay [...] has been a strong source of support."[26] He seems to refer to encouragement from his members, something which remained valuable in 2020. "I felt hopeless," Jimin stated in his speech at the 75th United Nations General Assembly, relating his personal hardships experienced from COVID-19.[27] "And then, my friends took my hand. We comforted each other and talked about what we could do together."[27] Expressed by Jimin as a hand reaching out for physical connection and comfort, emotional support is how we can hold each other up through strife.

JIMIN: A KALEIDOSCOPE OF FILTERS

He realised this more than ever in 2020, identifying in an interview with *The Atlantic* that "what keeps me going are the relationships and the energy I get from them."[28] Thus, Jimin not only depended on his relationships, but paid forward the sentiment through efforts to connect with ARMY. Through both his empathy and words of consolation for those struggling, Jimin embodied a filter of himself that could truly be described as a friend.

The compassion Jimin so beautifully exemplified is needed more than ever during a global pandemic, and he himself was a great advocate in extending that empathy out into the world. Jimin consistently tweeted ARMY messages to "make sure to wear your masks" and "be safe",[29] while also acknowledging the importance of self-care and kindness: "strengthening your immune system and being too hard on yourself I think are very different."[30] Further, he spoke up for children who can't fully understand the reasons for restrictions, encouraging all of us to "come together, to end this situation" in an October livestream.[31] The kind of unity Jimin calls for — realised through masks, social distancing, and vaccines — is the only way a pandemic may be overcome, and this requires compassion. A perfect example of how empathy like this works can be found in the dumpling incident, a memory from 2016 that Jimin and V frequently revisited in 2020. A silly, yet impactful fight they solved with healthy communication grew into the cultivation of a better relationship,[17,32] and taking the time to be compassionate with others will similarly benefit the pandemic. Just as Jimin and V, dumplings in hand, cutely agree to "not fight anymore" in their performance of *Friends*,[18] we must follow their example and use empathy to combat adversity.

Alongside teamwork, it's important to know how to strive for happiness even through strife. For ARMY, there is no greater spokesperson for happiness than Jimin himself. The word has become a brand for him, stylised as 'h^^py', with the two carets symbolising a pair of smiling eyes. This Jimin-ified version became popular among ARMY from when he was spotted sporting a Chanel bag with 'i'm so h^^py' embroidered upon it with bright yellow thread in December 2019.[33] Identical to how he is presumed to have threaded that phrase onto the leather, Jimin has woven the concept into his life. In a *Bangtan Bomb* ringing in 2020, Jimin created his goal for the year: "I want to make a firm path that allows for my happiness."[34] This was a simple, yet bold declaration, made harder as he and the other members experienced multiple disappointments due to COVID-19. Still, Jimin succeeded with flying colours.

"Every time I sing our music, I'm always happy;"[35] "I felt happy when I got back home;"[36] "making this album was a very happy period of time."[37] Jimin explicitly expressed his joy on numerous occasions, even depressing ones, such as when BTS had to perform for shadowy voids throughout the year. But more frequently, he expressed his desire for ARMY to find happiness, too. This became his most significant message throughout 2020, starting even before the pandemic as Jimin answered during the *ON* music video filming that he wanted to hear "I'm so happy!" from ARMY the most.[38] In the summer, this changed to words of reassurance with "all you have to do is to keep laughing where you are",[30] and in the fall a hope that "you could find happiness."[31]

These messages are honourable, strong testaments to his character, but so is his ability to recognise that happiness is not always possible. One of Jimin's best qualities is his emotional intelligence which allows him to empathise with many emotions, mirroring how he can change filters. In the pandemic, this intelligence helped him be hopeful without falling into toxic positivity. Toxic positivity refers to optimism gone overboard, labelling only happy emotions as 'helpful' or 'good' and dismissing negative ones.[39] When someone shares something weighing on their heart, a meaningless claim of 'it will be okay' or 'cheer up' can often do more harm than good. Instead, it is more comforting to validate and express compassion for those emotions, and Jimin did just that in 2020.

This appeared in the creation of *BE*, specifically in a conversation about the title track that would become *Life Goes On*. Jimin expressed concern about the song's theme, not wanting it to be too optimistic since "something intended to be consoling can make someone feel even worse."[40] By understanding positivity can be hurtful, this led to the members creating a quiet track that sat with emotions of sadness, nostalgia, and hope, rather than one superficially advocating for smiles and endurance. As shown through Jimin's comprehension of emotion, he honours a rainbow of filters both within others and in himself. Thus, he avoids toxic positivity, promoting healthy expression.

While Jimin recognises the validity of the pain the world experienced in 2020 and wants to help others, he knows healing everyone is far beyond his reach. In a March VLive, he regretfully expressed this, saying, "I might not be able to do anything for you."[21] Yet, Jimin continued to identify that he can "give [ARMY] a positive effect",[21] demonstrating it by what he does best — creating new filters through which to perceive life. Jimin claimed he wanted to become a "happy virus",[21] a term that denotes his desire to instil happiness in ARMY as well as his skills in redefinition. Because 'virus' has become a thing of fear, Jimin reinterpreted it to become a word associated with his sweet self.

This idea of shifting perspectives to cope with pain also appeared in *Fly To My Room*.[15] Jimin begins the track against a hard, constant beat imitating the repetition of quarantine, utilising assonance as he sings, "it's so suffocating that I'm going crazy" and "feel like it's still day one".[15] By starting the song with compassion for the listeners, who can likely identify with these emotions, he validates those feelings to avoid toxic positivity before offering another point of view. With V's line, "I'll just change this place to my world",[15] the room transforms from a place of confinement to a safe space of wonder. This concept of seeing the good in what we have is further emphasised when Jimin sings, "sometimes you get to know, broken is beautiful".[15] Broken is still broken, but sometimes, there's beauty in it. *Fly to My Room* encourages us to adopt a new mindset to ease a negative situation, which Jimin did in 2020 to achieve happiness. As much as h^^piness is Jimin's brand, this year he advocated for multi-faceted filters of expression, and through accepting those emotions without judgement, he was able to strive for joy.

Sexy: "You'll be wanting only me"[1]

In Jimin's hands, 'sexy' is not simply defined by bare skin or suggestive movements. Rather, it's a facet of him that is allure, charm, and power of his own creation. Most memorably in 2020, he expressed 'sexy' through his performances of *Filter*, inspiring conversations on gender and masculinity. Jimin also explored new filters of creativity behind the curtain, expanding his repertoire with his work as a producer for *Friends*, production manager on *BE*, and songwriter on *Dis-ease*. Jimin redefined 'sexy' in a healthy way that best suited himself, a quality exuded on stage through his dance and offstage in his life.

Black or white? Red or purple? Pristine fedoras, pressed jackets, sleek scarves, or expensive shades? The question may change, but the answer remains the same: Park Jimin. In his performances of *Filter* at the *Map of the Soul ON:E Online Concert*, the 'stage commander' awed ARMY with his stunning vocals, dancing, and visuals.[41] Jimin claimed he was "really ambitious",[31] words made indisputable with complicated, energetic choreography. What was most incredible, however, was his ability to filter *himself* by showing various sides of his personality within the same stage.

As a dancer and performer, Jimin is gifted in his ability to interpret. On stage, interpretation refers to the ability to take a set piece of music or choreography and make it one's own. Depending on the genre or intention of a piece, one's freedom may be limited, but interpretation in art is always encouraged. However, for an excellent interpretation, foundational skills are essential — and, here, Jimin is perfect. With his precise musicality, trained technique, and refined muscle memory that produces effortless lines, once a routine has been learned, he can focus on interpretation.

In *Filter*,[41] Jimin interpreted the choreography to not only stand out from his backup dancers, but also to contrast with himself. On Day One, his movements were quick and powerful, hitting poses with high energy and professionalism. Day Two's performance felt more coy, comfortable, yet dangerous as he glided through the choreography. A moment that best demonstrates Jimin's interpretation ability is *the* move — a body roll, sit, and sway motion where Jimin trailed a hand down his chest, stealing the hearts of ARMY. Some backup dancers' interpretations made it complex, thrusting their hips or leaning into the motion, while Jimin made it simple. As he bent his knees in plié, his lifted spine let him remain tall, hips perfectly still in a wide, second position. With a slow, side-to-side shift emphasised by his shoulders and two fingers curved delicately around his inner thigh, Jimin's rendition of this move was not only sexy, but elegant. Throw in attitude differences between days — Red Jimin throwing a smirk to the side and Purple Jimin challenging the camera with piercing eye contact — and the result was two unique, equally captivating pictures. Through these subtle differences, Jimin showed his excellence in skill and self-confidence as a performer. Small alterations in movement and facial expressions can shift the entire tone of a piece, and while Jimin remained 'sexy' throughout all of *Filter*, he did so in multiple ways. Picking a favourite 'Jimin' is nearly impossible.

But, is picking even an option? With how *Filter* is written and performed, Jimin appears to be at the audience's mercy, singing "I will become anything for you".[1] However, this perceived choice is just an illusion. *Filter* encapsulates Jimin's ability to entrance any audience through presenting himself in countless ways, which calls back to Carl Jung's concept of persona. Jimin can choose to filter himself through his persona as cute, sexy, lovely, rugged, aloof, innocent, etc., and at least *one* style will appeal to each viewer. As they are further enraptured by his appeal to their specific desires, "neither tastes nor standards matter" anymore, since they "want [him] and only [him]".[1] What he wears, what he looks like, how he dances — none of it matters. The only true choice is Jimin himself.

Jimin is undeniably attractive no matter his form, the epitome of 'sexy' — yet not necessarily in the stereotypical sense expected for men. But as Jimin himself has so concisely stated, "What *is* men?"[42] Masculinity and gender expression are not topics unfamiliar to Jimin, who, along with BTS, has had a visible journey in transforming those socially-defined concepts into self-defined ones. Worldwide, gender role expectations tend to cater to the patriarchy, and while they are more oppressive for women, they are also harmful to men in leading to toxic masculinity. In their 2020 interview with *Esquire Magazine*, Suga described it as a "culture where masculinity is defined by certain emotions, characteristics."[43] These 'characteristics' are stereotypically male traits such aggression, emotional repression, and giving off a 'strong' air. This makes men believe they must exude these characteristics to be a 'man,' an ideology which, at its worst, can lead to violence or homophobia. Generally, it results in an unhealthy mindset where men feel they must be callous, tough, or macho.

Jimin and the other members of BTS are perfect examples of healthy masculinity — they are openly affectionate toward each other, and have been so since before debut in 2013. However, the stage then was a different story. Their rookie years delivered concepts influenced by traditional masculinity and hip-hop culture, with the members decked out in black-and-white, baggy t-shirts and flashy, gold rings and chains for *No More Dream*.[44] Jimin's physical masculinity was even a focal point of that performance, where he flashed his abs at the camera with a smirk. This 'bad-boy' persona persisted on stage, also making an appearance at the 2014 *Mnet Asian Music Awards (MAMA)*.[45] There, Jimin executed a hard-hitting krump routine with j-hope, ripping through his white tank top with a roar to reveal a bare chest with fake tattoos.

In these early years, the members consistently voiced a desire to be 'cool'. Jimin specifically lamented in several logs that he "could have shown [a performance] much cooler",[46] and wanted to "show a lot of cool images" in the future.[47] It can only be presumed that 'cool' refers to this type of sexy, macho image Jimin displayed — aggression at *2014 MAMA*,[45] a built body, a rogue demeanour. While not necessarily toxic, these expressions of masculinity seem to have stemmed from the expectations of that culture, as alluded to by Jimin himself in 2019. "I think I wanted to appear like a strong man. Now," he smiles, "I can just be myself."[48] And Jimin *is* himself, having developed own healthy version of what it means to be a man both on and offstage. Often, he carries himself with an ethereal beauty and soft air that some would describe as feminine, rejecting gender norms by sporting layers of jewellery and sometimes clothes marketed towards women. Still, he gives off an air that is intense, confident, and, most importantly, entirely Jimin.

Sometimes, being 'entirely Jimin' means redefining gender expression on his own terms, as he did in *Filter*. On Day Two of the performance, sharp-eyed fans spotted two distinct words adorning Jimin's palms:

JIMIN: A KALEIDOSCOPE OF FILTERS

'illecebra' and 'arcanus'. Both terms, fans uncovered, were in Latin, with 'arcanus' referring to the idea of mystery and even being defined as a "confidant",[49] and 'illecebra' meaning alluring or enticing.[50] These two words seemed to be perfect for his final performance of the song, highlighting the true, alluring mystery that the *Filter* stage embodied. But there was more significance to them when fans looked a little deeper; while 'arcanus' was a masculine form, 'illecebra' was feminine. Whether or not these terms were chosen with that intention, the importance of them lied in conceptualising how Jimin perfectly embodies both the masculine and feminine energies that the terms construct. Jimin shifts our understandings of what can be defined as "masculine" or "feminine" in the same way he challenges us to go beyond our preconceived notions of 'cutie' or 'sexy' or 'lovely'. His performance of *Filter* as described above is an entire example of this blending, but the 'arcanus' and 'illecebra' also extend beyond the song itself, representing rather how Jimin fuses both energies into his own expression of who he is. Somehow these two words perfectly illustrate how Jimin flows between not only what we understand as 'feminine' and 'masculine', but even going back to the definitions of the words themselves. His 'arcanus' side revealed through the mystique of his stage presence and focused gaze, but offstage is translated into his role as a confidant for those around him. The 'illecebra' arises in his innate onstage charisma, but also transfers into his charming and captivating offstage personality.

Jimin's *Filter* stage[41] was inspiring and validating to many ARMY as he interpreted gender on his own terms — yet another example of him expressing a filter wholly his own. He thus defined 'sexy' for himself in an effective, healthy way, but this was hardly the only moment in 2020 where he resisted toxic masculinity. One of Jimin's strengths is his ability to be vulnerable with his emotions, and he voiced them genuinely throughout the year, especially his feelings about being unable to perform. Before the final *ON* promotional stage, he expressed being "a bit sad" for not feeling like he had connected with ARMY, and as time passed, these emotions grew.[36] "It's a tough time for us;"[17] "I'm kind of fragile right now;"[40] "I felt very dejected and helpless."[51] Reflecting on 2020, he described that coronavirus' effect on BTS' plans for the year was "as if you poked a balloon with a needle."[52] In these quotes, Jimin's feelings come out so clearly, it is painful. However, he was never more candid than in one moment during the *ON:E Online Concert*.

Days before his 25th birthday and barely an hour after revealing *Filter*, Jimin cried. This was not the first time he had grown tearful during a concert, but this particular ending comment was distinct.

> "I think there were a lot of things I was frustrated about/things that were a bit unfair to be honest. As corona[virus] broke out, more than anything else, happily doing a concert like this with the members and playing around, being happy, and spending time with you all like this...doing this was what I wanted to do the most, but I...I didn't know why I had to go through something like this… "[53]

Those final words especially were heartbreaking to view in real time as Jimin repeatedly wiped his tears with his sleeve and paused to breathe, trying to keep from breaking down. He gazed out at the sea of ARMY's pixelated faces cheering him on, displayed on screens surrounding the arena as a virtual audience, with a look of sadness, pain, and love. It was this final emotion Jimin later described as what pushed him over the edge. Apparently, he wasn't aware the concert would feature ARMY watching in real time until several numbers in — "since then," he stated, "I couldn't get it together."[31] Jimin then recounted how stifling his emotions about not seeing ARMY, the opposite of his true nature, led him to that point.

> "At first, I let go [of] everything. Next, I tried to accept the reality, telling myself that it's okay. But when I saw your eyes during the concert, I realized it was not okay. I think I wasn't feeling good all along. The moment I saw you, the tears just poured down."[31]

JIMIN: A KALEIDOSCOPE OF FILTERS

It was the way he could "feel [ARMY's] hearts through the screens" that led him to tears,[31] and Jimin's reaction touched those same hearts with piercing understanding. His words became one of the most significant moments of the night, and many ARMY commented on social media about how deeply they were affected. While also feeling "there would've been people who were going through way more serious difficulties than we were",[52] words that demonstrate his humility, Jimin ultimately had a positive effect on ARMY by showing his emotions and being honest with himself. Thus, there is strength in vulnerability despite what toxic masculinity dictates. Just as by displaying filters of himself on stage, Jimin is an inspiration in real life through showing filters which are true to himself, and authentic, healthy expression is refreshingly 'sexy'.

But offstage, Jimin continued to showcase a 'sexy' side of himself through venturing down new avenues of creativity. While *Map of the Soul: 7*'s *Friends* was his duet track with V, it also displayed Jimin as both songwriter and producer, representing a new layer in his innate artistry. In BTS' comeback special for the album,[54] he confessed he was nervous to reveal it to ARMY, it being the first time he participated in the creation of a song for the group. But he felt confident in the synergy between V and himself, claiming that he believed ARMY would appreciate the stories the song relays. In his "I'm here~!" VLive on March 26th of 2020,[17] he disclosed the process that the song underwent to get to where it was, explaining how he wrote the melody of *Friends* alongside two other tracks that were presented to be chosen. Oddly enough it was the song he least preferred. But somehow it was meant to be; the song that Jimin believed "wasn't that special to begin with" ended up becoming "the most emotional song in the entire album."[17] It was even more special that the track that marked Jimin's debut as a songwriter and producer for BTS also happened to be the one that meant the most.

Through his role as both producer and songwriter for *Friends*, Jimin was able to showcase how his talent does not only lie in singing or dancing, but extends into all realms of the creative process. That urge to create, to translate a story through a medium outside dance or performance, that coloured his discussion of how *Friends* came about revealed yet another expression of Jimin. It was 'sexy' to see Jimin talk passionately about the process of constructing the track in his VLive, ARMY getting to see a new side of him in relation to his work and creative outlets. It was igniting to witness how his creative talents translate into the arena of production, showing that he truly can do it all. Expression through songwriting seems a natural fit for him, as it became a new means through which he could convey emotion or tell a story for the world to see.

When the pandemic hit, Jimin, along with the rest of BTS, inevitably felt a loss. But it was in that feeling of darkness that BTS decided to create a completely self-produced album, *BE*. Here, Jimin took on the challenge of a new role behind the scenes: project manager. And what a fitting role it was. Acting as the intermediary, Jimin's responsibilities as project manager seemed to play to all of his teamwork strengths, requiring him to facilitate discussions, combine ideas, encourage the members, and relay their concepts back to the company.[40,37,55] He, though, brushed it off on more than one occasion, claiming his job was "nothing special."[55] But this role allowed us, as ARMY, to see how Jimin's ability to unify and relate to people translated into the production side of his artistry. It afforded him the ability to discover a new side of his creativity that was cathartic in a time with so much chaos, disconnection, and uncertainty. And he admitted that it brought him a lot of pride to be able to organise the group's ideas to create a cohesive album.[55] Acting as a mediator, the one checking in, giving updates, and encouraging others, seems a natural fit for Jimin being the empathetic Libra that he is, but this act of unity was central to the construction of *BE*. It was symbolic. It was natural. It was Jimin.

Being able to not only try out a new role but also find happiness through it was another key tenant of this new position as project manager. Through the process of organising ideas and fostering collaboration, Jimin was able to work alongside his teammates in a way that was healing. Throughout his *201111* YouTube livestream,[37] Jimin constantly talked about the joy this project and role brought to him. During a period where so much emphasis was put on production, despite the toll the pandemic was taking on the world's mental well-being, Jimin found solace in the collaboration, creating rather than working on a project that came from the soul. He even disclosed how the process gave him a chance to understand and acknowledge himself in relation to the current situation, but also offered him some reprise through creation. In the same stream, he shared that "the process, asking the members to listen to [new ideas], the way we used to work, the way the other guys used to work before. It's been a while since we worked this way, so it was a very joyous time."[37] Collaboration and working through creation in a new way gave Jimin the chance to find *happiness*.

The album's sixth track, *Dis-ease*, relates directly to this idea of how work becomes an illness through the endless need to produce. The group sings and raps about how the process of production is blurred between love and hate, necessity and passion, not knowing if it's *them* that are sick or the world itself.[56] It is only in the bridge portion of the song that, you guessed it, Jimin wrote where we see an acknowledgement of continuation and an acknowledgement of strength.[13,57] Jimin disclosed that the process of creating this bridge took a matter of mere minutes; he was playing around in the sound booth, doing some ad libs, when the producer asked him to write something down.[13] Within four minutes, it was complete. ARMY were, of course, blown away: here was just another testament to how Jimin really can do anything.

But this bridge is significant in its lyricism, as well. It embodies the story of how Jimin has truly honed into his power in 2020, having journeyed "through the fire" to step into his own, walking "in [his] own style"[56] today more than ever before. Just as he reflected on his own experiences in *Friends* and *Christmas Love*, so too do we see a bit of that here with the lyrics "when the night comes, I'd close my eyes and believe in myself that I used to know".[56] In the darkness, in the hardest part, turning towards his old self and *trusting* him is a recognition of the journey Jimin has been on to get to where he is now. This is followed up a few lines later with what is almost a reply, stating that while Jimin trusts his past self, he knows that he has become stronger today. Jimin is both acknowledging the past, understanding that the experiences and hardships have made him who he is today, but also recognising that he is now stronger than ever. Trusting his past self instead of rejecting it takes courage.

For Jimin, his past self was constantly focused on work, a patient of the questionable illness described in *Dis-ease*. Even in his very first log, he stated that BTS had "to be even more hard-working."[58] With Jimin's many accomplishments and perfectionism, he has always possessed this devoted work ethic. And he is not alone — the capitalist ideology that dictates our worth equals our production pervades societies worldwide. This mindset can be so deeply embedded within us that when we find ourselves with no work, to use Jimin's words, "you start aching".[30] The pandemic brought with it circumstances where this sting became clearer than ever, and these are the emotions explored in *Dis-ease* as the members question their identities outside of their careers.

But in creating this track and the entirety of *BE*, Jimin and the other members allowed themselves to voice their emotions and struggles, transforming work into healing. After this catharsis turned production becomes hopeful when the vocalists recognise their empowerment, then it is where Jimin's spectacular bridge comes to a climax as he belts, "I will never fade away".[56] This line is a definitive statement of confidence, a fierce declaration of legacy — for all of BTS, and notably for Jimin. He delivers the culmination of the entire song, acknowledging his dedication and passion by validating himself, which is, if anything, the epitome of 'sexy'. This is the masterful, collected poise he embodies throughout *Filter*[41] and offstage as Park Jimin, the artist tirelessly searching for new modes of self-expression.

Lovely: "I want you to be your night, baby"[59]

'Lovely' — meaning delightful, enchanting, the quality of love itself. Jimin is 'lovely' in the truest sense, making this final descriptor the most powerful. From the words he spoke to ARMY with exuberant joy on October 10, 2018 — "I'm so lovely, you're so lovely, we're so lovely"[60] — it's clear it's a term Jimin also identifies with himself. During that exact same weekend in 2020, he best expressed 'lovely' with a dance

JIMIN: A KALEIDOSCOPE OF FILTERS

solo to the orchestral version of *Black Swan* for the *ON:E Online Concert*.[61] Metamorphosing into the black swan, Jimin showed another filter of himself that mirrors him offstage. With an examination of this performance, his music, and his past and present, we can most clearly see who Jimin is as the embodiment of 'lovely'.

Seven shadows decrease to one as a haunting violin shudders to life, leaving Jimin's single silhouette stark against a sea of blue light.[61] A swan stripped of its wings, he collapses to the ocean floor, struggling before falling onto his back in exhaustion. With one hand, Jimin delicately reaches up to the overhead camera as if towards the surface, yearning for the sky that lies just beyond his grasp. Thus begins a fight between light, shadow, and self-acceptance. Throughout the piece, Jimin dedicates himself to this story, embodying the black swan to perfection with his contemporary training. Contemporary is a special style of dance — it utilises technique based in ballet, but doesn't adhere to ballet's rules; it takes the invention of modern, yet seems less strict with boundaries in movement. Contemporary borrows from numerous types of dance to create a style defined by freedom of expression, and this is precisely why it is the perfect style for Jimin. Although he has performed contemporary before, his *Black Swan* solo stands out as he used all of his abilities to create a stunning performance.

Jimin, in this solo, is perfection.[61] His technique is evident in his entire body, from the impressive forced arches of his feet to the delicate positioning of his fingers. More impressive are his lines — the creation of beautiful shapes with the body through extensions of limbs, ones that can be easily broken by a slightly bent leg or a neck tilted too far. Yet Jimin's are always effortless, years of muscle memory taking over to let him focus on other skills. And focus he does in this piece, flying through barrel turns and aerials, spotting nothing but blue light, and shifting from isolated to elongated movements as if breathing. Jimin uses all of his music, *always*, connecting the motions to truly *dance* them, and, through this, he becomes music itself. This solo showcases all of Jimin's talents as a dancer and demonstrates exactly why he is so 'lovely'. Still, the most incredible ability he shows here is expression, or, his capability for storytelling.

As he dances, Jimin creates a narrative of himself as the black swan, mirroring the original song's lyrics. Yet, "cry[ing] out a silent cry",[62] Jimin does not speak, instead twisting and turning his body to tell a story. Dance is a visceral language used to convey feelings that can only truly be felt and expressed through the physical body. It is through this language that Jimin experiences "first death",[62] telling a tale of ups and downs as he repeatedly falls to the floor and picks himself up. Just like an artist void of passion, a swan does not belong at the bottom of the ocean. Regardless, Jimin still finds a way to fly at the climatic point of the routine, extending his arms behind his back — out, out, out, *out* — as he finally spreads his wings and accepts his shadow. This narrative is evoked not just from the choreography, but from how Jimin embodies it. His control, musicality, technique, facials, and the way he *throws* his entire being into every moment of the dance, make the performance the evocative piece it is. It's identical to how in his life, Jimin uses numerous filters to create an image that is entirely loveable and fully him. By showcasing movements both light and dark, in this solo Jimin expressed metaphorically how he may be understood — as multi-faced and wholly 'lovely'.

On stage, Jimin manifested the core theme of *Black Swan*, voiced in his own words as a "self-confession of the artist."[35] His offstage journey bears a striking resemblance to this sentiment, particularly with the word 'confession'. This is most easily perceived in his songs *Lie* and *Promise*. Each with lyrics written by Jimin, they are similar in how they refer to a 'you', discuss suffering, and centre around truth. However, their differences demonstrate Jimin's efforts to accept his 'lovely' self without reservation.

Lie is brimming with torment. "Please get away, away, away from me", Jimin cries out, wanting to be freed from "these lies [...] this hell [...] [and] [...] this pain".[63] Yet, his torturer appears to be a shadow-filled side of himself. In 2016, RM described that Jimin wrote about his past and how he fell into a mindset "deep in lies" where he always "blamed [himself] [...] [and] always thought about [his] flaws."[64] Within the music, Jimin is both the victim and perpetrator of his suffering, and even though he knows these hurtful words are indeed lies, Jimin remains helpless against his own mind in a conflict without resolution. These parts of him are separate, but coexist in chaos as stifled and unhealthy filters of expression, respectively. However, Jimin worked hard to find peace within himself, as evidenced in his first original song, *Promise*.

According to Jimin, 'peace' wasn't his original goal, initially intending to make "a song that scolds [himself]."[65] The concept was dark and harsh, stemming from a quality Jimin disliked. "I'm not… not honest," he confessed a month after the song's release in December 2018. "I can't be honest with myself, that's what made me feel so suffocated."[65] But then, Jimin described that eventually he came to "a resolution and a promise" that centred around the self-addressed message, "'I want you to love yourself.'"[65] Utilising expression positively, in *Promise*, Jimin sings to the part of him that is unkind, candidly empathising with himself about his pain. Further, he encourages himself to accept both his good and bad sides without judgement through the lyrics, "I want you to be your light […] [and] I want you to be your night".[59] Jimin's journey, from causing his own suffering to promising himself to strive for self-love, shows how important genuine and free expression is to him. He has always been 'lovely,' but it's the progress Jimin made by embracing all of his filters, as the artist does in *Black Swan*, that enabled him to fly. By being honest, Jimin defined himself as the embodiment of 'lovely' in 2020, loving the light, dark, and everything in between.

But part of that light stems from looking back to the past in order to look forward. While Jimin brought in elements of childhood glee to work through internal empathy this year, another source has been through his embracing of narratives of the past to run even harder into the future. During BTS' interview with *Pitchfork* in 2020, Jimin chose *Epilogue: Young Forever* as his favourite song from the group's discography, claiming it was "a song that really means a lot to me."[66] This isn't the first time Jimin has mentioned his attachment to *Epilogue: Young Forever*, often referring to it as a source of comfort. In his previous Vlog from 2018, *180413 Jimin*,[67] he has even mentioned that he often goes back to watch clips of the group's performance of the track, wanting to hear the voices of ARMY as they collectively sing the song. While this instance was from several years ago now, the fact that Jimin still mentions this track as his favourite really is telling about the impact the song has had on him. And how fitting that this song, one that was released on a 2016 album about finding yourself and running towards a dream, was what Jimin mentioned in a year that has brought with it an impossibility to look toward the future at times.

In a serendipitous way, *Epilogue: Young Forever* seems to embody the variety of emotions that 2020 has brought Jimin. There was the initial feeling of abrupt change, the inability to perform, but it was blended with the courage to continue. This year more than ever, the words of "even when I fall… I run endlessly to my dream"[68] seemed to be the most pertinent for Jimin. Just as he found comfort in the soft falling of snow through *Christmas Love*, so too did *Epilogue: Young Forever* represent a means through which Jimin took comfort in the past and its connection to ARMY in order to look forward. Jimin's loveliness in this way manifested in an expression of holding onto the most important of times in our past to understand who we want to be going forward. He found comfort in that, embodied it even. His loveliness extended beyond the confines of the stage and became a loveliness defined by finding comfort in the past.

Of course, *Epilogue: Young Forever* is a song that means a lot to ARMY, too. It's the song we come back to, the one we chant for encores, and the song we often look to for words of encouragement as well. It's the song that represented their first Daesang-awarded album, *The Most Beautiful Moment in Life: Young Forever.*[69] And that's exactly where the connection stems from, this connection of a past song that binds Jimin to the fans, and us back to him. Jimin has stated he cried while watching videos of ARMY singing along, understanding why ARMY have such an attachment to this song and to BTS. It makes perfect sense, then, why Jimin still in 2020 feels attached to this song. The desire that Jimin expressed even three years ago of wanting to return to the stage after watching *Epilogue: Young Forever*, wanting to feel that physical and emotional connection again with ARMY, seems to echo the same sentiments expressed in 2020.

Conclusion: "I run endlessly to my dream"[68]

This year was not only a journey of redefining boundaries and expectations, but it was also a continuation of Jimin's projection of self-love and acceptance. Through the explorations of his varying filters and the expression of redefining himself through his performance, Jimin continuously demonstrated how loving himself was an act of strength in more ways than one. Empathy has been his superpower time and time again, whether it be with his members or with ARMY through VLives, tweets, or even Weverse posts. But this year also saw Jimin loving himself through finding and redefining the means of expression. Self-love was not just about loving who he was, but also understanding his own worth in relation to others. It was about Jimin realising that he is someone who loves to express love, but also loves to *be* loved. In his November *Weverse Magazine* interview, he expressed that this took the form of understanding who was *worth* his time, and who wasn't, stating:

> "I also saw some people for -who they really are, some people who don't really care about me. Rather than pushing those people away, I learned how to react less emotionally to them. Likewise, I was able to be more emotionally honest with people who are very considerate toward me."[13]

Jimin has always been honest about his journey of self-love, but disclosing how he has learned to react with less emotion towards those that do not extend the same levels of understanding towards him struck a chord with ARMY. Here, Jimin showed that understanding himself first and foremost was his biggest strength. Putting himself first, putting his emotional well-being at the forefront before others was a means of translating his self-love into self-compassion. Deciding to react with distance rather than disdain was a direct act of this self-compassion and a declaration of knowing his worth. To Jimin, empathy is something that is relational, a dialogue of understanding that resides in interactions with others. It even, as the quote above reveals, exists in the creation of boundaries.

Through this exchange is also where Jimin showcased this year how external love can also be a reflection of the internal. At the end of his note for *Christmas Love*, Jimin shows this in saying that all of us "always deserve to be loved."[19] While this sentiment was directed at ARMY, it also translates back into Jimin's own understanding of his self-worth and acknowledgement that he is deserving of love. 2020 was the year Jimin realised that love, not only of others but of himself, can truly make him stronger. This ultimately translated into his own work, as he stated that upon reflecting on his own position as a performer and artist, he wants to continue to create not only for the sake of the craft itself, but also to receive love from those around him. It is easy to say creation stems from a position of passion and desire, but it is courageous to say that the desire itself is a desire of love and acceptance.

Jimin's journey in chasing after love is powerful, and 2020 was a year where he achieved this goal by being honest with ARMY and himself, baring his filters through onstage performances and offstage expressions of the heart. He showed empathy, connection, and the importance of happiness, similar to that seen in *Friends*,[18] redefined masculinity and productivity, mirroring his *Filter* stages,[41] and reflected on growth and self-acceptance, themes he discussed through movement in his *Black Swan* solo.[61] 'Cutie', 'sexy', and 'lovely' are all Jimin — both sides of him and the artist himself. Like an opal, he cannot be described with one colour as he holds a multitude of shades, each glittering, dynamic, when light shines upon them. And so, we must give him the spotlight he deserves, capturing all the facets that complete him.

2020 was more than difficult, but Jimin persevered. Further, he flourished, expressing a kaleidoscope of filters and continuing to sprint toward his dream — which, currently, is "performing in front of you all in person."[52] Jimin has labelled his motivation as not only ARMY, but

JIMIN: A KALEIDOSCOPE OF FILTERS

"the thought of [his] future self who will have grown into an even better artist."[70] Many ARMY, it is easy to assume, are just as excited for his future accomplishments and what new filters of expression he will embody. Whether they fit 'cutie', 'sexy,' or 'lovely,' each and every side will be loved as Jimin himself is meant to be loved and *is* loved — incredibly so. This chapter is an attempt to vocalise that love and project it outwards to him, a love typically represented through screams and shouts at concerts. Jimin has described this sound, the sound of ARMY's voices, as "the most beautiful and happiest sound."[71] Even through infinite distance, we hope that as he asks us to "apply [him] to [our] heart[s]"[1] in *Filter*, Jimin, too, can hear our love and hold it close to his own.

References

1. BTS. (2020). Filter [Song]. On *Map of the soul: 7*. Big Hit Entertainment.; Doolset. (2020, February 21). *Filter* [Translation]. https://doolsetbangtan.wordpress.com/2020/02/21/filter/
2. Serendipity_page. (2020, March 26). BTS new interview about on 'map of the soul: 7' 방탄소년단 [Video]. https://youtu.be/77gO1EcG07Y
3. Hwang, J.Y. (2019, June 13). *Busan recommends tour following Jimin (BTS)'s footsteps*. https://m.vlive.tv/post/1-11232581
4. Grauso, A. (2020, August 6). *Who Is BTS?: Your crash course on the band that's suddenly everywhere*. https://atomtickets.com/movie-news/who-is-bts-your-crash-course-on-the-band-thats-suddenly-everywhere/
5. Channel Korea. (2020, January 29). *What did the vocal coach say about BTS' singing skills?*. https://channel-korea.com/about-bts-singing-skills/
6. KOREA NOW. (2019, June 14). *BTS Jimin's highschool teacher and classmates reveal Jimin as a student* [Video]. https://youtu.be/8IBHrkmNr1g
7. Fairchild, M. & Bongbong. (2019, March 15). *Interview where BTS members describe each others' personalities!*. https://mnews.joins.com/article/23412069?IgnoreUserAgent=y#home
8. NME. (2018, October 11). *BTS vs. NME | Get to know the K-Pop sensations* [Video]. https://youtu.be/L993jVyE1I4
9. BTS. (2019). *BTS KKUL FM 06.13 : Comeback special* [Video]. https://www.vlive.tv/video/122415
10. 방탄소년단 [@BTS_twt]. (2019, February 26). 오늘 여러가지 정말 큰 상을 많이 받았습니다. 진심으로 감사드리고 앞으로도 더 좋은 음악과 무대로 여러분과 함께 나누고 싶다는 생각이 많이 [Tweet]. https://twitter.com/BTS_twt/status/1100449341200773121?s=20
11. Morin, N. (2020, December 2). *BTS helps the world feel a little smaller — & we need it more than ever.*

https://www.refinery29.com/en-us/2020/12/10163161/bts-be-album-songs-pandemic-group-interview

12 Bangtan Subs. (2013, May 9). *[ENG] 130426 Jimin's log* [Video]. https://www.youtube.com/watch?v=LfMOglXt4w0
13 Weverse Magazine. (2020, November 23). *Jimin "I'm the kind of person who likes to be loved."* https://magazine.weverse.io/article/view?num=56&lang=en
14 Big Hit Music. (2020, November 2). *BE | BTS | Big hit entertainment* [Video]. ihttps://ibighit.com/bts/video/be/bqHCnnbOQe5Bqt4AB9ICeb9M.php?l=kor
15 BTS. (2020). Fly to my room [Song]. On *BE*. Big Hit Entertainment; Doolset. (2020, November 20). 내 방을 여행하는 법 (Fly to my room) [Translation]. https://doolsetbangtan.wordpress.com/2020/11/20/fly-to-my-room/
16 BTS. (2020). Friends [Song]. On *Map of the soul: 7*. Big Hit Entertainment; Doolset. (2020, February 21). *Friends* [Translation]. https://doolsetbangtan.wordpress.com/2020/02/21/friends/
17 BTS. (2020, March 26). *I'm here~!* [Video]. https://www.vlive.tv/post/1-18241350
18 Jimin & V. (2020, June 14). *Friends* [Performance]. BangBangCon the live. Kiswe Mobile Studio: Seoul, South Korea.
19 Jimin. (2020, December 24). Christmas love [Song]. On *SoundCloud*; Learn korean with sel. (2020). *Christmas love lyrics* [Translation]. https://www.learnkoreanwithsel.com/soundcloud-songs/christmas-love-by-jimin
20 BTS. (2020, March 26). *Hello, I'm here* [Video]. https://www.vlive.tv/post/1-18241349
21 BTS. (2020, March 30). *My brilliant appearance* [Video]. https://www.vlive.tv/post/0-18231744
22 BTS. (2020, April 14). *Today's guest is?* [Video]. https://www.vlive.tv/post/1-18241346
23 BTS. (2020, June 21). *Today, we're gimbap chefs* [Video]. https://www.vlive.tv/post/0-18231728

24 BTS. (2020, June 21). *Today, we're really gimbap chefs* [Video]. https://www.vlive.tv/post/0-18231727

25 BANGTANTV. (2020, June 7). *BTS commencement speech | Dear class of 2020* [Video]. https://www.youtube.com/watch?v=AU6uF5sFtwA&t=552s

26 Big Hit Entertainment. (2020, May 26). EP6. *Now and tomorrow* [Video]. https://www.weverse.io/bts/media/2135

27 BANGTANTV. (2020, September 23). BTS (방탄소년단) Speech at the 75th UN general assembly [Video]. https://www.youtube.com/watch?v=5aPe9Uy10n4

28 Cruz, L. (2020, December 26). *The astonishing duality of BTS*. https://www.theatlantic.com/culture/archive/2020/12/bts-2020-borahae/617521/

29 claire ⁷ ⌟ [@btstranslation7]. (2020, December 11). [TRANS] *The situation outside only seems to worsen with every passing day.. Please make sure to wear your masks, and please* [Tweet]. https://twitter.com/btstranslation7/status/1337608859242926085

30 BANGTANTV. (2020, June 16). *200616 Jimin (+ENG)* [Video]. https://www.youtube.com/watch?v=DYaj3NLIOQU

31 BTS. (2020, October 20). *I'm here* [Video]. https://www.vlive.tv/post/1-19344698

32 BTS. (2020, April 23). TaeTae FM 6.13 ② [Video]. https://www.vlive.tv/post/0-18231741

33 BTS Frontman JIMIN ①③ is Kpop's Best Dancer [@AnyaSpade4]. (2019, December 2). *Today vs 4 months ago* [Image Attached]. https://twitter.com/AnyaSpade4/status/1201690134258700288

34 BANGTANTV. (2019, December 31). [Bangtan Bomb] Happy new year 2020! - BTS (방탄소년단) [Video]. https://www.youtube.com/watch?v=zDP_EQYmT6U

35 BANGTANTV. (2020, February 25). *BTS global press conference 'map of the soul : 7'* [Video]. https://www.youtube.com/watch?v=akn5Uemr4Wc

36 BTS. (2020, March 8). *Live before last performance~*□ [Video]. https://www.vlive.tv/post/1-18241354

37 BANGTANTV. (2020, November 11). *201111 Jimin (+ENG)* [Video]. https://www.youtube.com/watch?v=xIzBCXEdmEo

38 BANGTANTV. (2020, March 8). BTS (방탄소년단) 7-second interview [Video]. https://www.youtube.com/watch?v=LF7Fm52OwV0

39 Chiu, A. (2020, August 19). *Time to ditch 'toxic positivity,' experts say: 'It's okay to not be okay.'* https://www.washingtonpost.com/lifestyle/wellness/toxic-positivity-mental-health-covid/2020/08/19/5dff8d16-e0c8-11ea-8181-606e603bb1c4_story.html

40 BANGTANTV. (2020, May 11). *2004** BTS (+ENG)* [Video]. https://www.youtube.com/watch?v=D7HPWv4apDA

41 Jimin. (2020, October 10 & 11). *Filter* [Performance]. Map of the soul ON:E online concert. Olympic Gymnastics Arena: Seoul, South Korea.

42 Bang, S (Executive Producer). (2016). *BTS bon voyage* [TV Show]. Big Hit Entertainment.

43 Holmes, D. (2020, November 23). *The boundless optimism of BTS.* https://www.esquire.com/entertainment/music/a34654383/bts-members-be-album-interview-2020/

44 HYBE LABELS. (2013, June 11). BTS (방탄소년단) 'No more dream' official MV [Video] https://www.youtube.com/watch?v=rBG5L7UsUxA

45 Mnet K-POP. (2015, November 30). *2015 MAMA [Boys in battle] BTS vs BlockB (2014 MAMA) 151127 EP.5* [Video.] https://www.youtube.com/watch?v=fnjQB4xpYG8

46 (2014, February 13). *[ENG] 130726 Jin & Jimin's log* [Video]. https://www.youtube.com/watch?v=MXiKfqg6cKA

47 Bangtan Subs. (2018, November 23). *[ENG] 140103 Jimin's log* [Video]. https://www.youtube.com/watch?v=JKyuyfL_0EQ

48 Big Hit Entertainment. (2019, January). *BTS world tour: Love yourself in Seoul: Commentary film* [Film].

49 Latdict. (n.d.a). *Latin definition for: arcanus, arcana, arcanum.* https://latin-dictionary.net/definition/4457/arcanus-arcana-arcanum

50. Latdict. (n.d.b). *Latin definition for: illecebra, illecebrae.* https://latin-dictionary.net/definition/22645/illecebra-illecebrae
51. PICKCON / 픽콘. (2020, August 21). 【ENG】 방탄소년단 BTS "Dynamite" Online global press conference (글로벌 기자간담회) [Video]. https://www.youtube.com/watch?v=3K7J7oXEDmw
52. BANGTANTV. (2020, December 31). [Bangtan Bomb] Happy new year 2021 - BTS (방탄소년단) [Video]. https://www.youtube.com/watch?v=49qk_V6uW-M
53. 스튜디오 [@STUDIO_0613]. (2020, October 10). *201010 jimin ending ment* [Image attached] [Tweet]. https://twitter.com/STUDIO_0613/status/1314916611078402055
54. BTS. (2020). *[Full] BTS comeback special: Let's do a viewable 'purple' radio* [Video]. https://www.vlive.tv/video/175309
55. Bangtan Subs. (2020, May 1). *[ENG] 200501 Jimin's live log* [Video]. https://youtu.be/C0ePHI494cQ
56. BTS. (2020). 병 (Dis-ease) [Song]. On *BE*. Big Hit Entertainment; Doolset.병 (Dis-ease) [Translation]. https://doolsetbangtan.wordpress.com/2020/11/20/dis-ease/
57. BTS. (2020). *BTS 'Live goes on'* [Video].https://www.vlive.tv/video/223615
58. Bangtan Subs. (2014, February 3). *[ENG] 130125 Jimin's log* [Video]. https://www.youtube.com/watch?v=avjAIUnveBE&t=7s
59. BTS. (2018, December 31). 약속 [Song].On *SoundCloud*. Big Hit Entertainment; Doolset. 약속 (Promise, Jimin) [Translation]. https://doolsetbangtan.wordpress.com/2018/12/30/promise-jimin/
60. Big Hit Entertainment. (2019, March). *BTS world tour: Love Yourself in Europe* [Film].
61. Jimin. (2020, October 10 & 11). *Black swan: Orchestral version* [Performance]. Map of the Soul ON:E Online Concert. Olympic Gymnastics Arena: Seoul, South Korea.
62. BTS. (2020a). Black Swan [Song]. On *Map of the soul: 7*. Big Hit Entertainment; Doolset. (2020, January 17). *Black swan* [Translation]. https://doolsetbangtan.wordpress.com/2020/01/17/black-swan/

63. BTS. (2016). Lie [Song]. On *Wings*. Big Hit Entertainment; Doolset. (2018, June 16). *Lie* [Translation]. https://doolsetbangtan.wordpress.com/2018/06/16/lie/
64. BTS. (2016, October 20). *WINGS behind story by RM* [Video].. https://www.vlive.tv/video/15694?channelCode=FE619
65. BTS. (2019, January 19). 내가 왔다! [Video]. https://www.vlive.tv/video/109729?channelCode=FE619
66. Pitchfork. (2020, October 5). *BTS break down their albums, from Dark & Wild to map of the soul : 7 | Pitchfork* [Video]. https://youtu.be/Tt9x61AL50E
67. Bangtan Subs. (2019, March 8). *[ENG] 180413 Jimin's log* [Video]. https://youtu.be/EwM24PQOj_Q
68. BTS. (2016). Epilogue: Young forever [Song]. On *HYYH: Young forever*. Big Hit Entertainment; Doolset. *Epilogue: Young forever* [Translation]. https://doolsetbangtan.wordpress.com/2018/06/01/epilogue-young-forever/.
69. Jeong, G. (2016, November 19). *BTS wins best album of the year at the 2016 Melon Music Awards*. https://www.soompi.com/article/916995wpp/bts-wins-best-album-year-2016-melon-music-awards
70. Chakraborty, R. (2020, November 9). *BTS: The rolling stone interview*. https://rollingstoneindia.com/bts-the-rolling-stone-interview/
71. 스튜디오 [@STUDIO_0613]. (2020, October 11). *201011 jimin ending ment* [Image attached] [Tweet]. https://twitter.com/STUDIO_0613/status/1315230251593719808

j-hope

CROSSING LINES WHEN IT COMES TO MUSIC
Nikola Champlin

Part one: Art for hope and peace

Jung Hoseok. Sunshine *j-hope* of BTS. The group's third-oldest member, one-third of its multi-talented rap trio, and a dance prodigy who left his home city of Gwangju for Seoul in order to follow his passion for dance when he was only a teenager,[1] j-hope is a person who seems born to be on the stage. Confident, charismatic, and perpetually peppy, j-hope has, since the group's debut in 2013, been known for his energetic live performances and for his outstanding dancing. As BTS' global popularity skyrocketed from 2017 onward, j-hope has often caught the eyes of casual viewers who comment on his bright personality and world-class dance skills.[2] Among BTS' devoted fans known as ARMY, j-hope (lovingly nicknamed Hobi) is universally adored for his kindness and his doting care for the other members, appreciated for his stunning on-stage flair, and idolised for his bold fashion sense.[3]

Yet, oftentimes, Jung Hoseok, the person behind the larger-than-life performer who is j-hope, is an enigma. Many ARMY have told me that j-hope is one of the harder members for them to understand, to feel like they really know what's going on in his mind and in his heart behind that bright, toothy smile and loud, excited voice. While, on the surface, j-hope is someone we hear from a lot — always boisterous in interviews, easily smoothing the way even with limited English during BTS' first set of eclectic American media circuit appearances — many ARMY seem to find him harder to understand than, say, Jung Kook or Suga who are often described to be wearing their hearts on their sleeves.[4] For casual listeners and fans, Jung Hoseok may be entirely and fully *j-hope*. Yet, j-hope has repeatedly shown multiple sides of himself and he has asked ARMY to see the depths of his thoughts, character, and personality. He has alluded to the responsibility he feels to be an entertainer and to the influence of his stage name that made "hope" indivisible from his identity.[5] j-hope has spoken openly about times in his BTS journey that were not easy nor happy, and when he was not always able to be positive.[6] j-hope should not be reduced to a handful of skills or to a sunny personality. j-hope may be harder to access than some other members of BTS because his onstage energy shines so brightly, but, therefore, the process of closely analysing his words, his songwriting, and his actions is all the more rewarding.

This examination is, of course, with limits. j-hope has chosen to share so much of himself with ARMY, but we don't know him personally and we don't know those things he chooses to keep private. Yet, he has generously given fans and the public so much of himself — through his words, his songwriting, his performances, his humorous commentary in BTS' reality show-style content like *Run BTS!*[7] and *In the Soop*,[8] as well as direct addresses to fans on VLive and YouTube. As a j-hope-biased fan who has never swayed from this choice of bias, there are numerous things that I find relatable in j-hope's art and in his character and these are the things that have inclined me toward him for years, while never lessening my love and appreciation for each of the others in their own special ways. As one of many j-hope-biased fans who feel resonance with j-hope's character beyond his skill set and sunshine personality, I like to talk about all the ways I feel connected to our Sunshine, Hobi.

In the challenging year of 2020, these emotional points of connection I felt with j-hope only grew and took on new layers. Before 2020, one of the largest windows I felt I had into j-hope's personality, character, and thinking was his solo mixtape *Hope World* which was released in March

J-HOPE: CROSSING LINES WHEN IT COMES TO MUSIC

of 2018.⁹ This mixtape paints a picture of the boy Jung Hoseok who would become j-hope and the shock j-hope still feels at the dramatic changes that have occurred in his life as he faithfully followed his dream of dancing. In the song *Airplane* on *Hope World*, j-hope tells us:

> It's still not believable to me
> That this Gwangju kid could get wrapped up in flight
> From my place in this high, high dream
> I'm flying above the beautiful world.¹⁰

In these lines j-hope expresses disbelief at the contrast between his origins, his humble beginnings, and the life he lives as an international celebrity, a life defined by travel and the beautiful richness of experiences, languages, food, and cultures — all made accessible, although still dream-like, by this airplane. When j-hope writes of travelling in an airplane, feeling that awe and hope when actualising his dream of seeing the world beyond his own familiar hometown ("That was what launched my dream /That was what made 'now'" he sings of his very first international trip with his members to Japan),¹⁰ listeners get to know the things that he appreciates and that he chooses to immortalise in verse.

j-hope's focus in his songwriting pre-2020 reflects his character and his public personality: one that is focused on the positive and hopeful things in his life. In the second track on his *Hope World* mixtape *P.O.P. (Piece of Peace) Pt. 1*, j-hope writes:

> If I
> Someone's strength
> Someone's light
> I wish I could be a
> Piece of peace¹¹

This song expresses his longing for his life and his work to contribute positively to society, a central pillar of who j-hope is as a person and one that is reflected in the topics and themes on which he focuses his writing.[11] Repeatedly, j-hope chooses to write about hope, about peace, about his dreams and aspirations, about his upward journey alongside the other members of BTS. Writing about these topics does involve sharing his emotions — his wonder, his shock, his awe, as well as some aspects of these changes that were challenging for him — but the songwriting on *Hope World* reveals less about j-hope, I would argue, than what we saw through his songwriting in 2020. In 2020, j-hope's songwriting went through a poignant evolution as he chose and embraced a new level of public vulnerability, talking about topics that would previously have felt "off-limits" for j-hope.

In a nutshell, j-hope in 2020 was both consistent and new, the same and different. He continued to show ARMY the personal characteristics and messages we have always loved and identified with him: resilience, hard-work, positivity, hope, encouragement of others, and self-confidence. On top of this consistency, he additionally showed new sides of himself, crossing into territory that was new and challenging, as he tackled tougher topics in his songwriting, as he stepped out of his comfort zone as a performer, and as he explored areas that showed he is increasingly comfortable taking risks.

Part two: Embodying ego

j-hope began 2020 in the minds of ARMY by examining and living the Jungian concept of ego. The more I reflect on the idea of ego as defined in the writings of the early 20th century, Swiss thinker Carl Jung, the more I feel this concept is the ideal fit for j-hope, among the members of BTS, to explain and embody.

In Jungian philosophy, the soul has three components: persona, shadow, and ego.[12] BTS' iconic rap trio tackled these three components in turn, exploring and examining how they each understood and expressed these ideas in their public and private lives. After RM's *Intro: Persona* in 2019, in 2020 Suga took the lead on the song *Interlude: Shadow* and j-hope starred on the song *Outro: Ego*, continuing a pattern of solo tracks

J-HOPE: CROSSING LINES WHEN IT COMES TO MUSIC

fronting albums that really got started with RM's *Intro: What Am I to You* on 2014's *Dark & Wild*.[13]

j-hope was the third of the three rappers to release his song. On January 8, 2020, Big Hit Entertainment shared a comeback map for BTS' highly anticipated *Map of the Soul: 7*[14] album that showed the imminent release of both *Shadow* and *Ego*.[15] This gave ARMY the opportunity to dream about and anticipate these upcoming tracks and music videos and to reflect on the ways in which each member of the diverse, dynamic rapline might embody their respective Jungian concept.

Before reading Carl Jung, whenever I heard the word "ego" it always had a negative connotation. Someone might be accused of having a big ego, or being egotistical, when they put themselves above others or myopically focused on themselves and their achievements. But for Jung, ego is the conscious Self, the synthesis between public and private versions of ourselves.[16] None of the Jungian archetypes of the soul, I learned, are bad things. Instead, they are natural aspects of ourselves.[16] The persona is our public self, the person we are socially, adjusting ourselves to fit our various social roles: parent, child, student, employee, boss, community volunteer, activist, and even ARMY. The shadow is our private self, our instinctual thoughts and feelings that we cannot control, and includes the feelings we have relegated to our subconscious because we fear they are not socially acceptable. The ego, our conscious "self" as we understand it, draws on our subconscious and designs our persona, forming the healthy synthesis of external and internal life.[16]

Throughout the song *Outro: Ego*, j-hope uses a refrain of self-trust. "Just trust myself" he sings, paired with another English line, "wherever my way".[17] As he bops along to an upbeat track that seems firmly centred in the unique style and sound he showcased on *Hope World*, he dances in front of images and objects that show his identity.[18] Some of these images are parts of his public persona: from the unique "Hobicore" style[19] I instinctively try to emulate, including smiley faces, graphic tees, and jewellery by artist Hurjaboy, to his artistic accolades (as he passes in front of a record shop, images from his solo video *Chicken Noodle Soup*[20] and the covers of BTS albums, as well as *Hope World*, appear in the window).

But some of these images and objects show more personal parts of j-hope. As he raps about the life of Jung Hoseok (his "self" without the public life of BTS), he shows photos of himself as a small boy, enjoying his favourite type of cake (strawberry), looking quizzical, and dancing.[18] I believe that the role of these visual elements is to demonstrate j-hope's genuine enjoyment of his personal style and preferences. He is celebrating these things, he is gathering them around himself and showing them off as an act of self-love.

If I were to pick the single thing that I love and admire most about j-hope (a tall order!), it would be that, in his songwriting, in his interviews, and in his very essence as a person, j-hope seems *aware* of happiness. Being aware of happiness is not the same thing as being happy. Someone who is aware of happiness does not always feel it, but they treasure it when they do. They collect the things that make them happy — they wear them, they hug them, they enjoy them. Awareness of happiness seems, to me, to be a choice, an active decision to prioritise happiness and appreciate things, and people, and places that bring you happiness. The members of BTS and j-hope himself have repeatedly spoken of how the bestowing of j-hope's stage name gave him a deep-seated purpose that he continues to uphold. He is the member who brings, gives, and shares hope. As he's told us so many times, he's our hope, and we're his.

I would like to emphasise how effectively j-hope blends the public and personal as he shares his message of hope. j-hope is someone who has made the personal — everything from his fashion choices to his food preferences to his work ethic — public. He has assembled the things he personally and instinctively loves around him, creating a unique self-brand that is instantly recognisable. This is why j-hope wonderfully exemplifies the concept of Jung's ego. Even as an international celebrity he is down-to-earth, practically minded, and humble. His work ethic and perfectionism shines through in every BTS project. He's the member insisting on another run through, the member monitoring the recordings of their dance practices with the sharpest eyes in pursuit of perfection. After the ground-breaking success of *Dynamite* giving BTS their first Hot 100 #1 in August of 2020,[21] j-hope was the member who didn't want to forego dance practice that day to celebrate.[22] And while I admire Jung Hoseok deeply and overwhelmingly for each day of his deliberate dedication to his craft, it's his repeated choice to be positive and happy — to be j-hope — that, I suspect, takes the strongest will and firmest commitment.

One example of this, which seems tiny, yet incredibly important to me and in fact revolutionary the more I think about it, is j-hope words during the interview portion of BTS' James Corden appearance on January 28, 2020. Early in 2020, BTS promoted the release of *Map of the Soul: 7* through several American TV show appearances. During these lively and light-hearted ventures — from James Corden's popular Carpool Karaoke[23] to Jimmy Fallon's iconic Grand Central Station *ON* performance[24] — j-hope continued to embody the energy of the Jungian ego that he'd used to help launch the *MOTS: 7* era. j-hope has always been confident in English interviews, connecting with his audience across a language barrier, using even only a handful of English words to capture his personality, the things he loves (Sprite!), and his warm-hearted enthusiasm. Yet, in all these early 2020 American appearances, it was clear to me that j-hope had been working hard on his English, as he spoke for longer, threaded in new vocabulary, and debuted an accent that was notably more American. In the James Corden interview, James posed this question to j-hope: "you're the quickest to learn the routines, what do you do if you mess up?"[25] As the member who leads the choreography review and is, as described, a hard-working perfectionist, this question seemed fitting for j-hope specifically. In a slightly flustered moment, perhaps a bit flummoxed by finding the right English words for his answer, j-hope said, "I don't care" with a bit of laughter at himself.[25]

I thought about this moment frequently in the months that followed. It seems, at first glance, a misfit response for j-hope's persona as we know and love it. But this moment, to me reveals his ego more clearly: a synthesis of his public perfectionism and his, as explained by himself, at times negative inner voice. In saying he didn't care if he made a mistake, j-hope normalises mistakes. Mistakes are going to be made, by BTS, by all of us. Mistakes are part of the learning process, and as someone who has devoted his life to learning — both in areas that he excelled at from a young age, like dance, and areas that were new, like rap and song-writing — j-hope knows this. Mistakes are part of the process and you shouldn't care about them. This kind of realistic optimism, in this tiny moment, seemed to encapsulate a lot of who j-hope is to ARMY: someone whose brand of self-love is one of self-trust and hope. Hope does not require perfection. It looks to the future and relies on improvement. It brushes mistakes off and quickly tries again. j-hope was able to expand the circle of people who benefit from his positivity through BTS' long-anticipated *Carpool Karaoke* appearance. *Carpool Karaoke* highlighted the personalities of BTS as a whole, across a language barrier, in a really effective way, providing translations of their clever Korean commentary and appropriately-timed personal camera cuts to show their reactions and expressions.[23] I was so glad to see how well this revealed BTS' individual skills and characters, and, like many ARMY, I avidly read the comments on the video from "locals" praising BTS, beaming whenever anyone shouted out "the guy in the middle" for his energy,[26] his smile,[27] and his "straight up just vibing."[28]

In the chorus of *Outro: Ego*, j-hope ascribes BTS' success to both "choice" and "fate", as he says that the place he and BTS have arrived at is "all / choices by my fate / so we're here".[17] Choice and fate form another dichotomy, like persona and shadow, while the current existence of BTS and j-hope himself rests in the middle. It would be wrong, j-hope suggests, to attribute BTS' success entirely to their free will, as BTS has arrived at an incredible pinnacle of achievement through a combination of factors and something like destiny.[17] But it would also be wrong to ascribe their journey entirely to fate, as this undermines the incredible impacts of BTS' hard work, creativity, and inventiveness throughout their journey. The thing that allows for the maximisation of both great choices and a brightly shining fate, j-hope says, is trust in oneself.[17] In trusting himself, in striking the right balance between many competing forces in his life, j-hope shows us how to live an authentic life, and this is a life encompassed by the Jungian idea of the ego.

J-HOPE: CROSSING LINES WHEN IT COMES TO MUSIC

Part three: Remedies and rage in 2020

j-hope's 26th birthday, on February 18, 2020, occurred right on the hinge between normalcy and a worldwide lockdown. He appeared that day on VLive to talk to ARMY, sharing his reflections and his hopes for the next year.[29] Yet, j-hope's expectations for 2020 were so mismatched from reality, just like all of our own. As we were all glued to the news, isolated in our homes, as the case numbers and death tolls rose, I kept mentally coming back to *Outro: Ego* and j-hope's insistence that we all "look ahead, the way is shinin' / keep going now".[17] 2020 did not seem like a year that would be shining, I thought. But a key thing I learned from j-hope in 2020 is that happiness isn't situational, it's a state of mind.

j-hope, by nature of being himself and living with a daily appreciation of happiness, has long been a source of positivity for ARMY. His bright smile and loud, unrestrained laugh mean that anyone around him or watching him instinctively smiles in response. In 2020, j-hope applied this skill set with intention, not simply relying on his display of happiness to uplift others, he worked to directly encourage ARMY and to be a bright light during the pandemic, providing ARMY and casual listeners with a brief reprieve from the tough daily circumstances around the world. In the year 2020, j-hope continually used a theme of affirming self-confidence and consistently applied the language of self-love as he spoke to his fans.

j-hope's commitment to sharing positive and hopeful messages with ARMY shone through in BTS' *Commencement Speech* in early June at YouTube's virtual graduation ceremony. In his remarks, j-hope echoed the refrain from *Outro: Ego*, as he said "I decided to trust myself."[30] In contrast to *Outro: Ego*, which was released when the way forward was shining and BTS was on the brink of another international journey to see their fans live in concert, j-hope's *Commencement Speech* remarks on self-trust came, not in a time of promise, but in a time of deep hardship. He told us that in the moments when he felt he'd reached "a dead end," when he could hardly take "a step forward," these were the moments he relied on self-trust. Just like j-hope's brand of happiness, I know this is not an easy thing to do. I noticed that j-hope tells us that he "decided" to trust himself.[30] Trust is not always our instinct and it's not the easy way, but the difficulty of this makes trusting in ourselves all the more necessary and powerful. Speaking in the context of commencement, j-hope ties this idea of self-trust to the lives of students who, at times, he knows, will distrust their decisions, from their major to their career.[30] Even though I listened to this speech as a twenty-nine-year-old and felt my graduations were far behind me, I was questioning many of my life decisions in 2020, trying to reprioritise my friendships and relationships with my family members while separated by big physical distances. I felt j-hope's advice personally, in the midst of my questions, as he reminded listeners that, "you are the leader of your own life."[30]

In his songwriting and in his performances, j-hope has a powerful appreciation for what his audience needs to hear. The nuance and freshness with which he delivers each performance — even a song he's performed with BTS many times — demonstrates his awareness of context. In June 2020, following hot on the heels of BTS' powerful words at YouTube *Commencement*, BTS brought new live performances to their repertoire with *BangBangCon The Live* their anniversary event. j-hope's shared contribution, the haunting *Jamais Vu*, had debuted on *Map of the Soul: Persona* back in 2019,[31] but hearing this song performed live in June 2020, it seemed to take on a whole new meaning in the context of this year.

In j-hope's verses in *Jamais Vu*, he described exactly those moments he referenced in his section of the YouTube Commencement speech: the moments where you're at a dead end, where you want to give up. "It'd be better if it was a game / because it hurts so much / I need to heal my medic" j-hope raps.[32] Through a reference to the video game *Starcraft*, in which the "medic" is needed to heal the other players,[33] j-hope describes a real world scenario in which even the source of healing is hurt, is wiped out as a resource and a source of hope. The chorus of the song that repeats the phrase "please give me a remedy" continues the language of hurt and sickness that requires treatment and healing.[32]

J-HOPE: CROSSING LINES WHEN IT COMES TO MUSIC

In the spring of 2019, when this song was released, I had thought of sickness and healing in entirely metaphorical terms. In June of 2020, when j-hope, Jin, and Jung Kook performed *Jamais Vu* for *BangBangCon The Live*, I thought of sickness and of healing in entirely *literal* terms. "All I wanted was to do well / I wanted to make you smile" j-hope sings, and we know, here, is the heart of his mission in 2020.[32] He wants to be hope and happiness for ARMY, in our darkest moments, and for him, his darkest moment, is any place he feels he's failed to do this. In showing us that he, too, feels failure, experiences moments when he blames himself for his imperfections (another line from this verse), he relates to his listeners, he emphasises, and he uses music as catharsis. Through sharing and acknowledging pain, it loses, even just a little bit, its grip on us.

In *ON:E*, BTS' second online live concert series of 2020, we not only got a charming performance of *Outro: Ego* with j-hope beaming and dancing in his carefree way, but we also saw the rapline and vocal units perform the pieces from *MOTS: 7* for the first time, and I'm pretty sure my soul left my body during j-hope's live verse in *UGH!*, debatably one of his greatest verses of all time. From its growling tempo and spit-fire lyrics, *UGH!* doesn't immediately seem to be a song of catharsis and comfort. A casual listener wouldn't group this song with *Jamais Vu*. Yet, in a fascinating parallel, *UGH!* also relies on music to explicitly channel and process emotion. The emotion that's being processed is different — and that difference is reflected in the sound of the song — but the end goal is the same. *Jamais Vu* asks for a remedy and serves as one. *UGH!* calls out rage that "takes over" the world, that "nobody can live without", and channels rage at rage productively and processes it.[34]

By October 2020, rage was another word, like sickness, that had shifted connotations in light of the events of 2020. I speak from the context of life in the U.S., where our country was confronting its deeply-rooted, systemic racism as Black Lives Matter protests swept the country.[35] Citizens stratified along political differences, as a divisive presidential election churned forward.[36] Neighbours and family members felt rage and betrayal directed at one another, divided over once seemingly simple public health protocol like wearing a mask.[37] All across the world, as the virus raged, communities and family members were torn apart by death, unable to say final farewells. Each ARMY faced their own set of tragedies, both local and global. There were, as j-hope put it, "tens of thousands of reasons to be raging".[34] In this verse, j-hope tells us he can rage, and we should too. Angry is okay, anger is natural. But if this anger is misdirected and there is "damage done to others' lives" then the hurt begets only more hurt:

> Someone gets hurt at someone's actions
> Someone becomes gloomy at someone's speech and behaviour
> Someone's spur of the moment becomes someone's moment
> Someone's rage becomes someone's life[34]

UGH! offers us a timely reminder about how to effectively direct our anger, and, in channelling it, provide catharsis. Although crafted before 2020, and performed relatively early during tumultuous 2020, *UGH!*'s lyrical relevance provided a significant touchstone throughout the year.

I've spoken of how j-hope's prioritizes positivity and shares happiness with his fans, through his lyrics, through his words, and through his performances. Throughout their career, one of the spaces in which BTS has most directly worked to provide comfort and levity is through their self-made reality TV shows, such as *Run BTS!* and *Bon Voyage*.[38] In 2020, without the option of international travel, ARMY were instead gifted *In the Soop*, a glamping trip that featured the members hiking, boating, fishing, playing sports, cooking, and doing crafts.[8] As I watched *In the Soop* I was struck by j-hope's craft skills, as this came soon after another heart-warming highlight of the year: j-hope's friendship-bracelets VLive.[39] On that day, ARMY trended HES MAKING BRACELETS on Twitter, overcome by the simple, yet touching gesture of j-hope making bracelets for his members.[40] Many ARMY were inspired to make bracelets of their own, for friends and family members. During *In the Soop*, j-hope exhibited a similar kind-heartedness and patience, as he meticulously assembled a wooden airplane and painted a canvas with a heart reading *I'm Your Hope*.[8] Before 2020, I didn't think of j-hope as one of the 'visual art-inclined' members of BTS. It's obvious that he enjoys art, colour, and visual elements (just look at how much he excels at fashion), but something about seeing j-hope pouring over these crafts projects was new and emotional, and very comforting, for me.

j-hope is bright and happy throughout his crafting, chattering away to ARMY like he would to close friends on VLive, and talking to the other members in a similar fashion on *In the Soop*. He smiles widely with pride at his own handiwork.[8] He chases that wooden airplane with all the glee of a child.[8] He clearly enjoys what he's doing. At the same time, I could not believe how long j-hope was willing to spend on these projects (his patience with that wooden airplane, as he glues every piece precisely, was a bit shocking to me, even though I felt I appreciate just how thorough and persistent j-hope is).[8] I loved that j-hope showcased himself crafting and doing art projects in 2020, and he was not the only member to do so. As a whole, these acts of patience and care, that did not rely on expertise or mastery, were comforting and inspiring to ARMY. Try something new this year in this strange and unexpected time you have, j-hope seemed to be saying to us: you don't need to be an expert, you can make something for someone you love.

Part four: Creating music to cross boundaries

In 2020, j-hope continued to provide the comfort and inspiring energy that he and BTS as a whole have always prioritised. Yet, 2020 was also a year of notable growth for j-hope, as he continued to push himself and grow, and he did some things that departed from his past choices as an artist. I noticed j-hope striking new ground primarily in the latter half of 2020, and through the songwriting on BTS' self-produced *BE* album,[41] but I also saw a plethora of small innovations, places where j-hope tried new things with awesome impacts.

One small example (when it comes to j-hope, even the smallest details speak volumes, I feel, because j-hope himself loves details) of j-hope charting new ground is his vocal part in *Dynamite*. *Dynamite* was a risk for BTS as a group, as they elected to do a full English song for the first time, departing from the songwriting influence of the rapline that has formed the backbone of their music for years. This song also prioritised the role of the vocal line and asked the rapline to step out of their comfort zone in singing more than rapping, putting their voices to an upbeat pop track rather than some of the edgier or grittier soundscapes in which they've been more traditionally comfortable. j-hope, RM, and Suga happily charged out of their comfort zones to bring us *Dynamite*, which has been a sky-rocketing success and a bright spot of 2020. It's my most streamed song of the year on my Spotify, and I definitely listened to it on many days when I didn't feel much like "shining through the city" when I first turned on the track, only to have my mood quickly improved.

j-hope's vocal part in *Dynamite* is in a much higher range than he normally prefers, which he has commented on repeatedly in interviews when asked about the track.[42] Very literally, this pushed him out of his normal zone of operation, and his perfectionism meant he worked at delivering this short, but challenging part with aplomb. j-hope shone through *Dynamite*'s 33 performances (no surprise there!) bringing his unique flair to the *VMAs*,[43] *Tiny Desk*,[44] and the show-stopping *Melon Music Awards* dance break oozing confidence in that purple, velour suit.[45]

I also loved to see j-hope being forced to confront his own sexiness (this doesn't happen enough!) after the wild popularity of his *Dynamite* promotional photo sporting the iconic OBEY t-shirt and sunglasses on the back of his head.[46] In an *AskAnything* interview, an ARMY asked j-hope if he knew about the reaction among fans to his hot promotional photo. We got to see j-hope flustered (as he always is by compliments), but also clearly pleased.[47] While certain other members of BTS are often praised first and loudly for their good looks (which is a double-edged sword), I'm more used to the collective reaction of ARMY to j-hope focusing on his dancing, his charisma, his rap flow, and his positivity. It's

J-HOPE: CROSSING LINES WHEN IT COMES TO MUSIC

another small moment, but a beautiful one, to see j-hope pushed out of his comfort zone by everyone calling him hot.

j-hope skyrocketed into new territory again with his contribution to the *Savage Love Remix*, which earned BTS their second Billboard Hot 100 #1 credit,[48] and listed j-hope and Suga as the first Korean songwriters on a Hot 100 #1.[49] This huge achievement seemed to come somewhat out of left field for a group that rarely covers other artists' songs as a full group, and it was delivered with a spontaneity and enjoyment that seemed to say it was the product of j-hope, Suga, and Jung Kook saying "sure, let's try it!" In his lines, j-hope raps "whether I'm afraid of you or that time / I'll love you like a fire right now".[50] Referring to a supposed future parting/break-up when he says "that time," j-hope tells us that his response to the possibility of an ending is to love "like a fire right now". Again, taken within the context of 2020, when BTS, like all of us, were separated from loved ones, friends, and experiences we cherish, these lines felt to me like a reminder to live in the moment and cherish it. The only response to loss is to love more fiercely in the moment, I realised, feeling the depth of j-hope's deceptively direct addition to the song. Both j-hope and Suga's deep lyrics present an almost ironic contrast to the original lyrics of the song, recontextualising the idea of "fake love" and elevating it.[50] Both rappers focus on the theme of the fleetingness of love, acknowledging that love may not be something that lasts, which can be found in Jason Derulo's original words, as he tries to make a lover stay, but j-hope and Suga expand this idea to more universal concepts of love and loss, that are not underlined by a romantic relationship that exists to get back at an ex-lover.[50] As we've grown to expect from them, BTS takes the personal and makes it universal without losing any emotional specificity.

As the world wound down difficult, taxing 2020, ARMY knew we'd be receiving another gift from BTS before the year's end: BTS' *BE* album, their self-produced tour de force that they made in the darkest and most uncertain moments of 2020.[51] I am far from the first person to point out that the *BE* album is, in every way, a product of the pandemic. Hours and days that would have been spent on a world tour, were instead spent at home and at the studio, writing and producing these tracks. The songs speak to the experience of the pandemic, referring to loneliness and isolation, but also the importance and the power of connection in the face of these feelings and experiences. j-hope crafted the song *Dis-ease* for this album, a song that plays on the meaning of 'disease' as a sickness and the meaning of the word as literally the opposite of 'ease'. I also hear in this title the echo of BTS' rapline's history of writing diss tracks in the form of their multi-part *Cyphers*. Again, in the context of 2020, the word 'disease' has a whole host of associations and connotations. Yet, this 'dis-ease' looks at a very personal application of the concept: the seductive relationship j-hope has with overworking.

In *Dis-ease*, j-hope begins the song by capturing his anxiety that surrounds both working and not working. He tells us that he "relieves" this anxiety "with a sip of coffee",[52] but does this take place on a busy morning when he needs the caffeine or on a day he has free from work and is even more anxious? I wondered, pouring over translations of these lines. When j-hope has free time, he explains in the song, he's uncomfortable.[52] What reassures him is not really coffee, but work, the feeling that he's energised and getting stuff done. But, he knows, he easily takes this to the extreme. "I think I should work till my body breaks", he raps, an honest acknowledgement of his workaholic mindset.[52] He is not "at ease" (emotionally) with being "at ease" (physically), which connects to the second understanding of the title of this song: the opposite of "ease". j-hope's relationship with work is one that he wants to escape, it seems to me, but this fixation on working stays with him, infecting him like a disease. He doesn't feel he's done enough, but when he overworks, he also chastises himself. As an adult, working ARMY, these feelings of self-accusation and "not doing enough" were immediately familiar to me, although j-hope processes and expresses them in his own unique way. Poignantly, he realises the real problem: "insecurity, this is a disease".[52] It's neither working nor having free time that is really the problem for j-hope. It's his mindset, and his guilt, that infects him in either scenario. This is further spelled out in the pre-chorus, in the words, "I'm sick, yeah, because I think too much".[52]

J-HOPE: CROSSING LINES WHEN IT COMES TO MUSIC

In the chorus of *Dis-ease*, there is a line that I interpret to be speaking to j-hope's motivations, as a performer, an artist, an idol, an entertainer, a source of comfort and hope, and as a song-writer, all hats we saw him wear in 2020. The *Dis-ease* chorus claims "one for the laugh, two for show"[52] in an echo of an old children's rhyme "one for the money, two for the show,"[53] which has been previously quoted in popular music by performers and artists, including Elvis Presley in his song *Blue Suede Shoes*.[54] In j-hope's adapted version of the line, he explains what he works so hard for: it's for entertainment (the laugh) and it's for the artistry of the performance (the show). It's very clearly *not* for "the money", as j-hope has updated the original line. Does "the one" and "the two" included in this line reflect that j-hope will keep trying at everything that he does? That he will always have the mindset of working twice as hard in order to achieve as much as possible? In this song, j-hope acknowledges an unhealthy relationship with work.[52] I think this line "one for the laugh, two for show" reflects the mentality of someone who puts performance and output first, someone who is ready to turn up the glamour and the charm, to insist that — in the face of any hardship — "the show must go on." j-hope's willingness to live for the laugh and for the show, to work and work for the performance and the music and to keep putting these things first, is both a pillar of his achievement and a risky mindset. *Dis-ease* dissects this aspect of j-hope's mindset in a deeply personal way, without offering any easy solutions.

ARMY knows and loves j-hope for his positivity. j-hope has acknowledged that his purpose and his image — hope-bringer and sunshine of BTS and of ARMY — is not always an easy role to play. He does not always feel happy, and has felt, at times, pressure to maintain this image. But he has also allowed this image to slip when he is not feeling it, and with increasing honesty in 2020. *Dis-ease* is a perfect example of this in my mind. j-hope's Weverse interview from December 2020 includes a reflection on the writing of *Dis-ease*.[55] He says, "the nice thing about music is that I can say what's on my mind, even feelings of sadness or depression, in beautiful ways. I don't usually express those feelings but this time I wanted to try."[55] j-hope acknowledges that *Dis-ease* is new for him, thematically and lyrically.[55] He hasn't been one to draw on the darker side of himself and his feelings for his songwriting, but he does this for *Dis-ease*.[55]

j-hope describes moving away from his normal style as "refreshing", but this new approach leads him into a near identity crisis as it directly challenges some of the things most central to his public persona. "I thought if j-hope leaned too much to one side people might think that's strange, too," he says in his Weverse interview.[55] He acknowledges that, as j-hope, his public persona is strongly associated with hope, positivity, and optimism. But he also acknowledges that he is not always positive, and that his shadow produces anxiety, fear, and frustration at times.[55] He worries that if he were to focus too suddenly on the anxiety around his relationship with work, he'd be "crossing a line," moving j-hope's persona too far into the shadows.[55] Instead, he strikes a poignant balance, pairing a bright chorus and old-school hip-hop sound with lyrics that delve into something that's tough for him to face. He says of *Dis-ease*, "that's why I tried to stick to my standards, but since I'm also human I also expressed emotions I couldn't articulate into music."[55] He's got the power of both sunny tradition and innovative vulnerability at play in *Dis-ease*.

j-hope began 2020 with *Outro: Ego*, with a song squarely rooted in self-trust and self-actualisation. He ends 2020 with *Dis-ease*, a song that shows us what the process of synthesising your persona and your shadow and living your ego actually looks like: striking a balance between your standards and your emotions. Even though j-hope shares much of himself with ARMY, he's also someone who keeps the personal from becoming too public, at times, never letting his Jungian shadow shape his behaviour fully, which he explains in his Weverse interview, saying "in my life itself and in my mind, I always think if there's a line, it shouldn't be crossed."[55] This statement reinforces how much j-hope's hopeful outlook — both publicly shared *and* in his own mind — is an active choice. This does not mean his brightness is false or fake, if he believes he should not cross certain lines into negativity. Instead, it strikes me all over again that j-hope knows the value and power of happiness. By making an active choice to look at the world positively, to be a positive person, he knows

J-HOPE: CROSSING LINES WHEN IT COMES TO MUSIC

he can have a positive impact. This takes strength and courage, day in and day out.

Yet, for j-hope there is an exception to the rule of not crossing professional and positivity lines, and that's music. "But I'm becoming more generous to myself about crossing lines when it comes to music," he says.[55] This seems to be the heart of j-hope's growth and innovation in 2020. Music is a space where the professional and personal rules don't apply. Music is the space where j-hope is increasingly comfortable being the many versions of himself, letting himself confront and process tough things, but also celebrating the things that make him happy.

In so many ways, j-hope crosses lines when it comes to music. I love the idea of him as someone who crosses lines, and as someone who is increasingly willing to do so, because I think this accurately shows his self-awareness and his growth. Many people are not aware when they're crossing a line. To me, it seems that j-hope always is. He crosses *with intention*. He speaks his truth powerfully and personally, bringing his shadow into view and internalising his persona. He encourages ARMY all over the world, crossing lines of language, lines of country borders.[56] He weaves through diverse musical genres, bringing BTS' past into their present, trying out new territory as a singer and as a songwriter. j-hope's songwriting is also, I've always felt, very thematic: he draws on many ideas and experiences associated with certain central ideas and concepts in building his songs. Many of his songs internally reference other songs he's written, or other songs by BTS — from the genius of his remix of *Airplane* in his verse in *Airplane Pt. 2* to *Outro: Ego*'s lift of *Intro: 2 Cool 4 Skool*. j-hope pulls ideas and images together across the lines of different songs, criss-crossing his words into a sparkling, multi-dimensional web.

While *Outro: Ego* and *Dis-ease* bookend j-hope's songwriting contributions in 2020, j-hope was also, in so many ways, an inseparable part of the fabric of BTS as a whole in this year. Just like how j-hope's backing vocals and creative sound effects (running the gamut from unbearably sexy to downright bizarre), appear in nearly every BTS song, he's ever-present in BTS' collective identity. j-hope is always seamlessly adding his flair, and his distinctive melodic rapping, to BTS' sound and his fresh ideas to BTS' lyrics. On the theme of happiness as something that is chosen, not given, and worked at every day, j-hope shared poignant verses in *Black Swan, Louder than bombs, Blue & Grey, Life Goes On*, and *Fly to My Room*, to name only a few examples where I'm slayed by j-hope's thinking and lyric writing. The more we listen to j-hope's words, the more we see how he operates in the world, the more we can internalise this theme of "happiness as a choice" for ourselves. Even the act of choosing to play a BTS track when I'm feeling down and exhausted, feels like something I've learned from j-hope. At each opportunity I have, and in each moment I can, I want to choose happiness.

How will we see j-hope's commitment to happiness, his trust in himself, and his increasing musical vulnerability directed in 2021, hopefully as BTS returns to the live stage? The possibilities are endless when the creator is j-hope. I hope he knows just how much ARMY trusts him to take us in unexpected, yet authentic creative directions. Given j-hope's statement in the *2020 ARMY Zip Interview* that his current challenge is his second mixtape,[57] we have a lot to look forward to and to anticipate from Jung Hoseok who continues to further share his emotional journey as a songwriter with the self-awareness, maturity, and positivity that are all integral parts of j-hope.

References

[1] Jang, Eun-kyung. (2015, November 7). *The star profile: BTS j-hope "My dream is to make 'my own idol.'"* https://web.archive.org/web/20170610033918/http://thestar.chosun.com/site/data/html_dir/2015/04/30/2015043001376.html

[2] L., Laís. (2020, June 9). *Our Hope.* https://medium.com/bulletproof/our-hope-804f9e61d12d

[3] Donbavand, Katie. (2021, February 17). *11 j-hope fashion moments I think we need to talk about more.* https://www.instyle.com/celebrity/11-j-hope-fashion-moments-i-think-we-need-to-talk-about-more

[4] @tamedwaters. (2020, March 2). *him [Jin] and hobi are the two we know the least about...* [Tweet]. https://twitter.com/tamedwaters/status/1234520931973943301?s=20

[5] Bang, S. (Executive Producer). (2019). *Bring the soul* [TV Show]. Big Hit Entertainment.

[6] Bang, S. (Executive Producer). (2018). *Burn the stage* [TV Show]. Big Hit Entertainment.

[7] Big Hit Entertainment. (2015, August 1 - Present). *Run BTS!* [Reality Show]. Weverse.

[8] Bang, S. & Lenzo, Y. (Executive Producers). (2020). *BTS In the soop* [TV Show]. Big Hit Entertainment.

[9] j-hope. (2018). *Hope world* [Album]. Big Hit Music.

[10] j-hope. (2018). Airplane [Song]. On *Hope world*. Big Hit Entertainment; Genius lyrics translations. *J-Hope - Airplane (English translation)* [Translation]. https://genius.com/Genius-english-translations-j-hope-airplane-english-translation-lyrics

[11] j-hope. (2018). P.O.P. (Piece of peace) Pt. 1 [Song]. On *Hope world*. Big Hit Entertainment; Genius lyrics translations. *P.O.P. (Piece of peace) Pt. 1* [Translation]. https://genius.com/J-hope-pop-piece-of-peace-pt1-lyrics

[12] Stein, Murray. (1998). *Jung's map of the soul: An introduction.* Open Court.

13 BTS. (2014). *Dark & wild* [Album]. Big Hit Entertainment.
14 BTS. (2020). *Map of the soul: 7* [Album]. Big Hit Entertainment.
15 Big Hit Music. (2020, January 8). #BTS #방탄소년단 MAP OF THE SOUL : 7 COMEBACK MAP #MAP_OF_THE_SOUL_7 [Tweet]. https://twitter.com/BIGHIT_MUSIC/status/1214957638623973376?s=20
16 Stevens, Anthony. (2001). *Jung: A very short introduction*. Oxford University Press, 1st edition.
17 BTS. (2020). Outro: Ego [Song]. On *Map of the soul: 7*. Big Hit Entertainment; Genius lyrics translations. *BTS - Outro: Ego (English translation)* [Translation]. https://genius.com/Genius-english-translations-bts-outro-ego-english-translation-lyrics
18 Big Hit Labels. (2020, February 2). Outro: Ego [Video]. https://www.youtube.com/watch?v=LmApDbvNCXg
19 Lopez, Amanda. (2021). *Hobicore — j-hope's iconic aesthetic serves looks and inspiration.* https://medium.com/bulletproof/hobicore-j-hopes-iconic-aesthetic-serves-looks-and-inspiration-5a05494c984
20 Big Hit Labels. (2019, September 27). j-hope 'Chicken noodle soup (feat. Becky G)' MV [Video]. https://www.youtube.com/watch?v=i23NEQEFpgQ
21 Trust, Gary. (2020, August 31) *BTS' 'Dynamite' Blasts in at No. 1 on Billboard Hot 100, becoming the group's first leader.* https://www.billboard.com/articles/business/chart-beat/9442836/bts-dynamite-tops-hot-100-chart
22 BTS. (2020, September 1). *1st in BILLBOARD! Gather ARMY!* [Video]. https://www.vlive.tv/post/0-18231721
23 The Late Late Show with James Corden. (2020, February 26). *BTS carpool karaoke* [Video]. https://www.youtube.com/watch?v=T4x7sDevVTY
24 The Tonight Show Starring Jimmy Fallon. (2020, February 25). *BTS performs "ON" at Grand Central Terminal for The Tonight Show* [Video]. https://www.youtube.com/watch?v=MZh-w2nysuI

25 The Late Late Show with James Corden. (202,0 January 29). *BTS recaps the GRAMMYS, looks forward to 'Map of the soul: 7'* [Video]. https://www.youtube.com/watch?v=6_dPHFg7lxo&t=139s

26 Tcmhh_. (2020). *There should be an energy drink call[ed] j- hope. I would drink that every day* [Comment]. https://www.youtube.com/watch?v=T4x7sDevVTY

27 Maitreyee Bhargude (2020). *The guy sitting in the middle is literally a ball of sunshine. He was smiling and laughing throughout the carpool karaoke* [Comment]. https://www.youtube.com/watch?v=T4x7sDevVTY

28 AlkaSeltzer. (2020). *the guy in the middle is straight up just vibing* [Comment]. https://www.youtube.com/watch?v=T4x7sDevVTY

29 BTS. (2020, February 17). *Hoba, love you~♥☐* [Video]. https://www.vlive.tv/post/0-18231757.

30 BANGTANTV. (2020, June 7). *BTS commencement speech | Dear class of 2020* [Video]. https://www.youtube.com/watch?v=AU6uF5sFtwA

31 BTS. (2019). *Map of the soul: Persona* [Album]. Big Hit Entertainment.

32 BTS. (2019). Jamais Vu [Song]. On *Map of the soul: Persona*. Big Hit Entertainment; Genius lyrics translations. *Jamais vu (English translation)* [Translation]. https://genius.com/Genius-english-translations-bts-jamais-vu-english-translation-lyrics

33 *Medic* [Article]. https://starcraft.fandom.com/wiki/Medic

34 BTS. (2020). UGH! [Song]. On *Map of the soul: 7*. Big Hit Entertainment; Genius lyrics translations. (2020). 욱 (UGH!) (English translation) [Translation]. https://genius.com/Genius-english-translations-bts-ugh-english-translation-lyrics

35 Taylor, Derrick Bryson. (2021, March 28). *George Floyd protests: A timeline*. https://www.nytimes.com/article/george-floyd-protests-timeline.html

36 Burman, Tony. (2020, November 6). *In the wake of divisive presidential election, an angry America polarized like never before.*

https://www.thestar.com/opinion/contributors/2020/11/06/in-the-wake-of-divisive-presidential-election-an-angry-america-polarized-like-never-before.html

37 Reynolds, Emma. (2020, July 22). *The mask debate is still raging in the US, but much of the world has moved on.* https://www.cnn.com/2020/07/21/europe/masks-debate-us-europe-asia-intl/index.html

38 Big Hit Entertainment. (2016, July 5 - 2020, January 7). *Bon Voyage* [Reality Show].

39 BTS. (2020, May 14). *If you're bored, watch (Be aware you might get frustrated!)* [Video]. https://www.vlive.tv/post/1-18241339

40 Ky @urgirlky. (2020, May 14). *i don't know who he is, or why hes making bracelets, but i've woken up at 4am to say good for him. you make those bracelets. hell yeah man.* [Tweet]. Twitter. https://twitter.com/urgirlky/status/1260849791640141824?s=20

41 BTS. (2020). *BE* [Album]. Big Hit Music.

42 MTV News. (2020, August 28). *BTS share their top 7 favorite music videos & talk 'Dynamite' | MTV News* [Video]. https://www.youtube.com/watch?v=g2rpmYtnLKw

43 MTV. (2020, August 30). *BTS performs "Dynamite" | 2020 MTV VMAs* [Video]. https://www.youtube.com/watch?v=zJCdkOpU90g

44 NPR Music. (2020, September 21). *BTS: Tiny desk (Home) concert* [Video]. https://www.youtube.com/watch?v=gFYAXsa7pe8&t=209s

45 BANGTANTV. (2020, December 6). BTS (방탄소년단) Black swan perf. + ON + Life goes on + Dynamite @ 2020 MMA [Video]. https://www.youtube.com/watch?v=PtaP4UkZKyc

46 Big Hit Music. (2020, August 10). #BTS #방탄소년단 #BTS_Dynamite teaser photo [Tweet]. https://twitter.com/BIGHIT_MUSIC/status/1292838131234873344?s=20

47 AskAnythingChat. (2020, September 5). *BTS' J-HOPE DANCES just like dynamite* [Video]. https://www.youtube.com/watch?v=SrKNjd1ikow

48 Trust, Gary. (2020, October 12). *Jawsh 685, Jason Derulo & BTS' 'Savage Love' soars to no. 1 on Billboard Hot 100.* https://www.

J-HOPE: CROSSING LINES WHEN IT COMES TO MUSIC

billboard.com/index.php/articles/business/chart-beat/9464165/bts-jason-derulo-jawsh-365-savage-love-number-one-hot-100

49 Nava, Colt. (2020, October 16). *BTS Suga, J-Hope are first Korean artists with songwriting credits on a Billboard Hot 100 #1 song.* https://www.btimesonline.com/articles/140510/20201016/bts-suga-j-hope-are-first-korean-artists-with-songwriting-credits-on-a-billboard-hot-100-1-song.htm

50 BTS. (2020). Savage love (Laxed - Siren beat) (BTS remix) [Song]. Big Hit Labels; Genius lyrics translation. (2020). *Savage love (Laxed - Siren beat) (BTS remix)* [Translation]. https://genius.com/Jawsh-685-jason-derulo-and-bts-savage-love-laxed-siren-beat-bts-remix-lyrics

51 MTV Fresh Out. (2020, December 4). *BTS reveals the meaning Of 'BE' & their favorite song* [Video]. https://www.youtube.com/watch?v=JZPsBtWmlbc.

52 BTS. (2020). Dis-ease [Song]. On *BE*. Big Hit Labels; Genius lyrics translation. (2020). 병 (Dis-ease) (English translation) [Translation]. https://genius.com/Genius-english-translations-bts-dis-ease-english-translation-lyrics

53 Bolton, Henry Carrington. (1888). *The counting-out rhymes of children..* D. Appleton & Company.

54 Presley, Elvis. (1956). Blue suede shoes [Song]. On *Elvis presley*. RCA Victor.

55 j-hope. (2020, November 24). *j-hope "Even just one, single love is beautiful, but we're getting love from all over the world".* https://magazine.weverse.io/article/view?lang=en&num=57.

56 Iyengar, Samyukta. (2021, January 7). *BTS: Music to change the world.* https://medium.com/bulletproof/bts-music-to-change-the-world-53371b7b41dd.

57 Big Hit Music. (2021, January 24). *BTS ARMY ZIP dream interview: j-hope.* Weverse.

Suga

SETTING INTO MOTION THE JOURNEY TOWARDS THE AUTHENTIC SELF

Rajitha Sanaka and Kate Koncilja

In June 2020, BTS gather around a table covered with party treats, glasses of champagne, and a passionately decorated cake to celebrate their seventh birthday as a group — a recurring event by the name of Festa.[1] Excitement is evident on the faces of all the members who naturally drape themselves over each other and speak to the camera with bright smiles — except one member who is nonchalant. Hair the colour of honey, he speaks a few words at his turn and then becomes quiet, as if there is an automated switch within him, timing the man's words and actions. At one moment, he is excitedly expressive, and in the next, he seems to quietly reflect on something else entirely. This same man appeared on a livestream just a month earlier, playing a wild game of *Just Dance* with fellow members Jimin and Jin.[2] In mere minutes, the audience saw his mood shift from, "oh, I have to do this?" to "this is how I rock!" giving fans a burst of energy as they watched him become goofy, cheerful, and motivated while trying his hardest to get the best score.

Expressive, talented, introspective, bold, dedicated, and honest — these are just some words to describe Min Yoongi, more commonly known under the stage name Suga, a rapper of BTS.[3] Sometimes, he appears as more distant and unemotional compared to other members; other times, he is the loudest and wildest of the group. ARMY are familiar with these diverse shades of Suga, coming together to paint a picture of someone who is simultaneously unique, human, and utterly inspiring.

Born in the city of Daegu, South Korea, on March 9, 1993, Suga had grand dreams and an even grander love for music and rap, writing his first song by 13.[3] Yet people dissuaded him from a musical career, his most significant adversaries being his own family. Unable to comprehend his love or talent for music, Suga has shared they were "completely against it. [...] my relatives said that I would most certainly fail."[4] However, boldly following his own conviction, the now global star steadily grew his career, engaging in underground rap battles with the name Gloss and mixing music for local crews in his home town.[3] At 17, he had his first job as a producer, eventually being recruited as one by Big Hit Entertainment and moving to Seoul.[3] It was when Suga was selected by Big Hit in 2010 to become the second member of BTS that all of his past experiences and tribulations culminated to realise his dream. In that moment, Min Yoongi was reborn as Suga: a global superstar, honest rapper, wordsmith, realist, practical dreamer, and swag-master. Many ARMY could not have imagined his pre-debut journey ending any other way. After all, as Suga has rapped when retelling his own story, "what kind of company would... say it doesn't want a genius like this?"[5]

Since BTS' debut in 2013, Suga has become an indispensable member of the group. He writes his own lyrics and produces many of the band's songs, which often are a mirror reflecting the voice, concerns, and confusions of young adults. Aside from his work in BTS, Suga has also extended his talent outwards to the K-pop industry as a producer and rapper featured on the tracks of many solo artists, the most recent and popular collaboration being with artist Lee Ji-eun, more popularly known as IU, for the track *eight* in 2020.[6] He has also worked with Shin Su-ran and the hip hop group Epik High among many others.[7] Most notably, he began his career as a solo artist himself under the moniker Agust D, releasing a mixtape of the same name in 2016 where he flaunted his success and intimately discussed his journey with mental health.[8]

SUGA: SETTING INTO MOTION THE JOURNEY TOWARDS THE AUTHENTIC SELF

Suga's personal evolution over the last eight years since his debut ultimately reveals he is as human as can be. Persevering despite adversity, his story is a well-balanced combination of love, luck, diligence, and endurance with a strong dose of unwavering belief in the self, and that continues into the present day. During 2020 especially, Suga influenced many ARMY with how he chose to live his life, courageously embracing his evolving self and facing the world as he is. Whether speaking as Suga or as Agust D — read backwards as 'DT' and 'Suga' as references to his hometown, Daegu, and current home as a member of BTS[8] — Min Yoongi carries that same honesty and acceptance. When he speaks, sings, or raps, he does it from the heart without embellishment, becoming a safe space where ARMY can feel heard, validated, and understood. This authenticity is one of his most notable strengths, and ARMY witnessed it in action more than ever this past year.

In 2020, Suga's authenticity was a prominent, defining trait of his as combined with his propensity for introspection — sometimes, introspection *itself* was how he showcased this authenticity. He demonstrated authenticity through his music, primarily his much-anticipated, reflective second solo mixtape that released in May, through his decisions, such as prioritising his physical health with an extensive shoulder surgery, and in the way he lived his day-to-day professional, personal, and creative lives, allowing himself to do what he wanted. Each choice Suga made and each way he expressed himself was genuine, even when reflecting on less-than-ideal situations such as the distance the coronavirus pandemic created with ARMY. "I'm used to an entire world shrinking in an instant," he said as part of BTS' speech at the 75th United Nations General Assembly in September, comparing the change in communication as akin to stepping into his hotel room after a lively concert.[9] "It was a precious time, unwanted but welcome," as "life became simple, maybe for the first time."[9] Seeing the light in such a dark situation, Suga was honest in relating how the pandemic gave him a breather from his whirlwind idol life despite the disappointment of having to be away from ARMY. No matter the circumstances, Suga has an authenticity in being honest and unafraid to speak on or accept his reality, showing tremendous courage. Further, his transparency about his fears and how he faces them head on to the point of prioritising himself is a beacon of hope to ARMY. By embracing his authentic self in 2020 and deciding to self-prioritise regardless of all the changes and struggles the year brought, Suga exercised agency by simply being who he wanted to be. As he chooses authenticity and accepts his humanity, Suga acts as not only an inspiration, but as a comforting and relatable figure to ARMY who makes all who look on him hope for the potential in their own lives.

Inspiring with authenticity

There is nowhere Suga better demonstrates his authenticity and introspection than in his music. ARMY know him as an expressive, genuine artist who finds ideas for music in daily life, "writing and taking notes" which turn into powerful lyrics as "every moment is inspirational."[10] 'Inspirational' may not be the ideal descriptor for 2020, but the pandemic made room for the expression of Suga's candid feelings in the self-reflective journey that was BTS' studio album, *BE*, released in November. Reflecting on their feelings and the sudden confusion the pandemic brought with it, the members seemed to say through their album, "in this situation, we are doing something for ourselves, so why don't you try it, too?" Sharing the message that despite the new normalcy, 'life goes on', Suga and the other members gathered to reflect exclusively on themselves, their current life, and the pandemic to provide much-needed comfort through what they know best — music. This was a step ahead in their personal journeys towards their true selves, and clearly catharsis for Suga as well. In fact, for him this journey started a little earlier in the year.

In May 2020, after releasing his second mixtape as Agust D, titled *D-2*, Suga discussed his relationship with music during a livestream, comparing it to an exercise from the book *About Grief* by Brian Shuff and Ron Marasco. To process pain, Suga recites, Shuff and Marasco tell their reader to "'go to a coffee shop [...] sit down, and write down painfully honest words'" before throwing them away.[11] "Instead of going to a new coffee shop and writing," Suga then says, "I make music. And I release my work."[11] With these few words, Suga gives great insight into the authenticity of his craft. By claiming he makes pieces to release his feelings, it only further emphasises his authenticity and practically confirms every verse comes from his heart.

BTS is the face of the Love Myself campaign in partnership with the United Nations which advocates for speaking your truth no matter what, and Suga clearly supports this notion.[12] It is unclear if the group's authenticity as artists was the reason they signed this exclusive, life-changing campaign that resonates with millions, but Suga's drive to speak himself is natural and inspiring. In 2016, a year before the group signed this campaign, Suga's first mixtape, *Agust D*, was released, providing an honest and pure vocalisation of his innermost feelings and truth at that time.[8] Sharing one's story like this can lead to new movements or amplify ongoing ones, and this is the vision both BTS and their company stand for. Suga speaking his truth through music, whether about his mental health, the pandemic, or society, is revolutionary as it reiterates his humanity and underlines the power of authenticity. Additionally, he helps ARMY accept life's struggles and feel safer, comforted, and not isolated through taking full advantage of creative licence as a musician.

For Suga, music is not only a release and comfort, but a voice used to attack, defend, and love. BTS have always been responsible artists — maintaining a fine balance between themselves as professionals and individuals and staying true to themselves while being sensitive to their diverse, global audience. Suga especially is known for this: he keeps calm when expressing his thoughts and combats adversity by erupting in flames through his music. The way he uses his craft as a weapon and shield for himself, the group, and for ARMY is admirable, and this was clearly demonstrated in 2020 on *D-2*.

In the track, *What do you think?* Suga as Agust D asks a rhetorical question to the jealous adversaries who try to shake him, flaunting his success and retorting, "whatever you think, I'm sorry, but I don't f***ing care at all".[13] The same message pervades the title track, *Daechitwa*, where Suga calls himself "a king [...] [and] a boss" who's "time is more expensive" than money.[14] After the mixtape's release, Suga discussed how these two songs are "traps" laid out for haters just like pesticide sprayed to lure and kill cockroaches.[11] Shrugging his shoulders, he chuckled and expressed his amazement at how some people "never learn" and keep falling into the "traps" he lays.[11] These enemies remain unnamed, but Suga fights back at their words with his hard-hitting, crisp lyrics — efficiently using what he knows best to defend himself. Channelling his disappointment and anger into his craft is powerful, but Suga also tells ARMY and the world that love is the ultimate answer.

An example of him pouring out love and comfort appears in his lines from the 2018 song, *Love Yourself: Answer*. The creative genius raps, "loving myself might be harder than loving someone else / let's admit it, the standards I made are more (sic) strict for myself".[15] These words are a mirror to the reality of millions who have been fed the idea that self-love is selfish and may thus unfairly judge themselves. As ARMY show Suga and BTS they have reasons to love themselves, they accept that and remind us in return that we should be more loving towards ourselves. By using his words and music to attack, comfort, and love, Suga speaks his truth and inspires many.

In 2020, Suga continued using his voice to speak his truth, and one theme that consistently stood out in his music was the truth of being human. The track *People* on *D-2* is a principal example of this, where Suga muses alongside a dreamy beat what it means to be a person and "what kind of person" he is himself.[16] His conclusion in this specific song is that making mistakes and falling down are natural parts of life,[16] but across the whole album and throughout 2020, the most prominent human truth Suga emphasised was change. "People change — like I have [...] [and] like you have" he asserts in *People*;[16] "there would be no eternity for anything" he claims in *Moonlight*.[17] Suga sums the concept up best in his final line of *D-2* on *Dear my friend*, a track where he articulates his pain and mixed feelings on an old, faded friendship that has left only memories: "it's all so transient".[18] Change is natural, and "there's nothing that lasts forever",[16] even us as human beings ourselves.

SUGA: SETTING INTO MOTION THE JOURNEY TOWARDS THE AUTHENTIC SELF

Suga furthered this concept in his collaboration with fellow K-Pop artist IU in the 2020 spring single, *eight*.[6] As interpreted by fans, *eight* is about singer IU's feelings after losing her friends and fellow K-pop stars Choi Jin-ri and Kim Jong-hyun — known professionally as Sulli and Jonghyun, respectively — to suicide.[19] A deep, lovely, touching, and realistic track, it makes us hopeful and serves as a reminder that we are not alone, life is beautiful, and everything is ultimately impermanent. In his verse, Suga raps, "the word forever is a sandcastle", using metaphor to say nothing is eternal, even though we may dream of an island where we are "forever young".[20] Suga has also noted the pervasiveness of change in several 2020 interviews, claiming in an article with *Esquire* that "people's conditions vary day by day,"[21] and saying "it wasn't easy to accept that we eventually change" when sharing his opinion on BTS' growth in his personal interview with *Weverse Magazine*.[22] "But," he continues, "I think it's a good thing that we changed."[22] Thus, this idea that change is a natural, authentic, and human part of living we must accept is evident in Suga's honest lyrics and candid responses in 2020. Further, he made it visible in his own self-reflection.

Since joining BTS, Suga has experienced a personal evolution leading to where he is today, and he commented on this in 2020. The most surface-level change is his journey from "rags to riches", going "from a basement in Namsandong / to a penthouse in Hannam the Hill", as he plainly raps in *D-2*.[17] However, these gains were not easy to acquire. Suga has said in the 2018 docu-series *Burn the Stage* that as a teenager training pre-debut, his financial difficulties forced him to work part time as a delivery boy.[23] They were so dire, he once had to choose between having a meal and walking for two hours, or taking a bus and starving.[4] As he braved those stressful circumstances and prioritised his career and passion for music, Suga decided to keep going at his own pace. "Born a slave / [and] risen to a king",[14] he now owns a luxury flat in the most expensive complex in Seoul[24] with the "big house, big car, and big rings" he claimed to desire in BTS' debut song, *No More Dream*.[25]

Along with this transformation, Suga's evolution in personality and outlook is evident while his humility remains intact. Since BTS' early days, he has shown layers and proved he can be rowdy or composed, loud or quiet, and goofy or serious. Still, there is a distinction between that Suga and the one of today. In 2020 alone he claimed to have undergone a "change in personality [...] [and] interpretation and attitude toward life,"[22] and when reflecting on past years, he described the distinction between his past and present selves as a difference in maturity.[22,26] These feelings of maturation are evident in songs on *D-2* such as *28*, titled after his Korean age at the time of its release, where Suga reflects on his life and realises, "perhaps, I'm gradually becoming an adult".[27] As constant as change is, it is only natural that the Suga of today would contrast with the one who arrived in Seoul a decade ago. Nonetheless, Suga has always shown his true self, and if those selves appear to vary, that is only greater evidence that he is presenting his authentic self to ARMY at all times. We all learn and change as we live our lives, and Suga is no different.

His awareness of his development as a person also extended out into the physical world in 2020 through art, specifically involving the colour blue. It appeared alongside Suga several times, such as when ARMY witnessed him paint a huge canvas[28] as well as in his self-curated room for *BE*.[29] Each member took care to carefully design a space reflecting their state of mind and personality at the time, and Suga chose to douse his in blue. Clad in blue velvet and seated atop a blue couch bathed in blue light, the colour choice is clearly one reflecting Suga himself in 2020, as blue represents calmness, introspection, depth, and wisdom. Further, he denoted the concept of change with the "highlight" of his room — a mirror placed under his feet.[29] Suga explained it as a visible reminder that we exist, come what may, at that time and in that space.[29] By telling us that honouring our time and space of existence is important, Suga emphasises the notion that we are constantly evolving and must treasure ourselves, always. Just as Suga has accepted all parts of his authentic self over time, whether sarcastic, stoic, funny, or reserved, we must love and care for our changing selves, too.

While there has been evident growth in Suga's character, 2020 revealed this specifically with his first comeback as Agust D. Suga has labelled Agust D as "one of the many sides of me [...] [that] might even be a more accurate depiction of who I really am [...] it's just one of the many methods I use to freely express my thoughts."[30] With this description, Agust D may be viewed as an uncensored, extremely authentic version of Suga. The passionate and intense Agust D has forever been raw, but the artist we see in 2020 is different from the one who debuted in 2016. In *Agust D*, his first mixtape, the rapper is cocky, intense, and aggressive — *D-2* has moments of these feelings, but Suga appears more careful and calm, reflecting his maturation.

The differentiation between the Agust Ds of then and now is something Suga has brought to light himself, particularly in the music video for *Daechwita*. In it, Agust D appears as two characters — a blonde, greedy king with a thirst for violence, and a black-haired, undercover criminal on a mission to assassinate him.[31] "Initially," Suga recounted in a livestream, "I wanted to do both as blondes [...] because I was blonde for [*Agust D*]."[11] But then, he decided to change his hair to black: "I wanted to show a contrast [...] between them."[11] It is unclear whether Suga intended to have these hair colours denote a change within Agust D, but when *Daechwita* ends with the criminal firing a shot intended to kill the king,[31] it is easy to presume that the old one — named by Suga as "'anger'"[11] — is dead. Still, Suga stated, "The bullet might have missed him."[11] Therefore, the hostility fuelling Agust D may or may not be gone, but with Suga himself claiming he no longer possesses that "emotion called rage,"[11] the former is more likely. With these transformations, it is apparent that Suga has embraced much change over the years. Yet, he simultaneously appears apprehensive about this growth.

Embracing fears and the shadow of self

Throughout 2020, Suga was consistently authentic in relaying his musings, feelings, and personal introspections to ARMY, and this began at the start of the year. In early January, the comeback trailer for *Interlude: Shadow* was released as the beginning of *Map of the Soul: 7* promotions.[32] Both the song and the music video capture Suga's deepest fears as an idol and an influential artist while he reflects on the magnitude of his growth and success. Evolving from someone who dreamt of being a musician to one who has now achieved superstardom, he sings of anxiety and self-doubt regarding this change while using Carl Jung's concept of the shadow. The shadow, as described by Jungian Analyst Murray Stein, is "our coldest egotism, our most profoundly selfish part."[33] It is the mantra Suga chants in the beginning of the song — "I wanna be a rap star / I wanna be the top / I wanna be a rockstar / I want it all mine"[34] — seeming to express his motivation for becoming the artist he is today. Throughout the track, he vocalises discomfort at the revelation of the shadow within himself, one "that gets darker as that light gets brighter", referring to the spotlight of success and fame.[34] Rapping as his shadow, Suga first taunts himself for his anxiety, but eventually there is a reconciliation as he accepts his darkness and fear as forces that will always be there — "we're you and we're me".[34] Because we all have a shadow, this human presentation of fear and overcoming that fear is inspiring, providing a sense of hope and validation for many ARMY. "You must face your inner shadows [...] and move on forward," Suga said in an interview for *Map of the Soul: 7*,[35] noting it is good to accept that fear will never leave. However, for Suga, this anxiety appears to be something not just universal, but incredibly unique to him and his journey.

After the release of *Map of the Soul: 7*, Suga revealed the album is not just a compilation of good, inspired music, but a collection ridden with BTS' personal stories.[36] *Interlude: Shadow* is no exception, and similar themes relating to change continue to appear in many tracks on *D-2*, specifically about upwards growth and the fear of flying and falling. "Going higher, higher, and only higher, higher / it makes me dizzy," he sings in *Interlude: Shadow*, "don't let me fly / now I'm afraid".[34] Flying can only be surmised as a metaphor for Suga's growth to get to the top as an idol and with BTS, and even if he desired it as a teenager, now he is "afraid" when facing the reality of that elevation.[34] This sentiment pervades *Interlude: Shadow*, but appears more subtly in *D-2*, still using the imagery of vertical growth. In *Moonlight*, Suga tells of his journey from "a basement [...] / to a penthouse",[17] and *What Do You Think?*'s final verse ends with a claim that he's ascending "so high that you can't even see me".[13] The track *Honsool* also utilises flight with the phrase, "now I'm feelin' like I'm flyin'",[37] describing intoxication as Suga washes away his anxiety — ironically, this feeling is where his fears stem from in the first place. Even boastful, assertive *Daechwita* has a quiet moment where Suga rhythmically contemplates in the second verse, noticing his height and expressing desire "to just look down and put [his] feet on the ground".[14] What goes up must come down, and here, the potential of falling appears to be something Suga deeply fears — by reiterating it so many times, it seems he is also preparing himself for the same. ARMY has witnessed Suga embrace changes in his personality, status, and ambition, and he has been consistent in his career throughout 2020 by continuing to share his authentic reflections about these developments, even if they aren't always positively empowering.

This sentiment about Suga's honesty and authenticity has also been proven repeatedly over the years, especially regarding one topic where he has always been transparent: his mental health. In terms of his music, this has never been more apparent than on the most emotive track of 2016's *Agust D*, titled *The Last*. For close to four minutes, Suga discusses the exhaustive, daily battles of the mind, such as his thoughts that have led to social phobia, depression, self-loathing, and the loss of self-meaning he experienced as an 18-year-old.[38] He talks about the pain, hurt, and helplessness that come with having a mental illness,[38] rapping so powerfully with such passion, many ARMY may feel the need to take a seat after listening to the song. Even then, Suga expressed words that are nearly a premonition for the theme of *Interlude: Shadow* as he reflected, "the greed that used to be my weapon now swallows me, ruins me, and puts a leash around my neck".[38] Suga seems to have learned to better cope with these lasting feelings of anxiety as, like with his shadow, they will not leave. "Anxiety and loneliness seem to be with me for life," he commented in a 2018 interview with *Naver*, and so through "the lyrics [of *The Last*], I wanted to tell people 'I am anxious, so are you, so let's find the way and study the way together.'"[39] Although it is impossible to know how his personal journey is going, it appears Suga has made progress, stating in 2020 that his "self-esteem is at the maximum level these days."[11] There are likely many factors for his increased happiness, but a prominent one stems from his authenticity and prioritisation of the self.

Accepting self-evolution and leading with self-prioritisation

2020 has shown that Suga's authenticity extends inward as something he benefits from by embracing the changes he has undergone and the choices he has made. As he muses in *Moonlight*, "changes are fated to happen […] [but] perhaps, how we change is what matters",[17] and Suga has changed by choosing to accept and prioritise his honest and transient self. This change didn't happen overnight — we have seen him talk about embracing his evolving self from time to time, particularly in terms of his creation process. In June 2020, sitting alongside the leader of BTS, RM, for their *Respect* sub-unit interview released as part of 2020 Festa, Suga shared how his process of writing songs has changed. "I used to squeeze and wring things out, but now, if it doesn't come, it doesn't come. If it does, it does. […] I learned to enjoy it. Before, I was really hard on myself."[40] With this development, there is a visibly improved awareness and understanding of the self that Suga possesses, and his choice to trust his instinct and not berate himself is surely a form of self-care. Watching Suga continue on the journey towards his authentic self is empowering for ARMY, too. With his words and actions, he constantly reiterates that when we serve ourselves enough, we will become equipped to lend a hand to others. Improving as people must begin with self-prioritisation and care, and by embracing himself with all his human traits, changes, and flaws, Suga has thus created a safe space for millions of fans to do the same. Only those comfortable with knowing and receiving themselves unconditionally allow the same for others, and so the acceptance of the authentic self seen in Suga is extremely validating for ARMY and the world.

Suga's journey of self-prioritisation appears primarily through his repeated efforts to voice and release his authentic emotions through

SUGA: SETTING INTO MOTION THE JOURNEY TOWARDS THE AUTHENTIC SELF

music. In 2020 and earlier years, he has frequently used his words and music to inspire ARMY and others to prioritise our mental and physical health. In the commencement speech BTS gave for YouTube's virtual ceremony for the class of 2020, Suga spoke of feeling as if he'd "fallen to the ground during a race," left alone in the dust as a result of the pandemic.[41] And then he shone a light, stressing on a positive aspect of the quarantine the pandemic forced on the world. He said, "there are some things you can only do in isolation, such as focusing on myself and breaking my own barriers."[41] Here, he relates the importance of caring for the self and focusing on its growth — something ultimately not selfish at all, but rather selfless, as one is then able to be their best both for themselves and others — while prioritising one's own boundaries, emotions, and health.

Suga demonstrated this once more in November of 2020, when Big Hit Entertainment announced he had undergone shoulder surgery for an injury he suffered in 2012. It was the result of a road accident from when Suga was working as a delivery boy, a job he was forced to have due to his aforementioned financial difficulties.[23] While giving his all on stage to perfectly sync with BTS' power-packed, intense choreographies, Suga had to manage the shooting pain he regularly felt in his shoulder for close to eight years. He has even shared that while on tour, he regularly took shots to ease the pain and struggled to hold a microphone that weighed merely 500 grams.[42]

With his injury affecting him to this extent for nearly a decade, it is understandable that Suga would want to improve his health. However, the result of the surgery was him missing promotional activities for *BE*, at a time when BTS had just made history as the first non-English band to top the Billboard Hot 100 chart with *Dynamite*.[43] The band's popularity and demand had risen to a new scale in this time.[43,44] For Suga to take a break during the most crucial time of BTS' career was not only bold, but a sign for millions of ARMY across the globe — to try and take a chance on oneself. Taking necessary, sufficient time off to heal and come back stronger and healthier can be seen as a step towards the journey of self-prioritisation, and by making the choice to heal despite potential setbacks, Suga demonstrated the value of trusting the self and giving space for personal needs. Getting surgery was not something that only benefited himself, but benefited BTS' quality and longevity as a whole and was ultimately for the better. However, ARMY at first responded to the news with an outpour of mixed emotions — social media was filled with messages describing disappointment about missing Suga, hope for a positive recovery post-surgery, and worry about his overall health. As expected for someone who wears humility on his sleeve, Suga genuinely apologised for his absence, along with a mature and thoughtful request: "Please understand this time as being my chance to prepare to meet you again strong and healthy, and even if I must be away for a short while, please wait for me to come back to you."[45] Suga thus chose to do what was best for him by prioritising his physical health, inspiring ARMY to also develop habits of self-care and put the self first for a brighter future where we can live with full authenticity.

Throughout his career, Suga has been an advocate for mental health care and started many conversations on the topic which have been beneficial to many. It is unique that he chooses to address subjects like mental health care through his music, particularly with songs like *The Last*, where he candidly discusses his depression, OCD, anxiety, and suicidal thoughts.[38] Further, he has been open about his treatment, such as in 2019's Festa where he mentioned an interaction he had with his therapist that allowed him to fixate less on everyday events and happenings that don't go how he imagined.[46] "'It happens'" is what he was told, and Suga shared those same words — all feelings and emotions are valid, but they happen, and then they pass.[46] Dwelling less on stressful situations, while accepting that they are inevitable, Suga has grown to be happier and more healthy.

As he is casually vocal on 'taboo' topics and encourages discussing them as we do the common cold, Suga not only comforts and validates millions, but helps ease the discomfort and stigma attached to those illnesses. He is building a safety net for people, especially from parts of the world where these topics are hastily swept under the carpet. As Suga related in his interview with *Naver*, this is ultimately his aim — to share with others that these issues are common so that we can deal with the pain together.[39] Suga taking the first step by speaking authentically about how he prioritises his mental health urges ARMY and others to openly discuss their feelings and emotions as well. Comments on YouTube on tracks like *The Last* act as proof that he is successful in easing pain for many.[47] With no definite solution for mental illness, easing and validating suffering through empathy, normalising discussions around these topics, and encouraging self-prioritisation in this way is the least that can be done, and Suga is undoubtedly a leader of this movement.

Additionally, Suga encourages authenticity by breaking and speaking out against unreasonable societal stereotypes that confine people into boxes, demonstrating self-prioritisation by embracing the self as is. He and the rest of BTS have been redefining masculinity and male friendships while combating stereotypes on expectations through their music, the ways they present themselves on camera, and how they interact with one another. In 2020, these subtle rebukes went a notch higher when Suga verbally discarded labels on masculinity during an impactful interview with *Esquire*. Claiming a culture exists "where masculinity is defined by certain emotions [and] characteristics," he said, "I'm not fond of these expressions."[21] Suga followed up by saying that it is foolish to set standards, and worse, to struggle to fit into them because human minds and emotions vary day by day.[21]

Echoing the sentiment he expressed in the track *People* that transience is human nature,[16] these words are a necessity in our time where gender-related violence and inequality exist all over the world. Instead of forcing ourselves into limiting, harmful stereotypes, Suga seems to say that we should accept and prioritise loving ourselves as we exist here and now. This message is again one that holds the authentic self above all else, and may be a source of strength for those trying to understand themselves. By prioritising and speaking on his mental health, physical health, and how he wishes to exist in these ways throughout the year, Suga has ultimately exercised agency in the quest to be true to himself.

Utilising his voice, exercising agency

The acts of discussing personal feelings in his music, sharing his fears and struggles, and employing self-prioritisation have all been enabled by one thing in Suga's life, and that is freedom of choice. He has constantly chosen to be his authentic self and to follow his heart, even in his early debut days as evidenced in 2013 where he and RM were dissed and ridiculed for making the 'glamorous' choice to become mainstream pop idols instead of remaining underground rappers.[48] Bravely, honestly stating that his decision to become a K-pop idol was his desire to amplify his voice, Suga has since utilised that same voice to send a message to ARMY and the world: you can do anything you want. 2020 saw him inspire many as, during the *YouTube Commencement*, he encouraged viewers to "get your hands on the changes you can make, because your possibilities are limitless. After all," he softly smiled, "I also had no idea I would become BTS either."[41] Not giving into fear and self-doubt or being worried about what others think has allowed Suga to have pure agency and make authentic choices to develop into the best version of himself. These words and the way he lives his life are an inspiration for ARMY and others to take a chance and stay true to our goals and our truth, since there is no end to the greatness we can achieve — both individually and collectively.

It appears that surrounding oneself with people who believe in this same sentiment can be helpful, as Suga has been further able to embody authenticity due to his company's futuristic, progressive, and compassionate work culture. There are several instances where BTS has shared that Big Hit Entertainment provides artists the freedom to express their truest and deepest thoughts and ideas through music. Suga discussed this after the release of *D-2*, specifically regarding *What Do You Think?*[13] He first contemplated including the track in the mixtape, as it was written a couple years prior to its release and he wasn't then feeling the "rage" he had felt before while writing it.[11] Although some of the strong, explicit lyrics Suga had originally written had to undergo several revisions, his decision to eventually add it in as the third track was backed by CEO Bang Si-Hyuk, who told him to "'just do whatever you want to do.'"[11] Big Hit's artists are always encouraged to be sincere and genuine towards themselves and their work, and so, with this support, Suga is able to be authentic both in his life and his artistry.

Along this same line, 2020 was a year where Suga was empowered in his choices to do what he desired simply because he wanted to do so, following his instincts and being his true self. Before, as described in his Festa interview with RM, he would push himself when it came to producing music and lyrics,[40] but now he has "started knowing the fun of music" by creating as he likes.[22] When asked about how he tried to be innovative with *D-2*'s musical style, Suga confessed that "it's more that I made the music I wanted to make [...] I just do what I want to do."[26]

This more lowkey, less pressured approach to artistry has yielded great results and even prompted him to experiment with different things in 2020, such as creating a melody "for the first time" with *Telepathy* on *BE* and taking singing lessons.[22] Most notably, he picked up the guitar in July, practising daily for hours and taking song requests from ARMY during a calm livestream to show off his skills.[49] Why take on these new hobbies? Other than to deepen his understanding of music,[22] "I simply want to be able to sing while playing guitar when I get older," he said in an interview with *Rolling Stone India*.[30] "That's all."[30] Doing what he wants to do, Suga now "choose[s] to simply play the music and write."[22] Utilising that freedom of choice makes all the difference, and by taking full advantage of it without being hard on himself, Suga is able to follow his heart and be as authentic as possible.

However, not all of his new endeavours involved music — Suga also tried out painting, and his reaction to the result of this venture revealed a message about the connection between choice and fighting adversity. In April and May 2020, Suga appeared live on YouTube painting a gigantic canvas, giving ARMY a chance to witness the process of his first piece from start to finish.[28,50] The final stream was just after *D-2*'s release, and Suga worked almost silently while playing the mixtape in the background.[50] However, just as he finished, he said something remarkable:

> "It's done. Didn't go exactly the way I wanted it. It's a lesson on life. It doesn't always go the way I want it. But in the middle of that, something new came out. Paint over your life to your heart's content. You never know. All of a sudden, something might pop up on its own."[50]

With these candid words, Suga encourages everyone to keep striving for what they want — life is unpredictable, but remaining authentic, trusting your heart, and continuing to persevere can lead to great results. This sentiment is one Suga has emulated before, most starkly in his verse on *MOTS:7*'s title track, *ON*. "Even if my knees drop to the ground", he raps, "unless they are buried under it / it will just be an ordinary happening".[51] In other words, we may fall, but unless our choice to stand tall again is revoked, falling is just another part of life. If there is agency, the choice to persevere always exists, and as much as Suga emphasises that truth, he knows there is power in the decision to desist as well. *D-2*'s *Burn It* clearly communicates this as Suga raps to his past self who he wants to incinerate, "I hope you don't forget that giving up decisively also counts as courage".[52] In this way, whether electing to endure something or walk away from it, Suga validates the power of choice that is authentic and prioritises the self — whether you want to keep going or give up, either are okay, as "the choice and decision is yours to make".[52]

Sharing his life truths: A source of comfort for ARMY

Ultimately, the most influential choice Suga has made is sharing the wisdom he has gained from living authentically, and through doing this in 2020, he was an inspiration and comfort to ARMY. In his music, interview responses, livestreams, and all other communications, he has spoken truthfully of his innermost opinions and feelings, including simple, everyday struggles which seem daunting for some, as well as thoughts which are hard to live with for others. "I think it's the same with everybody," he revealed in early 2020, "I think everybody goes through the same things."[53] Identifying this human commonality of shared life experiences, Suga seems to channel his personal emotions — whether anxiety, happiness, ambition, or depression — out into the world. This act of "send[ing] messages that [young] people [...] can all relate to and giv[ing] comfort through [their] music" is what Suga considers to be his and BTS' greatest strength, and this belief is far from false.[54] By being honest with himself and projecting that honesty outwards through speaking his mind, Suga makes us feel heard.

Suga also employs these acts of authentic empathy outside of his words, caring for the world by sharing his time and money to make a positive impact. When BTS were interviewed by *TIME Magazine* in 2020 after acquiring the title, 'Entertainer of the Year', he revealed his belief in the importance of giving compassion and care, especially during a pandemic. "There are times when I'm still taken aback by all the unimaginable things that are happening," Suga said. "But I ask myself, who's going to do this, if not us?"[55] This final, rhetorical question is nearly identical to Suga's verse on *MOTS:7*'s *Louder Than Bombs*, a song which discusses the struggle of holding accumulated grief from worldwide tragedies.[56]

Literally putting his money where his mouth is, in 2020 Suga was among one of the first few celebrities in South Korea to make a substantial donation to the Hope Bridge Korea Disaster Relief Association to help his hometown, Daegu, which was one of the cities most affected by COVID-19 in the country.[57] He also donated more for the treatment of children suffering from cancer to a local Daegu hospital for his birthday,[58] and, alongside BTS, gave one million dollars to fund the Black Lives Matter (BLM) campaign in June.[59] Suga's acts of charity have also influenced ARMY to make a difference, as many worked to match BTS' BLM donation[59] while still others chose to give the money of their cancelled concert tickets to help Daegu's coronavirus relief, which reportedly saw around 8,000 listed donations.[60] By choosing to be authentic in his message to help the world and spreading it outwards, Suga becomes an inspiration for others to do the same.

Finally, Suga's comforting presence and both quiet and loud ways of showing care towards band members and ARMY are endearing to witness. With a soft and calm demeanour, Suga expresses his love for his bandmates in various ways. These range from rare verbal expressions of love[61] to acts of service like those we witnessed in 2020 on the show *BTS In the Soop,* one where the group used the pandemic's forced isolation to rest and relax.[62] Here, Suga repeatedly showed his caring, loving self who is openly accommodative of the member's needs as a thoughtful older brother figure. Besides cooking for the members throughout the show alongside eldest member Jin, he was also attentive and protective of them, such as during a comedic occasion in the penultimate episode when he endearingly attempted to sway RM from woodcarving for fear that he would hurt himself.[62]

In 2020, we also witnessed Suga's return as a DJ for *Honey FM,* a radio show he livestreamed weekly from April to June, inviting each BTS member to join him to tell stories and answer questions.[63] All of this was to "share emotions even though we cannot meet," and Suga often went further by offering words of reassurance and counselling to individual fans who expressed their personal struggles and pain.[63] Extending his time, laughter, and wisdom in this way, he showed great care for ARMY, and he amplified these feelings later in the year through music. In *Telepathy* on *BE,* a song Suga produced in half an hour,[22] he and BTS sent a message to ARMY about the stream of joy they receive from them even in the darkest of times. "In the days that feel the same, / I'm the happiest when I meet you", Suga sings.[64] In these ways, the rapper relayed love through his forte of authentic expression. Suga himself has proven change is unavoidable, both with circumstances and emotions. Yet, here, he reveals three constants — his authenticity, his care for ARMY, and his belief in our love for him, too. "Thankfully", he softly smiles in *Life Goes On,* "between you and I, / it's still the same".[65]

Holding our hands and leading the way

In 2020, Suga continued on his journey of authenticity, embracing himself for who he is without apology. Using introspection to identify change within himself, he came to terms with those changes while

SUGA: SETTING INTO MOTION THE JOURNEY TOWARDS THE AUTHENTIC SELF

voicing his fears in his music and giving consolation to others by doing so. Suga further made the decision to prioritise himself and his desires by exercising free will, and as he shares all of his honest lessons, thoughts, and wisdom with the world, he utilises his authenticity in a way that is comforting and inspirational. Many ARMY are thankful for him because of this, and as they express their deep gratitude, Suga has noted that this loving energy returns back to him. "Hearing our fans saying that we changed their lives changes our lives in turn," he said in BTS' 2020 interview with *Rolling Stone India*.[30] With this cycle of positive influence and appreciation, it is no wonder why BTS and ARMY share such a genuine connection.

In staying true to himself and accepting his humanness, Suga is an inspiration, but he is even more of a guiding light in how he encourages others to do the same by following their dreams. A popular phrase among ARMY is the saying, "what Suga wants, Suga gets,"[66] which came into existence after fans realised that all that he dreams and wishes for BTS comes true. In interviews or in lyrics, Suga utters what he desires for himself or the group, and then the universe, ARMY, and BTS work to make it happen. It is fascinating and jaw-dropping to see how he systematically has used this superpower-like form of manifestation from debut, achieving all his dreams from attending the *Billboard Music Awards* in 2017 to getting a Grammy nomination in 2020.[66] In particular, it is incredibly inspirational to ARMY, as watching Suga realise his ambitions makes us believe in our dreams and inspires us to work to fulfil them. This also extends outwards to BTS as a group with lifelong goals like self-love. With BTS by our side, encouraging us to build a strong sense of our authentic self that we can love and listen to, ARMY feel that achieving such a dream is not impossible. After all, if Suga and BTS can get what they want, surely ARMY can get what ARMY wants too.

Throughout the year of 2020, Suga held ARMY's hand, showing us how he took one more step in his journey of living as his authentic self. Further, he created a safe haven by speaking his mind and being honest with himself and with the world, validating the reality of millions as a permission slip to allow ourselves to claim a space and voice in the world, big or small. In this way, he and BTS have laid the path towards a safer, healthier, and freer world for generations to come. Suga inspires us to be better humans than we were yesterday, and by sharing his lived experiences, his hardships, his weaknesses, and his fears, he allows us to embrace all the shades of our human selves, too. For this, we as ARMY are grateful — for Suga's existence which completes BTS, and to be living at the same time as someone who so inspires us to love, live, and let live. So many of us in 2020 have been reminded by him to live our lives authentically and to the fullest, and so ARMY's love and respect for him will remain as true, pure, and real as Suga himself.

References

1. BANGTANTV. (2020, June 12). *[2020 Festa] BTS (방탄소년단) '방탄생파' #2020BTSFesta*. [Video]. https://www.youtube.com/watch?v=t9zPnWQIiuw
2. BTS. (2020, April, 27). *JinKiMin☐* [Video]. https://www.vlive.tv/video/188036
3. Dam-young, H. (2019, February, 11). *50 facts about Suga of BTS*. http://kpopherald.koreaherald.com/view.php?ud=201902110940113850171_2
4. Jeong, L. (2021, March 8). *How did BTS member Suga get where he is today? The K-pop idol known as Agust D almost quit Big Hit Entertainment as a trainee – until CEO Bang Si-hyuk paid his tuition fees himself.* https://www.scmp.com/magazines/style/celebrity/article/3124274/how-did-bts-member-suga-get-where-he-today-k-pop-idol
5. Agust D. (2016). 724148 [Song]. On *Agust d*. Big Hit Entertainment; Doolset. 치리사일사팔 *(724148)* [Translation]. https://doolsetbangtan.wordpress.com/2018/11/11/724148
6. Delgado, S. (2020, May 6). *IU and BTS member Suga release timely pop song "Eight."* https://www.teenvogue.com/story/iu-bts-member-suga-eight
7. Gurung, S. (2019, March 9). *3 of BTS K-pop star Suga's top musical collaborations.* https://www.scmp.com/magazines/style/news-trends/article/2189233/3-bts-k-pop-star-sugas-top-musical-collaborations
8. Herman, T. (2016, August 16) *BTS' Suga addresses depression & cost of fame on 'Agust D' mixtape.* https://www.billboard.com/articles/columns/k-town/7476080/bts-suga-agust-d-mixtape
9. BANGTANTV. (2020, September 23). *BTS (방탄소년단) Speech at the 75th UN general assembly.* [Video]. https://www.youtube.com/watch?v=5aPe9Uy10n4

10 크랩 KLAB. (2020, September 10). *[ENG SUB/Full Interview] BTS joins KBS News9 | 200910.* [Video]. https://www.youtube.com/watch?v=-PMVYa87Ftg

11 BTS. (2020, May 28). *D-2.* [Video]. https://www.vlive.tv/video/19380

12 *Home - Love myself.* (2021). https://www.love-myself.org/eng/home

13 Agust D. (2020). What do you think? [Song]. On *D-2.* Big Hit Entertainment; Doolset. 어떻게 생각해? *(What do you think?)* [Translation]. https://doolsetbangtan.wordpress.com/2020/05/22/what-do-you-think/

14 Agust D. (2020). Daechwita [Song]. On *D-2.* Big Hit Entertainment; Doolset. 대취타 *(Daechwita)* [Translation]. https://doolsetbangtan.wordpress.com/2020/05/22/daechwita/

15 BTS. (2018). Answer: Love myself [Song]. On *Love yourself: Answer.* Big Hit Entertainment; Genius English Translations. (2018). *BTS - Answer: Love myself (English translation)* [Translation]. https://genius.com/Genius-english-translations-bts-answer-love-myself-english-translation-lyrics

16 Agust D. (2020). People [Song]. On *D-2.* Big Hit Entertainment; Doolset. 사람 *(People)* [Translation]. https://doolsetbangtan.wordpress.com/2020/05/22/people/

17 Agust D. (2020). Moonlight [Song]. On *D-2.* Big Hit Entertainment; Doolset. 저 달 *(Moonlight)* [Translation]. https://doolsetbangtan.wordpress.com/2020/05/22/moonlight/

18 Agust D. (2020). Dear my friend (feat. Kim Jong Wan of NELL) [Song]. On *D-2.* Big Hit Entertainment; Doolset. 어땠을까 (Dear my friend; Feat. JW of NELL) [Translation]. https://doolsetbangtan.wordpress.com/2020/05/22/dear-my-friend-feat-jw-of-nell/

19 Kubrick, K. (2020, May 6). *Is Eight from IU and Suga a dedication to Sulli and Jonghyun?* https://www.somagnews.com/eight-iu-suga-dedication-sulli-jonghyun/

20 IU. (2020). eight (Prod.&Feat. SUGA of BTS) [Song]. On *eight.* EDAM Entertainment.; Doolset. (2020, May 6). *IU – eight (*

SUGA: SETTING INTO MOTION THE JOURNEY TOWARDS THE AUTHENTIC SELF

에잇) *(Prod. & Feat. SUGA)* [Translation]. https://doolsetbangtan.wordpress.com/2020/05/06/iu-eight-prod-feat-suga/

21 Holmes, D. (2020, November 23). *The boundless optimism of BTS*. https://www.esquire.com/entertainment/music/a34654383/bts-members-be-album-interview-2020/

22 Kang, M. (2021, January 4). *SUGA "I'm grateful that there are still unvisited areas in the world of music."* https://magazine.weverse.io/article/view?lang=en&num=96

23 Park, J. (Director), & Yoon, J (Producer). (2018) *Burn the stage: The movie*. Big Hit Entertainment.

24 VoomVoom. (January 1, 2019) *BTS SUGA purchases luxury apartment in prominent neighborhood for 3 million dollars*. https://mnews.joins.com/article/23314622?IgnoreUserAgent=y#home

25 BTS (2013). No more dream [Song]. On *2 cool 4 skool*. Big Hit Entertainment; Doolset. (2018, June 21). *No more dream*. [Translation]. https://doolsetbangtan.wordpress.com/2018/06/21/no-more-dream/

26 Bruner, R. (2020, May 22). *BTS's Suga reflects on his new solo mixtape as Agust D on D-2*. https://time.com/5839715/bts-suga-d2-mixtape/

27 Agust D. (2020). 28 [Song]. On *D-2*. Big Hit Entertainment.; Doolset. 점점 어른이 되나 봐 *(28; feat. NiiHWA)*. [Translation]. https://doolsetbangtan.wordpress.com/2020/05/22/28-feat-niihwa/

28 BANGTANTV. (2020, April 24). *200424 Suga*. [Video]. https://www.youtube.com/watch?v=hiLg74p4i8M.

29 Big Hit Music. (2020, November 6). *BE | BTS | Big hit entertainment* [Video]. https://ibighit.com/bts/video/be/CiKVONXC1287Rj1yVSGVUbN2.php?l=kor

30 Chakraborty, R. (2020, November 9). *BTS: The rolling stone interview*. https://rollingstoneindia.com/bts-the-rolling-stone-interview/

31 HYBE LABELS. (2020, May 22). Agust D '대취타' MV [Video]. https://www.youtube.com/watch?v=qGjAWJ2zWWI

32. HYBE LABELS. (2020, January 9). BTS (방탄소년단) Map of the soul : 7 'Interlude : Shadow' comeback trailer [Video]. YouTube. https://www.youtube.com/watch?v=PV1gCvzpSy0
33. Stein, M., Buser, S., and L. Cruz. (2020). *Map of the soul: 7: Persona, shadow & ego in the world of BTS*. Chiron Publications.
34. BTS. (2020). Interlude: Shadow [Song]. On *Map of the Soul: 7*. Big Hit Entertainment; Doolset. (2020, January 9). *Interlude: Shadow*. [Translation]. https://doolsetbangtan.wordpress.com/2020/01/09/interlude-shadow/
35. Zack Sang Show. (2020, February 4). *BTS interview*. [Video]. YouTube. https://www.youtube.com/watch?v=Hk2_A-rh7IM
36. Variety. (2020, February 23). *BTS talk identity crisis, new album 'Map of the soul: 7'* [Video]. https://www.youtube.com/watch?v=7fVQGcvgmEQ&list=PL-26BMf58kB_v_xwg7k8vn5H1NY0FPGca&index=3
37. Agust D. (2020). Honsool [Song]. On *D-2*. Big Hit Entertainment; Doolset. 혼술 (Honsool) [Translation]. https://doolsetbangtan.wordpress.com/2020/05/22/honsool/
38. Agust D. (2016). The Last [Song]. On *Agust D*. Big Hit Entertainment; Doolset. 마지막 *(The last)* [Translation]. https://doolsetbangtan.wordpress.com/2018/06/01/the-last/
39. SBS PopAsia HQ. (2018, January, 30). *BTS' RM & Suga open up about depression and anxiety*. https://www.sbs.com.au/popasia/blog/2018/01/30/bts-rm-suga-open-about-depression-and-anxiety
40. BANGTANTV. (2020, June 9). *[2020 Festa] BTS (방탄소년단) Answer: BTS 3 units 'Respect' song by RM & Suga*. [Video]. https://www.youtube.com/watch?v=bXyL34Enl2o.
41. BANGTANTV. (2020, June 8). *BTS commencement speech | Dear class of 2020*. [Video]. https://www.youtube.com/watch?v=AU6uF5sFtwA&t=287s
42. BTS. (2020, November 21). *Life goes on Min Suga*. [Video]. V LIVE. https://www.vlive.tv/video/224568

43. Lyons, S. (2020, September 28). *BTS's "Dynamite" makes Billboard chart history with new no.1 achievements.* https://www.koreaboo.com/news/bts-dynamite-billboard-chart-global-hot-100-200/
44. Moon, K. (2020, November, 20). *See the major highlights from BTS' momentous year in 2020.* https://time.com/5914034/bts-2020-highlights/
45. Kim, D (2020, November, 6). *Update: BTS' Suga undergoes surgery for his shoulder + to take break from most activities.* https://www.soompi.com/article/1436247wpp/bts-suga-undergoes-surgery-for-his-shoulder-to-take-break-from-most-activities
46. BANGTANTV. (2019, June 12). *[2019 Festa] BTS (방탄소년단) '방탄다락' #2019BTSFESTA* [Video]. https://www.youtube.com/watch?v=CPW2PCPYzEE
47. Jeonilysm. (2016, August 16). *BTS Suga (Agust D) - The last 마지막 [Lyrics Han|Rom|Eng].* [Video]. https://www.youtube.com/watch?v=DB_AP7DLQ0w
48. Abi Abroad. (2013, November 23). B-Free disrespecting BTS Rap Monster & Suga? | 방탄소년단 디스 비프리. [Video]. https://www.youtube.com/watch?v=EuliJWvytV8
49. BTS. (2020, October 21). *Long time no see.* [Video]. https://www.vlive.tv/video/219057
50. BANGTANTV. (2020, May 22). *200522 Suga (+ENG).* [Video]. https://www.youtube.com/watch?v=y2ym6aA-AZc
51. BTS. (2020). ON [Song]. On *Map of the Soul: 7*. Big Hit Entertainment; Doolset. *ON* [Translation]. https://doolsetbangtan.wordpress.com/2020/02/21/on/
52. Agust D. (2020). Burn it [Song]. On *D-2*. Big Hit Entertainment; Doolset. *Burn it (feat. MAX)* [Translation]. https://doolsetbangtan.wordpress.com/2020/05/22/burn-it-feat-max/
53. Bell, C. (2020, February 26). *BTS send heartfelt messages to their future selves: 'I just hope you're happy and healthy.'* http://www.mtv.com/news/3157677/bts-interview-future-selves-map-of-the-soul-7/?utm=share_twitter

54. The Tonight Show Starring Jimmy Fallon. (2020, February 25). *BTS on first impressions, secret career dreams and Map of the soul: 7 meanings* [Video]. https://www.youtube.com/watch?v=v_9vgidPJ8g
55. Bruner, R. (2020). *Entertainer of the year BTS.* https://time.com/entertainer-of-the-year-2020-bts/
56. BTS. (2020). Louder than bombs [Song]. On *Map of the Soul: 7*. Big Hit Entertainment; Doolset. *Louder than bombs* [Translation]. https://doolsetbangtan.wordpress.com/2020/02/21/louder-than-bombs/
57. Sunio, P. (2020, March 3). *Coronavirus in Korea: Daegu-born stars Suga from BTS, Son Ye-jin of Crash landing on you, Parasite director Bong Joon-ho and Red Velvet's Irene join the fight against Covid-19.* https://www.scmp.com/magazines/style/news-trends/article/3064798/coronavirus-korea-daegu-born-stars-suga-bts-son-ye-jin.
58. Kaufman, G. (2021, March 12). *BTS' Suga celebrates 28th birthday with donation to children's cancer charity.* https://www.billboard.com/articles/news/international/9539415/bts-suga-donates-childrens-cancer-charity-birthday/
59. Kwak, K. (2020, June 7). *BTS' fan ARMY matches group's $1 million Black Lives Matter donation within 24 Hours.* https://variety.com/2020/music/news/bts-army-matches-black-lives-matter-million-dollar-donation-1234627455/
60. Benjamin, J. (2020, February 28). *BTS fans inspired to donate concert ticket refunds to Coronavirus relief.* https://www.billboard.com/articles/news/international/9324851/bts-army-donate-tickets-refunds-coronavirus-relief-suga
61. BANGTANTV. (2018, June 11). *BTS (방탄소년단) '방탄회식' #2018BTSFESTA.* [Video]. https://www.youtube.com/watch?v=K4Melso7MPU
62. Bang S. & Lenzo Y (Executive Producers). (2020). *BTS In the soop* [TV Show]. Big Hit Entertainment.

SUGA: SETTING INTO MOTION THE JOURNEY TOWARDS THE AUTHENTIC SELF

[63] BTS. (2020, April 25). *DJ Suga's honey FM 06.13* [Digital audio]. https://www.vlive.tv/video/187843

[64] BTS. (2020). Telepathy [Song]. On *BE*. Big Hit Entertainment; Doolset. 잠시 (Telepathy) [Translation]. https://doolsetbangtan.wordpress.com/2020/11/20/telepathy/

[65] BTS. (2020). Life goes on [Song]. On *BE*. Big Hit Entertainment; Doolset. *Life goes on* [Translation]. https://doolsetbangtan.wordpress.com/2020/11/20/life-goes-on/

[66] Vee. (2019, February 23). What Yoongi wants, Yoongi gets. *Army's, Amino app* [Fan forum]. https://aminoapps.com/c/btsarmy/page/blog/what-yoongi-wants-yoongi-gets/1JVb_3JlU6uzlXplZwXxd62X3XYq7rRlR2w

Jin

IT'S DEFINITELY THE FOREHEAD, BUT IT'S MORE THAN THAT TOO

Padya Paramita

"Sort of free, do-whatever-I-want personality"[1]

Kim Seokjin, better known as Jin from BTS, is the oldest member, part of the vocal line, and a big brother figure to the rest of the group. When one thinks of Jin, the first thought that usually comes to mind is his signature moniker, 'Worldwide Handsome', a title he proudly proclaims. The nickname stems from his good looks, similar to Adonis, the god of beauty and desire. Some of his most-talked-about physical features include his wide shoulders, and his sharp forehead revealed when his hair is pushed back, which sometimes makes a difference in how he looks. It makes sense that he was recruited from a bus by Big Hit Entertainment when he had been an acting student at Konkuk University in South Korea.[2] Jin is also often thought of as the chief comedian of the band. Despite being the oldest, he has one of the more carefree personalities, and isn't afraid to show his inner child. He is also known for being the caretaker of the group. It's common knowledge that Jin is an introvert, but when you see him competing his heart out on BTS' variety show *Run BTS!*, or wrestling youngest member Jung Kook, you're likely to forget that.

Jin takes pride in this fun-loving and caring exterior, his "sort of free, do-whatever-I-want personality",[1] as he described to *Weverse Magazine* in late 2020. In *Break the Silence*, a docu-series filmed during BTS' 2019 Speak Yourself tour, Jin said, "I don't really want to show people that side of me. So I try my best to not show my darker side. I try hard to act more cheerful so I tend to separate Jin from Kim Seokjin."[3] The video then cues to a montage of Jin having the time of his life at Six Flags, an American theme park, then contrasts with him alone in his room, gaming away for hours. While he can easily be mistaken for an extrovert, Jin is just an extraordinary example of someone with a very healthy work-life balance. He makes an active effort to make sure he's always 'on' for the camera — and that fans see a more energetic and cheerful side of him.

2019 closed with BTS' iconic performance at the *Melon Music Awards*. A lot of fans very clearly remember Jin, standing with his hair pushed back and revealing his famous forehead, on top of a wooden horse, where Jin represents Ares, the Greek God of War. We cannot think about epic horses without touching upon the Trojan Horse, used by the Greeks to enter Troy to win the war. The war started as Helen, the most beautiful woman in the world, was seduced and kidnapped by Prince Paris of Troy. Jin, similar to Helen, is known as someone who is worldwide handsome. His beauty is what Jin is known for, he's the handsome one, the funny one, the one with the forehead. But apart from that, it has always been difficult to place who Kim Seokjin, as opposed to Jin, actually is. Especially prior to 2020.

2020 began like any other year. BTS began the new decade by starting promotion for their album *Map of the Soul: 7,* which had a release date of February 21st. To promote the album, the members took on various interviews and television appearances, including participating in *Carpool Karaoke* with American late night TV host James Corden. Very interestingly, Jin was placed in the back row of the car with members V and Suga, perhaps because they were shy on camera or less confident with their English, perhaps more so due to their introverted natures, which is more apparent in the case of Jin when he has to communicate in a foreign language rather than his native one. However, that didn't stop

JIN: IT'S DEFINITELY THE FOREHEAD, BUT IT'S MORE THAN THAT TOO

Jin from keeping the entertainment going. When asked about members' nicknames, he proudly declared, "I'm WWH, Worldwide Handsome, you know?"[4] He also answered a question with how excited he had been to meet Post Malone, and the band began to sing a rendition of Malone's hit, *Circles*.

In another TV appearance with Corden, BTS played a game of hide-and-seek with actor Ashton Kutcher.[4] Jin chose to hide inside a photo booth and had been taking snaps of himself when he was found and carried out by Kutcher. It was later posted that Jin's photo had a wonderful place between photos of Tom Cruise and Mahershala Ali, and above a picture of Kutcher himself. Having studied acting, it seems completely fitting that Jin's face belongs among the stars of Hollywood.[5] Fitting his degree, Jin does an excellent job of maintaining a more distinct exterior persona, playing into the 'Worldwide Handsome' title rather than presenting as someone who is shy.

BTS also made an appearance on *The Tonight Show Starring Jimmy Fallon* and took a ride on an infamous New York City subway train. When asked how it has been coming to the United States, fellow member Suga says that the response never fails to amaze him, to which Jin adds, "It's all thanks to ARMY. I love you, ARMY."[6] And that is something that has remained consistent throughout the years. Jin may be an introvert, but he wants ARMY to see a side of him that gives them hope, makes them smile, and fills them with love. That's who he always plans to be, that's why he intentionally acts cheerful, and consistently differentiates Jin vs. Kim Seokjin.

Perhaps, if it weren't for the world shutting down due to COVID-19, Jin would have remained that way. Instead, we did end up seeing more of the real Kim Seokjin.

2020 was a year that every single person in the world faced adversity in some kind of way due to the pandemic, and they each reacted in varying ways. BTS was no different. For Jin, 2020 meant losing out on touring opportunities, but it also meant chances to showcase the different sides of him, whether it is BTS' Jin, or Kim Seokjin. This came in the form of opening up more in interviews, engaging in songwriting and challenging himself to go beyond just being a member and vocalist of the band, and, incredibly enough, to reveal more of who Kim Seokjin is, to let the audience into his world more. He divulged his inner struggles, with mental health, with imposter syndrome. We were reminded that Kim Seokjin is not just Mr. Worldwide Handsome, he isn't just a prankster, nor is he just a beautiful exterior with no nuance.

While Jin of BTS is seemingly perfect, an embodiment of a man who is good looking and he knows it, he is someone who isn't afraid to make himself look silly to make his friends and fans laugh. Kim Seokjin is human, and he is one with depth, thoughtfulness, and an abundance of talent.

"Space that made you think"[1]

Map of the Soul: 7 is an album that is impossible to talk about without diving into the ways Jin played a role in almost all of the songs. The album is one which grants the audience "space that made you think,"[1] a phrase Jin uses to describe demos without rap in his Weverse interview. It's ironic because the way Jin talks about himself later in the year, outwardly drawing boundaries between Jin vs. Seokjin, also created a space that made us think. The songs on the album as well, can be described similarly. The album tells a story of the members' growth, as a few of the songs parallel tracks from their very first album, while at the same time showcasing their growth. Jin played a crucial part in creating this space, as exemplified throughout the various tracks.

The first track BTS released from *Map of the Soul: 7* was *Black Swan*, an anthem about trying to maintain passion for music, the field the members are in, and the fear that one day the passion might die. With the debut of the audio, BTS also posted the *Black Swan Art Film,* where dancers performed to an orchestral version of BTS' song.[7] A week after the short film was released, BTS' YouTube channel, BANGTAN TV, uploaded a reaction video where the seven members watched the film and expressed real time reactions.

JIN: IT'S DEFINITELY THE FOREHEAD, BUT IT'S MORE THAN THAT TOO

As the band members see the dance troupe take centre stage, BTS' leader RM's eye immediately catches one dancer, who is shirtless among a group of dancers clad in black, and declares "he must be the white swan, the rest are black swans."[8] This prompts rapper j-hope to say, "That should have been Jin hyung right there,"[7] and causes Jin to laugh and say "what are you saying?"[8] It's clear here that BTS' members see Jin very much as a centrepiece, a standout face of the band, a white swan among black swans.

The way Jin laughs it off is a trait he has continually shown, a humility that often leans towards self-deprecation. However, just like j-hope held belief in him, the members always build Jin up because his statements underestimating himself are simply not true. He has been a centric part of BTS' previous narratives. In BTS' music videos from the *The Most Beautiful Moment in Life* (commonly known as *HYYH*) and *Love Yourself* eras, Jin is the timekeeper and the centre of the BTS Universe, as told through the official *Save Me* webtoon.[9] He has the members' fate in his hands, similarly to how they rely on him in their everyday life and look up to him as a centric figure.

When *Map of the Soul: 7* is released, the members' faith in Jin continues to resurface. In a panel hosted on VLive to celebrate the comeback, Jin announces, "I don't get familiar with choreography as fast as the rest," a heartbreaking statement that honestly doesn't account for how hard he's worked as a dancer over the years.[10] The younger members are quick to disagree with him on this, with V saying "That's not true!" and Jung Kook adding "you're good!" When Jin jokingly asks, "how would you guys know," V is solemn in his response: "Don't say such things!" Jimin agrees, saying, "We know, being beside you."[10]

BTS released a video titled *'ON' Kinetic Manifesto Film : Come Prima* on the same day as *Map of the Soul: 7* came out. In this video, Jin, sporting a mullet, performs the title track for this album alongside fellow members.[11] Hours before the video and album came out, Big Hit uploaded a teaser of the song on TikTok, where Jin's vocals singing the words "can't hold me down cause you know I'm a fighter"[12] could be heard loud and clear. Jin is very much a fighter — as we'd continue to find out through the ways he would take us through his struggles with anxiety and imposter syndrome later in the year.

The storyline that Jin conveys through the songs on the album portrays him as the reassuring presence we know he is. He is the one who tries to save others, makes his fellow band members and fans happy, and radiates comfort by centring himself around the people he loves. These are reflected in songs such as *ON, Zero O' Clock,* and *Moon*.

Jin's vocals are featured throughout. His high notes are a standout in *Jamais Vu*, a song he performs with Jung Kook and j-hope, about the phenomenon of performing a familiar activity but not recognising it. This might remind the audience of Jin's role in the *Save Me* webtoon, where, as previously mentioned, Jin's character is a time traveller who often repeats the same day over and over again to save his friends. In those videos, Jin is constantly filming the others, trying to make sure he remembers and keeps track of what is occurring. He doesn't want to experience jamais vu, he wants to hold on to them and make sure he gets the job done.

Another song where Jin's vocals stand out is *Zero O' Clock*, a vocal-line-only track which leader RM has described as being about the urge to move forward at the end of the day, no matter what happens. In a VLive he said "When the vocalists recorded the song, it felt like they were telling my own story as if they were trying to comfort me."[13] Jin's voice is the beacon of comfort as he reassures the listeners, and perhaps himself, "and you're gonna be happy".[14]

Of course, we cannot mention this album without talking about *Moon*, Jin's solo track, one he wrote with the help of Slow Rabbit and RM. In the first episode of the fourth season of BTS' travel show, *Bon Voyage,* Jin is shown on a plane flying to New Zealand, conceptualising this song. At that moment he says, "To us, ARMY is everything, that's what the song will be about."[15] And he delivered. *Moon* is, in every beat, every word, every note, a complete ode to the love that Jin has for the BTS ARMY. In the song, he directly acknowledges the way he is known for his looks, "Though they say I'm beautiful / my sea is all black / A star where flowers bloom and the sky is blue — /the one who is truly beautiful

JIN: IT'S DEFINITELY THE FOREHEAD, BUT IT'S MORE THAN THAT TOO

is you"[16] — this is very typical Kim Seokjin, deflecting comments about this beauty onto ARMY, whereas Jin would claim the title of being the beautiful one. As we'll see later in the year during *BE* promotions, he often takes compliments and turns them towards ARMY. *Moon* is a work of art. Jin's hold of metaphor is well at play here, as he compares himself to the moon, the celestial body which orbits around the earth, which is ARMY. In Jin's own words, "I am the moon and earth is ARMY, and written in the perspective of how the moon looks at the earth. I usually write dark songs, but this track is very bright."[17] This is such a brilliant comparison, since the moon orbits the earth, and Jin always prioritises making sure the others around him feel comfortable. The Moon's presence helps stabilise the earth's wobble, which helps stabilise our climate. At the same time, without the moon's gravitational pull towards the earth, it would be lost. Jin's reliance on ARMY is thus very much symbiotic. He didn't know it at the time, but in the dark year that 2020 would become, *Moon* would be the comforting hug in song form that numerous people would turn to for warmth and reassurance.

The official music video for *ON* was released a week after the album, and at the beginning, Jin can be seen interacting with a pigeon, a symbol of peace and hope on the battlefield where the video is set, and by the end he is holding an empty cage.[18] According to an analysis by Twitter user @Adorable_9790, as translated by user @haruharu_w_bts, "the MV starts by showing a world that lost its peace, when Jin takes the last pigeon and exits the room, you can see lots of empty bird cages. They seem to have fought for a new world many times, but they failed. It looks like he took the last opportunity and exits (the last pigeon)."[19] While this is one of the numerous ways *ON* can be interpreted, this has a meaningful implication. As mentioned previously, Jin's role as the last hope is synonymous with his position in previous videos, he is the one who tries to save others. He is the one who is the memory keeper, the one who observes the world around him. *ON* adds to that narrative, where the fate of the world — and his friends — rests on Jin's shoulders in the narrative conveyed by BTS' music videos. As the oldest member of the band, he is willing to take on the responsibility of making sure his friends are safe and that he sees the journey through. As he mentions in the song, he knows he's a fighter.

BTS dropped the music video for *Black Swan* as a surprise in early March. Although it is Jimin who plays more of that centre/white swan role, Jin still does hold a very interesting place in the narrative.[20] Most BTS music videos (and songs, too) have an arc and are usually left up to the viewers' interpretation, and *Black Swan* is no different. Many of the scenes in the music video allude to the film of the same name. The audience can see Jin standing in the centre of a room filled with six mirrors as he sings the words, "nothing can devour me / I sing with ferocity".[21] In a song about fear of losing true passion, Jin is faced with many reflections of himself, while his physical form stands in the middle, not quite facing any of them. While it's hard to gauge exactly what BTS means, one of the interpretations of Jin's segment can be seen as the depiction of a man who is faced with his egos, similar to how Nina, played by Natalie Portman, hallucinates multiple versions of herself in *Black Swan* (2010).[22]

The plan was for BTS to take this album — which unsurprisingly ended up being one of the highest selling albums of 2020 — and go on a world tour. Alas, in a matter of weeks after the album's release, the pandemic hit and one by one the shows started getting cancelled. While it was absolutely devastating on all fronts, one of the more positive aftermaths of the pandemic was seeing how much BTS' Jin started opening up the curtains to the real Kim Seokjin, when ARMY needed more reassurance than ever from the members of the group.

"A business trip for 10 months"[1]

As the pandemic hit, BTS decided to postpone their world tour. In May, when the group would have been in the midst of their journey in North America, the fans were instead greeted with *Break the Silence,* an eight-part docu-series reflecting the members' mindsets on their Speak Yourself World Tour. The documentary gave the audience a vivid picture of Jin, including bits of Kim Seokjin, as he delved into who he was. We learned that he was hard on himself, "you know the saying about how

JIN: IT'S DEFINITELY THE FOREHEAD, BUT IT'S MORE THAN THAT TOO

putting in the effort eventually pays off? Well I have never been really satisfied with myself, so I must continue to put in the effort."[23] He let us into his fears in performing: "You know, since I haven't done this in a while, I worry a bit. Like, 'what if I mess up the dance?' and 'What if I forget the lyrics?' So in my room, I looked over the words and ran through the movements one more time. But still it's hard to shake off the anxiety."[23] One of the most compelling things about BTS' members has always been how they are not afraid to remind us that they're human beings with legitimate fears. They've always been strong advocates for mental health, and that's always started with letting people know about their struggles as well. In 2020, particularly, Jin enabled us to understand his fears more so than ever before.

Prior to 2020, it seemed like Jin had to feel 'on' at all moments, play a certain role, fitting for someone with the aforementioned acting degree. While of course, what he shows us is his authentic self, in *Break the Silence* he admits to turning his energy up several notches to take the form of mood maker and the comfort figure. In the past he has been guarded, whereas now, in the face of a pandemic, he's shedding his layers, like the onions he had to show RM how to chop on the show *Weekly Idol*.[24]

In *Break the Silence,* he acknowledges how much the exterior is a part he's playing and elaborates on his introversion and the way he separates Jin from Seokjin. He says, "sometimes it feels overwhelming to meet up with people. I know that I haven't changed at all. But sometimes people who have known me for a while start to drift away because they aren't comfortable with me anymore. I lost a bunch of people like that… and losing them makes me sad."[23] This is a side of fame that not a lot of people talk about — as gratifying as his journey may have been, Jin lost people too. Perhaps the most revealing of them all, "I try to show my bright side on camera. I mean, the fans want to feel happy when they see me. Right? So if I were to break their hearts it would in return break my heart. I wouldn't be able to stand that. That's why I want the fans to see the best of me. At least on TV."[23] Jin explains why he's seen laughing and smiling and playing pranks most of the time he's caught on camera.[23] He's an introvert himself, but when he's being watched by ARMY he wants to make people smile, even if he might not be feeling his best. While Jin's personality often has him misunderstood by fans as just adding comic or visual value, there's so much depth and nuance going into every decision he makes, including his deliberate desire to be the centre of laughter.

Such a developed and introspective point of view highlights just how much kindness and generosity Jin has to offer, even if it compromises his own comfort level. This is resonant with the message of his song *Epiphany*, from their *Love Yourself* era, where he goes from singing "I adapted myself entirely to you, I wanted to live for you / But as I kept doing so, I became unable to bear the storm inside my heart",[25] to saying "I'm the one I should love in this world / The shining me, the precious soul of mine / I realize only now, so I love me / Though I'm not perfect, I'm so beautiful".[25]

BTS were invited as guest speakers for *Dear Class of 2020* a worldwide graduation organised by YouTube, featuring speakers and musicians from across the globe. Each member spoke during the event, and Jin's speech was as reassuring as ever. "Sometimes, I'd feel restless, watching my friends go on far ahead of me… I soon realized that their pace was not my own. What held me together during those times was a promise I made with myself: 'to take it slow.' I'd go at my own pace, steadily."[26] In a year where people reacted to the circumstances in different ways, imposter syndrome and self-doubt were regular company for most, even a bestselling artist. Jin's perceptive words would go on to comfort ARMY throughout the rest of the year.

June also gave us more relaxed sides of Jin. For BTS' 7th anniversary, Festa, he participated in one of the more fun events which was released as *Map of the Song: 7*. Jin and the other members performed intentionally poor karaoke versions of each other's songs.[27] When Jin sings *Seesaw*, a Suga solo song, alongside RM, he demonstrates a clear knowledge of the choreography, despite not being a part of the original song. Jin had previously memorised the entire choreography of j-hope's song *MAMA* from their 2016 album *Wings*. This was again another example of the way Jin showed love and support towards his bandmates. Jin was also featured heavily in commercials BTS starred in that were posted across

JIN: IT'S DEFINITELY THE FOREHEAD, BUT IT'S MORE THAN THAT TOO

the summer. One of these was a Samsung ad featuring Jin and Jung Kook in suits, fighting each other for their phones.[28] The commercial contains Jin in a nutshell — it showcases him as both classy and serious and yet, playful and fun. As an actor, he is able to adapt to whatever role necessary.

And of course, we cannot mention the summer without talking about *BTS In the Soop*, a series that replaced *Bon Voyage* for the year due to travel restrictions. Instead of flying to a different country, the men of BTS take a trip to a forest in Korea, surrounded by greenery and water.[29] Jin's request for amenities includes a large fish tank, where he can collect fish for dinner. *In the Soop* very much shows the big brother side of Jin, as he spends a relaxed time with the members, and often takes charge of cooking during meals as he is of course, the best cook, alongside Suga. However, what sticks out the most about the *In the Soop* version of Jin is his determination to catch a fish during his travels. "Will Jin catch a fish before *In the Soop* ends?" was a question on the minds of many. During the show, Jin playfully sings a song where he makes the words up as he goes, "Please let me catch one fish / What did I ever do wrong? / Dragon King please / Give me one fish."[29] His fishing partner Suga states that despite not being very interested in fishing, "The reason I still go is because Jin asks me to come along with him. Even if I don't catch anything, I just do it because Jin hyung loves fishing."[29] Jin's passion for the simple things he enjoys is contagious. Moreover, his bandmates' willingness to make him happy is extremely touching. Alas, Jin's wish wasn't granted, but that again is a lesson from Jin, to continue persevering, even if the endeavour may not be the easiest.

"Spectrum of emotions"[1]

At the 75th General Assembly in September of 2020, Jin was as wise as ever in his speech. He talked about the important things at a time of quarantine and distancing, "I found again the people I love. The other members, my family, my friends. I found the music I love, and I found myself. Thinking about the future and trying hard are all important. But cherishing yourself, encouraging yourself and keeping yourself happy is the most important. In a world of uncertainty, we must cherish the importance of 'me', 'you', and 'us.' That's the message of "Love Myself" we talked about for three years."[30] That's the thing about Jin — each time he speaks at a public event, he reveals just how introspective and thoughtful he is.

As the person who had thousands of fans across stadiums all over the world singing the words "I'm the one I should love in this world" along with his song *Epiphany*, Jin understands the ambassadorship that BTS holds as promoters of self-love.[25] It's very characteristic of Jin to use himself as an example to not only remind ARMY how human he is, but to remind them it's okay to feel down, or to doubt themselves — but ultimately come out stronger. His reflection on self-love is no different. During a 2018 episode of his show *Eat Jin,* Jin says:

> "Honestly it's very hard to love myself. I couldn't love myself that much during debut days. But I forced myself to love myself. Now, I am filled with self-love. I don't know if I should call this 'effort,' but I realized efforts themselves can increase self-love. I hope more people would self-compliment themselves every day with thoughts of self-love. There are things in this world that can be done or just can't be done. Don't be harsh on yourself when things don't turn good… I would like you to have this mindset and love yourself more."[31]

And his message has continued to be carried forward. When an ARMY on Weverse cited the lyrics of *Epiphany* and thanked Jin for helping them smile and feel good about themselves, Jin replied, "I feel so proud when I see ARMY working to love themselves and practicing 'love myself'."[32]

In the last week of September, BTS took over *The Tonight Show with Jimmy Fallon* in what was dubbed BTS Week. Jin joined the band in showcases of their songs across various years: including *Idol* at Seoul's Gyeongbok Palace wearing modernised hanboks,[33] *Home* in a more relaxed setting,[34] *Black Swan* clad in all black,[35] and *Mikrokosmos* which

JIN: IT'S DEFINITELY THE FOREHEAD, BUT IT'S MORE THAN THAT TOO

finished with the BTS symbols among the stars.[36] Fans were quick to notice that Jin had traded his signature pink mic for a white one, and many wondered why — Twitter user @eggiebabies even tweeted, "genuinely don't know how to live in a world where jin's mic isn't pink."[37] Perhaps a reason that Jin's mic stood out to fans so much because despite the colour pink often being associated with femininity, Jin made the style very much his own. Arguably, it helped break notions of toxic masculinity and associations of the colours. Without it, things felt a little amiss.

Many recalled that on a VLive previously, RM had mentioned that Jin doesn't like pink anymore, while others tied it to the *Moon* era — with white being a nod to that. Glowe, a customised microphone designer had even posted on their Instagram that this new mic had Swarovski crystals in them[38] (Jin and gems would come back as a symbol of the *BE* era soon). But the pink was iconic — ARMY had tied this piece of equipment to his essence, and even though it was a small detail, it was heavily missed. However Jin had not lost any of his flare or charm as on the third night he showed his acting skills once again by winning a game of charades titled Zoom Olympics.[39]

We cannot talk about October without diving into *Map of the Soul ON:E*, BTS' online concert that was livestreamed by nearly a million ARMY on October 10-11, 2020.[40] The group performed songs primarily from the *Map of the Soul* era. BTS always puts on a *performance,* incorporating never-before-seen choreography and each members' strengths into each song, and Jin's solo, *Moon* was no different. It was interesting to see that once again, he didn't have his signature pink microphone with him. However, that was far from the topic of discussion as the *Moon* performance was absolutely breathtaking.

The first night, Jin came out dressed in an all white outfit, and on the second day in a pink chiffon top. He stood atop a platform built like the moon and sang the first verse. Next, he walked down the spaceship-stairs of the moon structure and was greeted by a group of dancers dressed like foxes. Artist Oh, who had built the set for *Moon,* confirmed on his Instagram that this concept was a nod to *The Little Prince,* a famous French novella published in 1943.[41] As Jin sang among models of celestial bodies about how he and ARMY had become each other's moon and earth, the foxes danced around him. In *The Little Prince,* the character of the fox plays a significant role in teaching the prince about building relationships. The fox tells the prince:

> "To me, you are still nothing more than a little boy who is just like a hundred thousand other little boys. And I have no need of you. And you, on your part, have no need of me. To you, I am nothing more than a fox like a hundred thousand other foxes. But if you tame me, then we shall need each other. To me, you will be unique in all the world. To you, I shall be unique in all the world."[41]

Although the fox's role in the story is more of a cameo, the fox teaches the prince — and the reader — the importance of building trust and understanding with another, and therefore distinguishing that person from the others in the world. The fox and the prince's story relates directly to the message of *Moon* to include an added layer to the metaphor of Jin and the ARMY. If Jin wins ARMY over, he will hold a unique presence in their heart and provide the comforting presence he does. He hopes that ARMY will welcome him into their hearts, and the symbiotic relationship can continue to thrive.

As he performed the second chorus, Jin's movements translated into the exact meanings of the lyrics, and each particular word — such as moving his hands around his head for the word "wonder", and pointing towards his eyes when singing the word "looking".[42] In detailed moves and likening the song to *The Little Prince*, Jin reminded ARMY of the way BTS and ARMY support each other — how his love for ARMY is unique and he will always be there for ARMY.

"Was it a dream?"[43]

In the lead up to the release of their next studio album *BE* which was put together entirely by BTS in terms of curation, production, writing — Big Hit released concept photos of rooms designed by each of the members, along with an audio track explaining the reasoning behind their choices. Jin's room was simple in its contents — the photo showed him dressed in a light blue robe over a white shirt and light purple pants. The room itself was covered in lavender curtains in front of a lavender backdrop. There was a crystal chandelier above Jin, and next to him sat a lamp. In the audio accompaniment, instead of saying much about himself, Jin diverted his use of royal colours and gems towards ARMY. Jin started his explanation by talking about the importance of comfort, even in luxurious surroundings. "I chose silk pants that go perfectly with all the sparkle, a nightgown, and slippers to make myself absolutely comfortable in a room full of precious stones. Don't I look completely at home?"[43] he asked ARMY. Then, consistent with his message about self-love and love for ARMY, he added, "Have you forgotten along the way that each one of you is a unique and precious gem? Never forget to cherish yourself and always remember that you are a sparkling gem."[43] Again, he always tries to show love for others and ARMY. In a year surrounded by uncertainty, if one thing was certain, it was how much ARMY could rely on Jin to always be there.

Jin played a crucial role in the songs themselves within *BE*. He sang the reassuring chorus of title track *Life Goes On*, "Like an echo in the forest / Another day will come / As if nothing happened / Yeah life goes on".[44] Throughout the music video Jin appears in green pyjamas, counting the days till he next sees ARMY. The music video shifts from colour to black and white as Jin closes his eyes in his living room. When he opens his eyes, he is on a stage, performing with BTS. As the time travelling centre figure, Jin seems to be transporting BTS from the pandemic-struck world to a COVID-free universe where the band can reunite with their fans. Once again he is shown as the central character in the music video, and is essential to bridging the gap between the current circumstance and the post-pandemic return of concerts.

Jin has also been very vocal about his love for the song *Blue & Grey*, co-written by member V, about being lost at a time of despair. In multiple interviews, he has cited the song as being his favourite on the album, because perhaps he too connects with the repetitiveness of life after COVID-19 and the question of, "Where's my angel? / At the end of the day, casting its shadow / Someone come and save me please / is only the sigh of the exhausting day".[45]

In *BE,* Jin was also featured in a unit track called *Stay* alongside RM and Jung Kook. This song is another nod to the tug Jin feels in his heart for ARMY, and how much he cherishes the part of his life where he could tour and see fans. He told *Weverse Magazine*, "The song opens with the words, "Was it a dream?" and I came up with the theme. We used to see our fans and it was great, but now that's something we can't do anymore. I thought it all felt like a dream. I wanted to say, "We used to be so happy together, but now I feel like your very existence was a dream.""[1] I came up with the intro and then talked about it with RM. He really helped me a lot." *Stay* carries on the messages from *Life Goes On* and *Blue & Grey* as BTS continues reflecting on the current situation. Throughout the song Jin and Jung Kook sing about the emptiness not seeing ARMY has left them with — "Wouldn't it be possible for me to see you?"[46] They ask. They compare their state to one of repetitive chanting, of calling for fans, even if it's just a crumb. The line, "tomorrow that is unchanging" conveys the monotone of their ARMY-less world, while through the chorus, "Like a crazy person, I keep sayin' / Wherever you are / I know you always stay",[46] they remind themselves that no matter what, ARMY will always stay with them.

2020 gave us both *Moon* and *Stay,* two tracks filled with heartfelt messages that reminded ARMY that Jin was a constant in their lives even if nothing else was certain.

JIN: IT'S DEFINITELY THE FOREHEAD, BUT IT'S MORE THAN THAT TOO

"Wonder if I deserve any of this"[1]

In the same interview with *Weverse Magazine,* Jin discloses the imposter syndrome he encountered when *Dynamite* achieved successes such as #1 on Billboard charts and a record number of views on release day.[1] He told them, "I started to think, "Do I deserve all this congratulations and love? That's not me — I'm not that kind of person." I got over it a bit, but even until a few days ago, the pressure was so intense that I couldn't get any work done."[1] He went on to discuss how living in the present had helped him cope with quarantine, and with his self-doubts. "You can be happier finding 10,000 won on the ground now than earning 100 times that in the past. I think I'm living true to my feelings by living in the now rather than thinking about the future or the past."[1] Jin had never elaborated on his genuine questioning of his place as an idol this much before 2020.

The year saw him tackling fears around performance in *Break the Silence* and with this interview he was considering whether he deserved any of this at all. The shadows of fear in this man who has been, as previously mentioned, an Adonis figure, the visual of the group, the older brother of the band, was a revelation, a reminder that BTS members are human too. As much of a comfort figure as Jin was to both ARMY and BTS, he had fears of his own. He wasn't just Worldwide Handsome full stop. As he mentioned when talking about *Epiphany,* and through the Weverse interview, he has to reassure himself constantly. It's not easy being someone who balances self-love and imposter syndrome. In talking about them so openly, while still carrying himself confidently on stage, Jin shows us that it is possible to hold the duality of self-doubt and stride. He may have these fears, but he still manages to come up with a different cute expression during each of his *Dynamite* solos. One wouldn't be able to guess that he is the same man who questions his success, and that makes him admirable. His layers seem never ending. The comfort figure, the big brother, the confident musician — combined with the person who has imposter syndrome — make Jin who he is.

The pinnacle of a year that showed us the difference between BTS' Jin and the person Kim Seokjin arrived on December 4, 2020, on Jin's

28th birthday. Shortly before midnight, he released a new song, titled *Abyss,* alongside a note thanking ARMY for the support and love. In the note, Jin addressed the mental health struggles he had faced throughout the year — something a younger version of him, a Jin in an earlier era would never do — and he even discussed how he had sought help from professionals and how much Bang Si-Hyuk, the CEO of Big Hit Entertainment had supported him at this time:

> "Those were the thought I had, and the deeper I was submerged in thoughts, the more painful it felt, and that's why I think I wanted to just put everything down. I also got counseling on this and made it through each day. I then talked with Bang PD-nim, and he suggested writing a song on this emotion.
>
> To him I said, "I'm not confident to do a good job, and what if the outcome is not good when I'm already at a position where I shouldn't [fail]." And Bang PD-nim said, "Such things are not important. But if you give it a try, you'll surely do a good job. I'll look for someone who has a good fit for you."[47]

Mental health is a topic typically stigmatised in South Korea,[48] so to have an idol of Jin's stature talk so openly about this was groundbreaking.

The song itself was revealing, showing a part of Jin's mind and hearts that allowed fans to share his pain. The words "Still, I remain with myself / With my voice unable to come out, I just circle around him / That dark place, / I'd like to be submerged in it, I'd like to go to it"[47] are a testament to his strength and resilience, and once again a demonstration of how deeply he thinks, and how introspective he has always been.

Abyss was a present Jin gave fans for his own birthday — unravelling parts of him that we had never seen before. We take a trip into his heart, "With my breath held, I walk into my sea, I walk into it / I face myself who is crying beautifully and sorrowfully".[47] Jin is among the BTS

JIN: IT'S DEFINITELY THE FOREHEAD, BUT IT'S MORE THAN THAT TOO

members who cry the least in concerts, having to hold the position of the eldest, and usually being there to comfort the others. To see him frame crying as a binary of beautiful and sorrowful is noteworthy — he tells us there is no shame in facing anxiety and fears, and that crying is raw and powerful. Through the words, "Myself in that darkness / I'd like to go find him and tell him / that I'd like to know more about you today, yeah",[46] he confesses that he hasn't explored the side of him that has trouble with mental health and struggles to be happy. He wants to embrace that side of himself. As a celebrity, he is expected to put on a happy face at all times. However, via this song, and lines such as "I'd like to be submerged in it, I'd like to go to it", he is opening himself up to the possibility of not just discovering his inner sorrows, but revealing that side to the world as well.[47] As someone who proudly had declared before 2020 that he insists on hiding Kim Seokjin from BTS' Jin, this is absolutely groundbreaking. He is extremely attuned to what fans need, and he provides them with the ultimate comfort.

"It felt like a part of my life disappeared"[1]

The end of the year schedule for BTS is always packed with award shows and musical programs in South Korea. One of their appearances involved a performance at the KBS Song Festival hosted by the Korean Broadcasting System.[49] One of the songs they performed was *I Need U*, the title track from their 2015 album *The Most Beautiful Moment in Life Pt. 1*, a song that played a crucial part in putting them on the map as a group to watch out for in the K-pop industry. In the 2020 version of the performance, BTS paid tribute to the 2015 versions of themselves, wearing similar sailor-like costumes.[50] Just like how this performance highlighted the ways BTS have grown as a group since their first hit, we can also use it as a reflection of Jin's evolution. There are many differences between the 2015 and 2020 versions of Jin. He hadn't yet become a household name. He had less confidence in his dancing abilities. He hadn't written as many songs, though he was definitely still Worldwide Handsome. The 2020 version of Jin is one who is more dynamic, expressive, and unafraid to let ARMY in. The lines between BTS' Jin and Kim Seokjin became far less blurred at the end of 2020 than they were at the beginning. As BTS closed the year by performing at Big Hit's *New Year's Eve Live* concert, fans were delighted to see that Jin's pink mic was back. Whether the white microphone had been there as a symbol of the *BE* era, or perhaps Jin simply missed his microphone, it was the cherry on top to cap off the familiarity, comfort, and love that Jin had provided ARMY with throughout an otherwise very unsettling year. He is a man of nuance, depth, and perception — so yes, his forehead *is* noticeable. But there are so many more layers to him than that.

References

1. Jin. (2020, October 26). *"It feels like my memories of ARMY were all a dream"*. https://magazine.weverse.io/article/view?num=60&lang=en
2. 쟈근콩 [@tinyseokjinnie]. (2018, February 11). *something I found out from k-armys recently is that Seokjin actually had gotten accepted to Sejong univ. and Kunkook univ. Astonished face and then chose KU to go. the acting academy Seokjin used to go when he was in highschool posted congrats when he got in*. [Tweet]. https://twitter.com/tinyseokjinnie/status/962651213278756864
3. Bang, S. (Executive Producer). (2020). *Break the silence* [TV Show]. Big Hit Entertainment.
4. The Late Late Show with James Corden. (2020). *BTS carpool karaoke*. [Video]. https://www.youtube.com/watch?v=T4x7sDevVTY
5. The Late Late Show with James Corden. (2020). *Hide & seek w/ BTS & Ashton Kutcher*. [Video]. https://www.youtube.com/watch?v=JPS3QC86Jio
6. The Tonight Show Starring Jimmy Fallon. (2020). *BTS on first impressions, secret career dreams and Map of the Soul: 7 meanings*. [Video]. https://www.youtube.com/watch?v=v_9vgidPJ8g
7. Big Hit Labels. (2020). BTS (방탄소년단) 'Black swan' art film performed by MN dance company. [Video.] https://www.youtube.com/watch?v=vGbuUFRdYqU
8. BANGTANTV. (2020). [BANGTAN BOMB] BTS 'Black Swan' MV reaction - BTS (방탄소년단) [Video]. https://www.youtube.com/watch?v=LQK7tF1vH2w
9. *SAVE ME - Prologue*. www.webtoons.com. (2019, January 17). https://www.webtoons.com/en/drama/bts-save-me/prologue/viewer?title_no=1514&episode_no=1.
10. BTS. (2020). BTS comeback special: Let's do a viewable 'purple' radio [Video]. https://www.vlive.tv/video/175309

[11] Big Hit Labels. (2020). BTS (방탄소년단) 'ON' kinetic manifesto film : Come prima [Video.] https://www.youtube.com/watch?v=gwMa6gpoE9I

[12] BTS. (2020). ON [Song]. On *Map of the soul: 7*. Big Hit Entertainment.

[13] BTS. (2020). *Namjun's 7 behind* □ [Video]. https://www.vlive.tv/video/179339?channelCode=FE619

[14] BTS. (2020). 00:00 (Zero o' clock) [Song]. On *Map of the soul: 7*. Big Hit Entertainment

[15] Bang, S. (Executive Producer). (2019). *Bon voyage* [TV Show]. Big Hit Entertainment.

[16] BTS. (2020). Moon [Song]. On *Map of the soul: 7*. Big Hit Entertainment; Doolset. *Moon* [Translation]. https://doolsetbangtan.wordpress.com/2020/02/22/moon/

[17] K-pop idols BTS discuss 'Map of the Soul: 7,' their love for ARMY & more. (2020, February 21). https://blog.siriusxm.com/k-pop-idols-bts-discuss-map-of-the-soul-7-their-love-for-army-more/

[18] Big Hit Labels. (2020). BTS (방탄소년단) 'ON' official MV [Video.] https://www.youtube.com/watch?v=mPVDGOVjRQ0

[19] haruharu [@haruharu_w_bts]. (2020, March 2). @BTS_twt #BTS #방탄소년단 #On music video analysis by a k-army [Tweet]. https://twitter.com/haruharu_w_bts/status/1234628830335307776

[20] Big Hit Labels. (2020). BTS (방탄소년단) 'Black Swan' official MV [Video.] https://www.youtube.com/watch?v=0lapF4DQPKQ

[21] BTS. (2020). Black swan [Song]. On *Map of the soul: 7*. Big Hit Entertainment; Doolset. *Black Swan* [Translation] https://doolsetbangtan.wordpress.com/2020/01/17/black-swan/

[22] Aronofsky, D. (Director). (2010). *Black swan*. Fox Searchlight Pictures.

[23] Bang, S. (Executive Producer). (2020). *Break the silence* [TV Show]. Big Hit Entertainment.

[24] Lee, S. (Executive Producer). (2015, June 17). BTS (Episode 229) [TV series episode]. *Weekly Idol*. Genie Pictures.

25 BTS. (2018). Epiphany [Song]. On *Love yourself: Answer*. Big Hit Entertainment; Doolset. *Epiphany* [Translation]. https://doolsetbangtan.wordpress.com/2018/08/09/epiphany/
26 BANGTANTV. (2020). *BTS | Dear class of 2020* [Video]. https://www.youtube.com/watch?v=ErTgtL1Tjns
27 BANGTANTV. (2020). [2020 FESTA] BTS (방탄소년단) 'MAP OF THE SONG : 7' #2020BTSFESTA [Video]. https://www.youtube.com/watch?v=kBVQ1s_REzI
28 Samsung. (2020). *Galaxy x BTS: The strange tailor shop □ | Samsung* [Video]. https://www.youtube.com/watch?v=Pii224aV-jY
29 Bang, S. & Lenzo, Y (Executive Producers). (2020). *BTS In the soop* [TV Show]. Big Hit Entertainment.
30 BANGTANTV. (2020). BTS (방탄소년단) Speech at the 75th UN general assembly [Video]. https://www.youtube.com/watch?v=5aPe9Uy10n4&t=293s
31 Jin. *EAT Jin*. [Video] https://www.vlive.tv/video/87662
32 「claire ⁷ 」[@btstranslation7]. *weverse 210322 @bts_twt an army cited the lyrics of 'epiphany' and thanked jin for encouraging us to smile & feel good about ourselves* [Tweet]. https://twitter.com/btstranslation7/status/1373968875042246662
33 The Tonight Show Starring Jimmy Fallon. (2020). *BTS: IDOL | The tonight show starring Jimmy Fallon* [Video]. https://www.youtube.com/watch?v=MXFkjMNXfpY&t=3s
34 The Tonight Show Starring Jimmy Fallon. (2020). *BTS: HOME | The tonight show starring Jimmy Fallon* [Video]. https://www.youtube.com/watch?v=2rcKpY-4QBI&t=3s
35 The Tonight Show Starring Jimmy Fallon). (2020). *BTS: Black swan | The tonight show starring Jimmy Fallon* [Video]. https://www.youtube.com/watch?v=g1-sFn-j5D0
36 The Tonight Show Starring Jimmy Fallon. (2020). *BTS: Mikrokosmos | The tonight show starring Jimmy Fallon* [Video]. https://www.youtube.com/watch?v=oYpUZjxJOVg

37 eggie!! ♡□⁷□□ [@eggiebabies]. (2020, October 2). *genuinely don't know how to live in a world where jin's mic isn't pink* [Tweet]. https://twitter.com/eggiebabies/status/1311888529589506054

38 Glowe [@crystal.glowe]. (2021, January 3). customized microphone for Jin, BTS □Swarovski crystal by Glowe, Korea [Instagram photograph]. https://www.instagram.com/p/CJll-RdjibJ/

39 The Tonight Show Starring Jimmy Fallon. (2020). *Zoom olympics with BTS | The tonight show starring Jimmy Fallon* [Video]. https://www.youtube.com/watch?v=v1kjByPiCLE

40 *BTS' virtual Map of the soul ON:E concert garnered nearly 1 million viewers across the globe.* (2020, October 12). https://www.billboard.com/articles/columns/k-town/9464078/bts-virtual-map-of-the-soul-one-concert-recap-viewers/

41 Saint-Exupéry, A., Saint-Exupéry, A., Woods, K., & Harcourt, Brace & World. (1943). *The little prince.* Reynal & Hitchcock.

42 pha⁷[@bemyjinnie]. *moon by jin choreography; it's literal meaning* [Tweet]. https://twitter.com/bemyjinnie/status/1314953301968867328

43 BE | BTS | BigHit Entertainment [Video file]. (2020, November 06). https://ibighit.com/bts/video/be/QCgwKq7hwPbOoHJfpzr617x8.php?l=kor

44 BTS. (2020). Life goes on [Song]. On *BE*. Big Hit Entertainment; Doolset. *Life goes on* [Translation]. https://doolsetbangtan.wordpress.com/2020/11/20/life-goes-on/

45 BTS. (2020). Blue & grey [Song]. On *BE*. Big Hit Entertainment; Doolset. *Blue & grey* [Translation]. https://doolsetbangtan.wordpress.com/2020/11/20/blue-and-grey/

46 BTS. (2020). Stay [Song]. On *BE*. Big Hit Entertainment; Doolset. *Stay* [Translation]. https://doolsetbangtan.wordpress.com/2020/11/20/stay/.

47 BTS. (2020). Abyss [Song]. On *Soundcloud.* Big Hit Entertainment; Doolset. *Abyss* [Translation]. https://doolsetbangtan.wordpress.com/2020/12/03/abyss-jin/

48 World Health Organization. (2006). *WHO-AIMS report on mental health system in Republic of Korea.* https://www.who.int/mental_health/evidence/korea_who_aims_report.pdf?ua=1

49 KBS Kpop. (2020). 방탄소년단 (BTS) - I NEED U [2020 KBS 가요대축제] | KBS 201218 방송 [Video]. https://www.youtube.com/watch?v=Z3Ycg7FL718

50 KBS WORLD TV. (2015). BTS (방탄소년단) - I Need U [Music Bank K-Chart #1 / 2015.05.08] [Video]. https://www.youtube.com/watch?v=g70nl70cH-4

RM

ONLY HUMAN
Wallea Eaglehawk

Genesis: I'm a 27-year-old Korean. That's what I think[1]

In RM's 2015 mixtape, aptly titled *RM*, he penned "I've diligently walked like this for seven years, and now the path gets cleared up for me".[2] These words were true to him as an individual five years ago. But now as he stands on stage at *Dick Clark's New Year's Rockin' Eve* counting down to 2020, they seem more relevant than ever. With a new year now upon him it felt as if RM's future was unbearably bright, surrounded by the technicoloured landscape of New York's Time Square and his beloved BTS members. It was like the path had been cleared for him once again to shine, and fly.

Kim Namjoon, Namjoon, otherwise known as RM, was born September 12, 1994 in Seoul, South Korea. 2020 marked his tenth year with Big Hit Entertainment, and the seventh as leader of BTS. This passage of time is what he reflected on for his New Year's message:

> "I first entered Big Hit in April of 2010. I've spent an entire decade just for BTS. From when I was sixteen years old to now at twenty-six, I've spent it all on BTS. If I take away BTS, there is nothing left in my life. I will remember this decade as being the decade of BTS.

> Maybe that's why I feel refreshed yet restless for 2020 because everything from start to finish is with BTS."[3]

Refreshed yet restless, because despite achieving accolades and going from strength to strength as a member of BTS, and as a solo artist, it felt as though 2020 held the kind of infinite possibilities previously unattainable to him and the group. This was the same energy that was potent on New Year's Eve — triumph, celebration, relief… an anticipation of what would come next.

RM is a rapper, lyricist and producer for and with BTS. Within the fandom and further afield, he is also known for his patronage of the arts,[4] his rumoured IQ of 148,[5] and his English language proficiency in overseas interviews.[5]

In 2020 RM was recognised as one of ten Patrons of the Arts by the Arts Council of Korea[4] and became a full member of the Korea Music Copyright Association.[6] Yet listing his accomplishments alone does not give a clear, nor appropriately nuanced, picture of the artist who leads one of the most influential music groups[7] on the precipice of something big in 2020. This chapter aims to provide further depth to RM by juxtaposing an analysis of his creative work with his interviews, both which provide ruminations on his sense of self, with the experiences of the audience who watches on.

Through this analysis, a paradox will be explored, a contradiction, a complexity: being both Kim Namjoon and RM gives rise to a dualistic, or perhaps even multiplistic experience of identity and life as he negotiates being both idol and fan, artist and idol, revolutionary and human.[8]

Persona, who the hell am I?[9]

The question of who RM is, is a shared concern with the artist himself, who in his 2019 solo *Intro: Persona* (henceforth *Persona*) asked "persona, who the hell am I?"[9] Though being released in 2019, *Persona* provides the first building block for this profile as it remains, to this day, one of RM's most autobiographical works. Though on the surface, it may not reveal much about what he has done or where he has gone, it does provide a glimpse into the ruminations of an idol negotiating the complexity of contrasting needs and experiences.

> ""Who am I," a question that I've been asking myself for my whole life
> A question that I will probably never be able to find the right answer for
> If I were answerable with only few words,
> God wouldn't have created all those many beauties."[9]

Perhaps what can come as a surprise to many when first becoming acquainted with the work of RM is that there is a duality, a stark yet symbiotic contrast between the idol who commands the stage and the artist who asks who he truly is. Fan translator Doolset Bangtan notes that the "many beauties" RM mentions in *Persona* can be interpreted as the many "different "I"s, different personas".[10] Which can be taken as not only the many different personas of others around the world, but perhaps the many personas that exist within RM himself. Not only is RM saying he doesn't quite know who he is, he is also acknowledging that there is perhaps more than one persona within him.

It is here that we can see the emergence of the complexity that lies within something more than just duplicity: multiplicity. As previously mentioned, RM appears to exist at the junction of many competing and contrasting identities, which he acknowledges in *Persona* with "the 'me' who I want to be / the 'me' who people want / the 'me' who I love / and the 'me' who I craft / the 'me' who's smiling / the 'me' who's crying sometimes / living and breathing every second, every moment, even now".[9]

It's no wonder, then, that the line that follows "persona, who the hell am I?"[9] speaks not to who RM is, but perhaps reveals the true sentiment of the song: "I just wanna go, I just wanna fly".[9] Which, arguably, represents two things: RM's desire to be moving forward, propelled by the frustration of constant ruminations on who he could be, and; his acknowledgement that it doesn't matter who he is, because all he wants to do is be free and fulfil his own destiny.

One of RM's most widely recognised roles is that of leader, within it comes a range of complexities and competing interests. "I think RM is a genuine leader," says Suga at BTS' birthday Festa in June 2020, "it's not easy to make sure everything's in place. It's possible because he makes it possible."[11] RM as a genuine leader rarely, if ever, centres himself in the narrative, take this interview with *Esquire*, for example:

> "Our company started with twenty to thirty people, but now we have a company with so many employees," RM says. "We have our fans, and we have our music. So we have a lot of things that we have to be responsible for, to safeguard." He considers it for a moment. "I think that's what an adult is."[12]

Through statements such as these, RM sets the tone for the rest of the group. Instead of centring himself by saying 'I feel a great responsibility to my company and our fans, that's what I think being an adult is', he reframes it as a statement on behalf of BTS as a whole. Through this, we can see his professional integrity coming into play, he is a leader through inclusion. He is a leader for the betterment of BTS alone, and takes none of the spotlight for himself. But his leadership doesn't stop there.

In an interview with Weverse, RM shares "I try to integrate myself into our generation, try to understand what people like me are thinking, and try to work hard to capture that feeling without being a burden on them."[1] Which gives further light to his professional and artistic integrity; he is someone who thinks deeply about those around him and tries his best to channel universal experiences through the group and outwards into the world. Not only is he a leader of BTS, but because of his unique role within the group, he is the leader of an entire ARMY.

Any chance he gets, he offers his positionality, "I think millennials are charging into society stuck between the analog and digital generations, and what I chose is BTS",[1] and reveals the responsibility he undertakes for representing his generation — and beyond — through and with BTS. Perhaps, then, being a leader is not a persona, as much as a character trait — one which can be consistently found throughout the personas he shares with the world. However, this is not done loudly, nor explicitly. He is leading by example, by first being the leader of his own life.

Interestingly, when asked to represent himself, he typically opts to take a smaller role within his own narrative. Such as not wanting to take too much credit for writing on the majority of tracks for 2020 release *Map of the Soul: 7* during the behind-the-scenes look he presents with each album.[13] Or simply making a joke, like when he was asked to leave a message for his future self during promotions for *Map of the Soul: 7*: "Have you finally got your driver's license?"[14]

Juxtaposed against his role of leader are his experiences of loneliness, which give further context to who RM is. Examples of which can be found in his solo work, such as 2018's *mono.* which was described by MTV as "equal parts wistful and weary [...] the theme of loneliness is constant throughout".[15] On *Always*, a single released on SoundCloud the same year as *mono.*, he raps, "one morning, when I opened my eyes, I wished that I was dead / I wish someone killed me / In this loud silence, I live to understand the world, but the world has never understood me, why".[16] Though he is the leader of BTS, in some respects it appears he still feels on the periphery. In his Weverse interview he reflects on a quote from artist Whanki Kim:

> ""I'm Korean, and I can't do anything not Korean. I can't do anything apart from this, because I am an outsider." And I keep thinking that way, too. That's my main concern lately."[1]

Perhaps this is why the lyrics from his mixtape "I've diligently walked like this for seven years, and now the path gets cleared up for me"[2] have the same energy as "I just wanna go, I just wanna fly",[9] because after all this time, perhaps he is tired of ruminating and analysing, tired of asking *why*. Perhaps in 2020 with his group members sharing more and more of the responsibility typically shouldered by the leader — such as speaking English in overseas interviews and writing songs on *BE* — some of the pressure of growing is coming off and he now can spread his wings and fly, with all his personas in tow.

Irrespective of how Namjoon sees himself as both Namjoon and RM, it is clear through *Persona* that he is someone willing to critique and analyse himself as a means of artistic rigour and perhaps also emotional catharsis. His role as leader of BTS adds further meaning to this, as such a reflection on identity — along with his past work that sheds light on his loneliness — is honest and vulnerable. In this sense, his experience of loneliness has afforded him a unique perspective — like all distance does — and has, arguably, meant that he has taken extra care when working with others, and interacting with ARMY. It has meant that he surely must seek to understand those around him, and the world more broadly, in the same way he wishes to be understood. Presumably, such loneliness, in part, has shaped an empathetic and analytic man who has honed his creative voice to help people understand who he really is. Through this, he is enabling others to understand and communicate who they really are, too.

They say life is full of paradox[17]

This is the genesis of RM in the year of 2020. Genesis is a strange word, mostly because it has strong religious undertones. Such a comparison to a religious figure would surely not be how RM chooses to present himself, but it does play an important role in his story. When given the opportunity to speak about himself, RM, time and again, will present as someone humble and genuine. On his birthday he appeared on VLive to spend time with ARMY where he said "birthdays are... I try not to make a big deal out of it. I just call my mom and say thank you for giving birth [to me] and [for] raising me. I call mom and dad first."[18] Later on, he addressed a viral photo where it appeared his muscles were popping out of his shirt: "Everyone, I don't have big muscles. Please know, I just try to work out hard."[18] And when concluding the session, he gave thanks for all his birthday wishes, saying that they were "more than I deserve, [they are] over my worth in destiny. Still, I appreciate all of this."[18] These three instances show RM as a laid back, hard-working artist with no desire to be aggrandised.

Another strange word is paradox, which typically refers to a self-contradictory statement. This was the word RM chose to use when he featured on Younha's track *Winter Flower* which was released early January 2020. Perhaps what is more interesting is the context because in the line that precedes "they say life is full of paradox",[17] he says "I'm okay with whatever you call me".[17]

What is of interest to this chapter is that there are many paradoxes, or contradictions, that exist within the identity and experiences of RM. One being that he does not wish to be regarded as a god or anything that places him above others, especially those within his own group. Yet, by all means, he is revered throughout the fandom and further afield as a genius,[19] and a revolutionary.[8] But if we are to take his lyric of "I'm okay with whatever you call me"[17] into account, then perhaps he also is completely aware of the contradictions of his experience of self — someone who is just a regular human being — with his fans' experience of him — the leader, the genius, the revolutionary.

If you were to take RM's perspective of himself, he might say something like: I am the leader of BTS, I am an artist, I am human. However, if you were to take a fan's perspective they could easily say: he is the leader of ARMY, he is our idol, he is revolutionary. Through the concepts of catharsis, metamorphosis, and antithesis these two paradoxical view points will be juxtaposed, and through a creative and analytical synthesis, they will merge to show an interpretation of who RM in 2020 was, in the words of an ARMY. After all, you can't spell ARMY without RM.

> "This might be another kind of irony itself, but this is who I am. I'm a 27-year-old Korean. That's what I think."[1]

Catharsis: "Namjoon, it feels like you're becoming a lyricist"[1]

흔들리는 건 이놈인가
Is it this guy that is shaking
아니면 내 작은 발끝인가
or is it the tips of my small feet[20]

Over the years, RM has been spotted reading art books and commonly posts pictures from galleries and museums, admiring artwork. Though this patronage of the arts is something more likely to be found in the 'Namjooning' category firmly in the 'I'm just a normal human' section of this chapter, it has a special significance here. In November 2020, RM provided an insight to his intensifying interest in not only patronising the arts, but studying them as a means to hone his own craft:

> "I think it's helped me develop a way of thinking using all the senses. I used to be attuned to speech and focus on language and auditory textures, but now I can look at my thoughts from many different angles. That's why I spend more time studying art now. I'm waiting for the day that it all comes to the surface, like when you paint the base on a canvas over and over so the colors pop. It's hard to answer in one word if it has a direct influence on my work, but I think people who create music develop a way of seeing the world through their personal experience and their creative process. Painters naturally exhibit their art over a very long period of time. I think it gave me an eye for looking at the world in one long, continuous stroke."[1]

Through this it appears that RM has been looking at the world in "one long, continuous stroke"[1] for some time now, and further, as leader and lyricist has become the continuous stroke throughout BTS' music.

RM: ONLY HUMAN

To see this unfolding, let us look to March 10, 2020. RM sits eating a burger on VLive, waiting for viewers to join. He's at his desk in his studio inside the Big Hit building; his hair is purple, his shoes are off, and there appears to be a pile of folded clothes on the couch behind him. It's late in the afternoon, just two weeks after the highly anticipated release of *Map of the Soul: 7*.

"How many times do I say hello?"[13] he asks as he continues to greet people, waiting for the right time to start.

Soon enough, he deems enough people have joined him and he begins his yearly 'behind' where he discusses each track on the album, giving fans and critics a look inside the writing process.

First, comes an overview of the album as a whole: "This album is for me..." he begins, "it feels like an agreement with the seven of us."[13] And how it was made: "I had lots of conversations with [the] other members. I[t] felt very complicated. The album reminded me of our old days."[13] Here, we can begin to see that the way RM's, and by extension, BTS', work arises from conversation — which has echoes of RM's leadership style briefly touched on above — and prioritises inclusion of all members to whatever extent they can or wish to participate.

RM does not shy away from sharing the emotions that arose during the writing process: "I kept kind of reflecting on our past. Kind of reminisc[ing]. How have we walked all [this] way?"[13] Here we can see that the writing process for RM isn't self-serving, or about his issues or thoughts alone, rather as he mentioned in his Weverse interview he tries "to work hard to capture that feeling [of a generation] without being a burden on them."[1] This, undoubtedly, is how he approaches writing for BTS, too. This album in particular saw RM reflecting on the journey the entire group has been on: "[reminiscing] made me laugh and cry so hard. [...] So I worked on this album with all those emotions and vivid memories."[13]

Representing all of BTS through individual tracks and a collective album with a coherent theme surely is no easy task, as it requires the balancing of the needs of each member, the team, the company, and the knowledge that millions of people around the world will be wanting to emotionally connect to, analyse, and understand the lyrics' message and purpose. It could be argued, then, that through his lyric writing is where, in this instance at least, RM leads the most and continues to set the tone for the entire group through ensuring a consistent message no matter how many other non-members work on the track. It appears, especially from this behind in particular, that RM is indeed the continuous stroke throughout BTS' lyrical works.

What can be deduced from the behind is that RM wrote the first draft for most tracks — including three of the solos — which saw him receive credits for 17 out of 20 songs on *Map of the Soul: 7*.[21] A feat, true to RM's character, that was met with humility and gratitude: "the fact that I showed a piece of my music to the world as part of my heritage [...] makes me feel very [encouraged], relieved, and just... I feel so good. I feel very happy."[13]

고요한 너의 슬픔이
Your silent sorrow
나를 흔들어
shakes me
조용한 나의 바다에
In the quiet sea of mine,
파도가 일곤 해
waves rise from time to time[22]

The track *Louder than bombs* was inspired by letters that RM received, and posts he had read on Weverse from ARMY who were suffering. "When I read fans' postings about sad things in their lives, I thought about the feelings that we have or the emotions. [...] all of us can't be happy all the time."[13] The song, though inspired by the suffering of ARMY, also seems to represent the suffering of BTS, not just in response to reading such letters or posts, but in general. "'Louder than bombs I break' this part is somewhat poetic," RM reflects, "I break, louder than bombs."[13] This speaks to the reciprocal relationship between RM and his fans, and his desire to ensure they are seen, heard, and understood.

He goes on to explain that through reading about ARMY's suffering, he realised that the expression on their faces — the smiling, cheering fans at concerts, for example — were not always their expressions — that sadness and pain often lies beneath.[13] He also mentions that the original lyric was 'all the pain pouring out' to reflect the outpouring of pain that fans often intimately share with the group.[13] This sentiment can be found in the lines "Louder than bombs I break / The pains that pour down / The facial expression you made — since the time I learned that it's not what it meant".[22] Which can be interpreted not only as ARMY breaking louder than bombs, with pain that pours down, but also as BTS breaking louder than bombs at the pain that pours from ARMY, and the world beyond.

Further, and interestingly enough, the same realisation that RM had that ARMY's expression of happiness or excitement not always their constant state, causing him to break louder than bombs, is one that can be reversed when ARMY learn of BTS' suffering that pours down from their lyrics. In this instance, RM has managed to be a conduit not only for his own innermost feelings, but for the group and the fandom as well — and because the concept is so universal, it becomes something relatable to an entire generation, as per his Weverse statement, and everyone else who listens, too.

Not only was *Louder than bombs* a form of catharsis, for RM and BTS to be able to express how they feel about ARMY and the suffering of the world, his original intention appears to be much more sentimental than that:

> "It made me think about how I can embrace all the pain pouring out. Can I embrace them? Can I? Can I hear them all, at least? Is it possible for a person like me to embrace their pain? I'm just a person. Is it possible to comfort them? Is it possible? It's a question or a confession to myself. It's also a plea. That's sad. […] it felt so desperate and sad at the same time. I can't do

multiple things at the same time. [...] Very sad. I was sad."[13]

Though he feels that he is someone who cannot save everyone and do everything, RM is embracing the pain of ARMY and the world through this song. This desire to embrace ARMY's pain has echoes of lyrics from *mono.*'s *Forever Rain* "if I could kiss the whole world deeply, would someone welcome me? / Would someone embrace my weary body?"[23] Two years later, RM is still embracing the whole world, understanding everyone's pain in the way he wished he could be understood.

It is through this very experience that he is able to create a song that has such great capacity for universal understanding. The pain of not being able to help everyone, not being able to do multiple things at the same time, this plea to himself is held within the words "louder than bombs I break",[22] for it is that tension of competing wants, needs, and abilities while remaining only human that creates such a powerful breaking point. This is surely a universal experience, as it is one he has already observed within ARMY, within BTS, and more broadly throughout the world and channelled through his lyricism. There is pain in breaking louder than bombs, and great healing, too.

Is it my fault?
Is it my wrong?
답이 없는 나의 메아리만
Only my echo, with no answer[24]

00:00 (Zero O'Clock), a vocal line song, appears to be the most meaningful and personal track from *Map of the Soul: 7* which RM reflects on: "This song's theme was related to thoughts I have. When I come home I lie down on the bed and start thinking. 'I don't think it's my fault. Is it my fault?' No. But such things happen frequently."[13] Though he does not feature on the track, RM is clear that "some of me is in this song".[13] Which becomes clear, when comparing how he speaks about his involvement in other songs, and their meanings to him, that *00:00* is something he finds to be more representative of his inner feelings, as opposed to those of the whole group.

As he continues to speak, his experiences come through. Arguably, they seem inextricably intertwined with his experience of being a leader, an idol, and working with others: "There are many things, many damages we get regardless of our intentions. Hurtful words. I have thoughts about it."[13] Surely the pressure to not make mistakes, or upset others is far higher for RM who must balance his needs with the needs of his members, his team, his company, and the world around them. Within the lyrics is also a pressure to perform: "The beat slips off by a bit / I can't make an easy facial expression / I keep forgetting familiar lyrics / Nothing goes the way I want it to".[24]

"Anyway," RM continues, "a day goes by and your life goes on."[13] Laying in bed ruminating on whether or not it was his fault, or his wrong, he looks at the clock and it's nearly midnight. Which is where this song exists, in the promise of a new day, a fresh beginning. Like the snow that covers the ground, making it bright and white and new, that presses down on the senses and creates a new reality: "Some time ago it snowed heavily. When I saw the snow-covered field where nobody [had stepped], it made me gasp and breathe out,"[13] RM reminisces. This experience is what he wrote the lyrics thinking about, which can be seen in these lines: "Like that snow that just settled on the ground, let's breathe as if this is the beginning / And you gonna be happy".[24] Life goes on, and you're going to be happy; this is what RM tells himself.

A song that was personal then became one that was performed by BTS' vocalists, which made the experience more meaningful for RM: "When members sang this song which felt like what was deep down in my heart, it was like my own story [was being told] by others to comfort me."[13] What started as a way for RM to express himself, then became a comfort to him, his members, and ARMY. This particular instance of catharsis, much like *Louder than bombs*, provided another opportunity for others to feel seen, understood, and heard. A process which started with RM and expanded outwards; this was just another way for him to embrace his own pain, and the pain of ARMY and kiss the whole world, just like he wished he could in *Forever Rain*.

Let's reimagine our world[25]

Calling RM a songwriter doesn't fully encapsulate the importance or breadth of his work. To call him a lyricist gives rise to the poetic and philosophical nature of his work; yet he is more than those three things alone. Not only is he a lyricist, a poet, and a philosopher, he is an idol, an idol who is also a leader.

There is a reason for making the binary of RM as an artist the fact that RM is also an idol, instead of grouping the role of idol with that of BTS member or revolutionary alone. It is because the notion of an idol who is an artist often seems paradoxical, contradictory. For it is commonplace to believe that an idol is fabricated, mass-made, a marionette for a faceless conglomerate.[8] It is commonplace to believe that the very process of becoming and working as an idol strips one of their artistic integrity and autonomy.[8] Yet it is through RM that we can see that being an artist who is also an idol is what affords him a greater opportunity for catharsis, expression, and broadens his impact on a large global audience.

It is RM's lyricism and his unique situation as an idol that is an artist that provides the basis for him to be a conduit for all he bears witness to. This, in turn, fuels his art form which enables him to continue being an idol. The pressure to perform as an idol must surely impact his ability to create in the way he truly desires, yet it is this very pressure point that spurns forth his best work. For it is his unique perspective and situation that he utilises as a catalyst and channels to create lyrics and moments that are universally understood and healing. This binary of idol and artist affords his creative work the ability to be one continuous stroke for BTS and ARMY.

Last, but definitely not least, in this exploration of RM as both artist and idol comes an iconic moment that saw the realms of his poetry, lyricism, and philosophising merge with his role as idol leader. In 2018, not long after his 24th birthday, RM spoke on behalf of BTS at the

RM: ONLY HUMAN

United Nations General Assembly. In his speech, he called on everyone to speak themselves as part of a self-love process — he wanted to hear their voices, he wanted ARMY to speak for themselves, undoubtedly after reflecting on the many letters and messages he received from fans around the world.[26] In 2020, almost two years to the day, BTS returned to give a follow-up speech and RM reflected on how life had changed:

> "Two years ago here, I asked your name. I urged you to let me hear your voice. And I let myself be filled with imagination. [...] I imagined the limitless possibilities before all of us and my heart [was] beating with excitement. But COVID-19 was beyond my imagination. Our world tour was cancelled, all our plans went away, and I became alone. I looked up but I couldn't see the stars at night."[26]

He urged the audience to not forget the words "love yourself, speak yourself"[26] which he shared last time, saying that we must face ourselves and try to remember who we really are.[26] And then, he delivered lines which in many ways exemplify RM at the intersection of responsibility, a desire to understand and be understood, and artistic expression:

> "Our tomorrow may be dark, painful, difficult. We might stumble or fall down. Stars shine brightest when the night is darkest. If the stars are hidden, we'll let moonlight guide us. If even the moon is dark, let our faces be the light that helps us find our way. Let's reimagine our world. We're huddled together tired, but let's dream again. Let's dream about a future when our worlds can break out of our small rooms again. It might feel like it's always night and we'll always be alone, but the night is always darkest before the first light of dawn."[26]

It is here that we can see the competing and contrasting selves of idol/leader RM with artist Namjoon come into their true power. Speaking to a global audience that has since viewed the speech 7.7 million times[26] in a way that channels not only his experience, but the experience of BTS throughout the pandemic, and merging it with his observations of the world around him to provide a message for ARMY and anyone else watching on. This is done in such a nuanced, poetic, and philosophical way that is both strong, leads by example, and leaves space for interpretation, understanding, and healing. "Let's reimagine our world"[26] extends far beyond the realms of artistry alone and shows RM as more than just the leader of BTS; perhaps he is the leader of an entire generation. Yet it is only an artist who can weave such words, or reimagine the world in the first place. This is why RM's role as artist comes first in this investigation, because how he creates as a lyricist profoundly impacts all other components that make up who he is, with all his vulnerabilities and secrets hidden in plain sight. It is the tension between idol and artist that has created RM, but it was no accident, nor a passive act; this was all of his own making, which makes it all the better.

> "In—was it 2017? Pdogg was talking to Yoongi, Hobi and me about our style, and said, "Namjoon, it feels like you're becoming a lyricist," and it really stuck with me."[1]

Metamorphosis: I don't know a single thing about BTS[1]

어쩜 이렇게 한 번 죽겠지 아마
Perhaps this will be how I die once[27]

The song *Black Swan* from *Map of the Soul: 7* asks the question: What happens when an artist — in the case of the song, a dancer — dies their first death? This first death is brought about by losing love for performance, for dancing, for music. RM does not know how long this moment will last, how long he will stay the leader of BTS, being able to tour the world and connect with millions of fans each year. At the time of writing the song in 2019, presumably, the first death imagined by RM and BTS was just that, losing the love of performing, or dancing, or music, or perhaps everything at once. Yet by the time the album was released in February, a different death was taking hold — one which would arguably prevent Namjoon from fulfilling his duty as performer, as the fullest expression of the persona RM, on stage with BTS.

On New Year's Eve, the future looked unbearably bright for RM, he was finally able to fly. Now, in March as he presents his behind the album VLive talking about writing *Black Swan*, another question perhaps is pertinent: What happens when a black swan loses its wings? "I felt something desperate in the process of transforming from a swan to a black swan",[13] RM reflects on watching the movie *Black Swan* in preparation for writing the song. Little did he know, he too would soon be on a similar journey; a metamorphosis of sorts, if you like. The kind of transformation that being a member of BTS affords such an artist, leader, and idol. The group in and of itself is a synthesis of the binaries that traps its members, even more so RM who is the sole leader. BTS is the means of catharsis and metamorphosis available to RM, and the conditions of an unprecedented pandemic provided fertile, and complex, grounds for this to occur.

넘어진 채 청하는 엇박자의 춤
Lying fallen, I ask you to dance with me off beat[28]
When writing *ON*, RM focussed on the idea of how to stay sane as a member of BTS. Amidst the complexities, the conflicting interests, the pressure, and the general demands of being an idol in an idol group, he has a unique view on how to manage: "Not to be eaten away by such things like [our] shadow, we have to go crazy. […] You gotta go crazy, that's how you won't go crazy."[13] But perhaps it was touring and performing to a live audience that provided the space to 'go crazy' and truly cathart. In an interview with Zach Sang, RM is asked if he's excited for touring: "Of course, that's the main reason why we do this."[29] When BTS' world tour was indefinitely postponed, it's no wonder that RM began to experience a different kind of craziness:

> "Throughout the promotion [of *Map of the Soul: 7*], I felt powerless. [...] sometimes I felt so frustrated, like [I was] being crazy. I felt so furious, like a crazy one. I shouted alone. I was so angry. Too frustrated."[13]

To someone who has experienced great loneliness, and carries the responsibility of leadership and channelling an entire generation through his creative work, surely seeing ARMY in concert is a moment of euphoria. To see the results of hard work, and to hear his own lyrics and feelings sung back to him amidst a sea of purple lights; how healing that must be. How maddening it must feel to not see, or hear, the biggest affirmation of your existence as an artist and human. With the "main reason"[29] why he creates music (or "do[es] this")[29] with BTS on hold, and his ability to "go crazy for one thing"[13] heavily impacted, RM finds himself at a new tension point, perhaps the biggest that we will explore in 2020. No tours, no live performances, seemingly banished to empty rooms filled with cameras. The world watches on as he performs, but RM doesn't see anyone. Without ARMY to mirror who he is back at him, perhaps RM struggles to see himself, too.

When writing *Black Swan* RM reflected on the desire of artists to have their work last forever.[13] Immortalised through film and media represented in the song as "film it now, film it now".[13] When paired with the image of BTS performing in empty rooms to a sea of cameras, yearning to see ARMY before them once again, the lyrics he wrote in 2019 take on new meaning and represent his, and the group's, journey for 2020:

> "As if I'm bewitched, I slowly sink down, nah nah nah
> Though I try struggling, I'm at the bottom of the sea, nah nah
> Every moment becomes eternity, yeah yeah yeah
> Film it now

RM: ONLY HUMAN

Film it now
Do you hear me yeah"[27]

Pandemic or not, the show must go on, after all.

With no touring, RM had a lot more time for activities more synonymous with Namjooning. "All I do is read [...] painting books. When I get home I just read books. Mostly art or art history",[18] he says during his birthday VLive, "and I feel like I should read novels, too, so I read some novels, but not that much."[18] During *In the Soop*, filmed in June, he steals away to his bedroom to sit near his bonsai — which he brought with him to the countryside from Seoul — to read. During the day he moves down near the water with his copy of *Almond* by Sohn Won-pyung. "What I like about this place the most is that I can read my book while looking over at the scenery," RM says, "When I tried to read books in Seoul, I would try to find a park to read my book in. I would put on my mask and put in the effort to get some outside air but I like how I can feel the outside automatically."[30] "It's a daily life I didn't get to have for the last 6 or 7 years," says RM when reflecting on the pandemic in December, "I get to enjoy morning, evening, and dawn."[31]

This is how RM appears to be for most of the year, alongside the rest of BTS for that matter. Resting, waiting, passing the time. In many respects, it seems that RM is doing what he can to survive the year with his beloved members. His brothers. Waiting for the chance to return to ARMY. In October, RM stands on stage at *Map of the Soul ON:E*. Here, he spoke to just under one million people over two nights:[32]

> "I have no religion, but I thank God we're living in 2020. I thank God we have this technology so we can be connected with no latency, see each others' faces. You're literally here, it feels like you're here. I thank God that we can do this. At least we can do this. At this kind of stage, it's no one's fault. It's not your fault, it's not my fault, not our fault. It's not anyone's fault. we're just people, humans doing what we can do."[33]

Perhaps for one of the first times in 2020 it is on this stage that RM is back as artist, leader, and idol after stepping into these roles individually or in smaller capacities throughout the year. But the mood is tinged with sadness, it's sombre, the yearning is palpable. Though he may be back on stage as performer and leader, though he is surrounded by faces of smiling ARMY spread across the screens in the stadium, as he looks out to the place where an audience would normally be, all he sees, presumably, are cameras and crew.

It's important to note here, though, that although this chapter doesn't delve deeply into the live performances of RM's in 2020, they most definitely existed; and he most definitely shone. While commanding the stage as BTS performed tracks from *Map of the Soul: 7* and *BE*, RM was unparalleled, channelling charisma and power down the lens of the camera. His dancing was effortless and his stage presence was undeniably transcendent. That was who the world saw: RM the leader, the rapper, the born performer. Which stands in contrast to how he and BTS presumably felt, and often shared: They were missing ARMY, they were missing live audiences, they were sad. Though the show must go on and by all means, RM exceeded expectations, things weren't the same, nor would they be any time soon.

거울처럼 난 너를 확인
I check on you, like a mirror[34]

Not only is RM the leader of BTS, he is also the leader of ARMY. This often means that when people are watching events and performances, seeing BTS for the first time, it's highly likely that they will come to know RM as leader first — especially when he is speaking English on behalf of the group when they promote overseas. When he has felt alone, lonely, and misunderstood by the world, surely it has been BTS and ARMY who has helped him feel even a little better. To be so adored by millions of fans around the world who seek to understand and support him, surely must be an intense and transformative experience.

This relationship between RM and ARMY is symbiotic and mutual. Though they may not always be in the same place at the same time,

RM through the use of his lyrics, performances, and messages is able to communicate with ARMY. Further to this, he channels ARMY's experiences through his lyrics, as explored earlier with *Louder than bombs*. He is the one who shares his understanding of ARMY back to them, he is the one who sees them and hears them when they feel they are alone in the world.

ARMY, in turn, responds with support, trending hashtags, donations, and, of course, showing up to concerts to give the love back tenfold. Perhaps they write a book or two to show how they understand him, see, and hear him, too. In an interview with *Esquire*, RM reflects on this transformative, loving relationship: "We and our ARMY are always charging each other's batteries [...] When we feel exhausted, when we hear the news all over the world, the tutoring programs, and donations, and every good thing, we feel responsible for all of this."[12] Further, he acknowledges that this is indeed a love relationship that breaks away from preconceived idol/fan norms: "Our love life—twenty-four hours, seven days a week—is with all the ARMYs all over the world".[12] For RM, ARMY are both a comfort and a mirror, reflecting back to him his own words and thoughts through a million interpretations in a million different ways. They are also his responsibility, as are BTS: he is the leader after all.

Yet while RM is unable to see ARMY in the way he wants, the paradox or perhaps the irony, is that ARMY in 2020 were able to see him — and BTS — more than ever. A perfect example of this was with the making of *BE* which, according to RM, was a process they decided to share with ARMY for the first time:

> "We thought that we had to share the process because we couldn't meet the fans in person [...] We thought we were going to get disconnected from the fans [with tours and concerts being cancelled]. [...] We had no choice but to do that, and I believe it was the right choice."[35]

Though what stood out the most during this process, when it came to RM, is that his role was vastly different to that of being the main lyrical contributor on *Map of the Soul: 7*. Each member was supported and encouraged to bring their own songs for consideration for *BE*, but it was RM's work that didn't make the cut, which he shares with Weverse:

> "I've got so many questions, I feel like my hair's turning white. That's why none of my songs are on the album. I wrote some, but they were too personal to use there."[1]

However, his lyrics still featured on the album: "Excluding my rap verses, I wrote *Stay* and the bridge for *Dis-ease* […] and also *Fly to my Room* […] I wrote all the lyrics [for *Life Goes On*] except Yoongi's and j-hope's verses."[36] Arguably, this is not indicative of RM's lack of input, or leadership. Instead, it's showing that his role as leader and his influence in the group is so strong that they have each been able to step up in ways they haven't in the past. Instead of having one track that screams RM, the album itself screams BTS in the most cohesive way to date. This, arguably, is the next logical step in his trajectory as lyricist and leader where it soon becomes hard to see where Namjoon the artist and RM the idol stops, and the rest of the group begins.

"You were the first to come up with the idea of telepathy," says Jimin to RM in his *BE-hind* video.[36] "I was thinking it might be useful someday," RM replies.[36] Though *Telepathy* is a song primarily written by Suga, RM's verse gives an insight to how he feels about ARMY:

> "In the days that feel the same, / I'm the happiest when I meet you / In my everyday life that is different every day, / the person that is you is the most special to me / Waking up like the wild grass in the morning, / I check on you, like a mirror / Instead of sleep, in my eyes it's full of you."[34]

This, paired with the concept of telepathy, paints a picture of immense connectedness with ARMY. Where RM either feels he can hear their thoughts, or wishes that he can, or perhaps it's a mix of both. When asked how he feels about people reaching out to him to tell him his songs have saved their lives by *Rolling Stone India*, he replied: "It's those very people who have pulled me back from the edge of the cliff down to 98, 97, so you can say we are saving each other's lives."[37] There is no doubt that the relationship between RM and ARMY is complex and deeply meaningful. Where love freely flows between them no matter the distance.[8] As the lyrics suggest, RM checks on ARMY "like a mirror",[34] undoubtedly looking for his own reflection, too.

Perhaps then, the first death of RM came when the pandemic shattered his mirror, his ability to perform to a live audience. Perhaps then he had to foster different avenues of connection and communication with ARMY by turning inwards, honing his telepathic, intuitive abilities; by reconnecting with himself. Perhaps, when turning inwards, and spending more time away from the stage, it was Namjoon who rose to the surface and began to occupy more space alongside RM. A harmonious balance, though born out of necessity and factors far out of his control, that has seen what appears to be a reconciling between competing personas and experiences.

Like an echo in the forest[28]

RM had his feet in two worlds throughout 2020: one where he was a member of BTS, a leader, an artist, an idol, a human being trying to negotiate the complexities of the pandemic; the other, which importantly exists because of BTS, where he was painfully aware of the suffering of ARMY and the rest of the world. Undoubtedly he would have felt pressure, pressure to find a way to see ARMY again for the sake of his group and the fandom itself.

The paradox is that, amidst the heartache and yearning, this was a year that provided space for normalcy. A different reality which he hadn't experienced since BTS' debut. Time and space to just… be. In many respects, the world that BTS had built for themselves, the means by which they connected with their fans and generated revenue for their company, was crumbling. Yet by the end of the year, the group were thriving with more accolades and achievements than ever before.

The unique situation of living through a pandemic, seemingly disconnected from fans, brought about a new way of connecting and relating. In the beginning, it presumably felt like an echo chamber — performing and only hearing his own voice instead of ARMY's. How disconcerting that must be. Yet it was this very experience of hearing an echo as his only answer, as he writes in *00:00* ("Only my echo, with no answer"),[24] that led to his metamorphosis.

During this transformative, albeit not entirely joyful journey, RM was able to channel his feelings and experiences through his lyricism once more for *Life Goes On*. A process which was able to keep him going through difficult times: "But back then (after the shows got canceled), that was the only thing we could do at the edge of the cliff. So [working on *BE*] was kind of like… the only thing I could do."[36]

Earlier in the year when talking about the message behind *00:00*, RM shared: "A day goes by and your life goes on."[13] Which was then echoed in his United Nations speech: "Life goes on, let's live on."[25] This sentiment, of course, then became the foundation from which *BE* sprung forth. *Life Goes On* is RM's greatest contribution to *BE*. Within the lyrics are his pains, his perspective, and his poetic look on life: "It looks like it'll rain today as well / I'm completely soaked / It's still not stopping / I run faster than those dark clouds / I thought that'd make it alright / But, it turns out I'm just a mere human / It hurts so bad".[28]

The sentiment of 'life goes on' speaks to RM's leadership and how it continues to permeate every aspect of his work; because it is an integral part of who he is, irrespective of persona or group. It's a reassuring message that is empowering, which can be hard to deliver when such a call can be interpreted as condescending. Perhaps the reason why it works is because it comes from the heart. This is not RM's message to the world, it's a message to himself and his group. One which they used throughout the pandemic: "I said that to members and said that repeatedly like a spell. We have to smile. We need to be okay. If we don't, it will make our fans lose their energy."[13] It is his sincerity that shines through and sets him apart as a born leader, for he first is leading himself through the darkness and out the other side, time and again.

In past years it felt perhaps as though RM has stridently led BTS around the world as they continued to reach new heights. The urgency for him to represent BTS well, to ensure he was their spokesperson, to ensure they were understood while touring overseas, was potent. At the start of the pandemic, it undoubtedly would have felt like all this hard work was not going to pay off. Without being able to tour, how would BTS communicate who they are to the world? Especially in the US as they remain perpetual outsiders.

Yet, what we have seen is that the pandemic has led to a metamorphosis of an unexpected kind; more of a transcendence… an inner peace. One of the entire group, with RM leading the way. His hard work in the past has meant that the entire group has been able to step up and contribute in realms he would typically stand alone; writing more on albums and speaking more English in interviews, for example. This, paired with the success of *Dynamite*, has resulted in a leader who appears to be more free.

Though he has always led from the middle of the group, it seems that now he is able to take more steps back as BTS lead together in ways they haven't before; ways which the pandemic made time and space for. He no longer has to try as hard to make the world understand him and BTS, because during a time where he likely thought they would lose momentum, more and more people have found him and become ARMY. Perhaps, the telepathic connection has strengthened through the global shared experience of COVID-19, which has taken the burden of responsibility, at least a small part, from the shoulders of RM.

Maybe this was the clearing of the road RM spoke of in his 2015 mixtape happening again, perhaps this was indeed the year he was free to fly. It just wasn't in the way anyone expected, least of all RM. If anything, being in BTS and leading an ARMY has shown that anything is possible, and nothing is as he thought it to be. A metamorphosis, a change, one which is surely painful and riddled with complexities and contradictions. Not only is "life goes on"[28] a suitable lyric for this peculiar transformation, but perhaps more so is "To remain sane, one must go insane [...] I throw all of myself into this two-sided world [...] The beautiful prison I walked into on my own [...] Bring it, bring the pain oh yeah".[20] This perfectly encapsulates many complexities within the life of an idol, and speaks to the dualistic and multiplistic nature of RM's experiences. In catharsis we have explored the two-sided world of being artist and idol, and here we have journeyed through 2020 with RM's experience as BTS and his relationship with ARMY, now comes antithesis… the beautiful prison of paradox that sees a human become a revolutionary, even when he doesn't want to be.

> "When BTS started out, I thought, "I know everything there is to know about BTS," but now it's, "I don't know a single thing about BTS.""[1]

Antithesis: I realise that maybe I can't do more than what I am[1]

모진 겨울 네가 흘렸던 피에서 빨갛게 나는 태어났지
I was born red, from the blood you shed in the harsh winter[17]

On March 30, 2019, two days after the release of RM's *Persona*, a log was uploaded to YouTube. RM is in his studio, reflecting on what makes him happy and where he's headed in life: "They say there are two ways of changing the world. The first is to be a revolutionary. The second is to see the world more positively. I want to do both. I will do both."[38] An article claiming BTS are changing the world cites this moment being one that "provides important insight to the intention behind the work of RM."[39] The article turns to BTS' *Love Yourself* trilogy, RM's UN speech, and his self-analysis on *Persona* as evidence of his revolutionary work.[39] The author muses: "It is unclear whether RM is an anomaly amongst a growing sea of idols, or if he is merely one of many millennials feeling the need to alleviate the heavy burden of a suffering planet."[39] Which, in the context of this chapter, remains true for 2020; RM is creating out of a need to express himself and understand the world in a way he has at times felt he has not been understood.

This, paired with his statement that he wishes to be a revolutionary, suggest that his lyrics and leadership are no serendipitous, whimsical art form that have coincidentally come to fruition. Rather, they are made with a clear intention: to be revolutionary. A revolutionary who is already inspiring change: the aforementioned article was the first published by a company called Revolutionaries, named after RM's desire to be a revolutionary. The same company which, a year later, entirely owned and operated by ARMY, began to publish books on all things revolutionary.[40]

Since the release of his log, there has been a growing discourse on RM being a revolutionary.[41] Some which explore his — and by extension BTS' — leadership and revolutionary relationship with ARMY: "This is the positive power of BTS and ARMY, together they are revolutionary."[42] Which has led to the creation of the concept of BTS as 'participatory revolutionaries' where "BTS enter into this revolution as equals with their fan base. They are both leaders of ARMY, but equal participants as human beings in an increasingly divided world."[43] All it took was one video for this new realm of thinking and theorising to emerge, all inspired by RM's revolutionary wishes and capacity.

In the eyes of ARMY, there is no doubt that RM is a revolutionary. Throughout the publication of Revolutionaries, and its imprint Bulletproof there is evidence of this ranging from opinions to analyses and beyond. One writer reflects on how RM speaks self-love into the lives of young people through his work,[44] another analyses the ethical standpoint of *Persona*.[45] Above all else, they share their views on RM's lyrics:

> "Namjoon bares his soul; he pens down how he genuinely felt during that season of his life. His openness in talking about his feelings of loneliness, sadness, darkness, and eventual hope, provides a safe space for his audience to know that it is okay to feel."[46]

Where they write about RM being a lyrical genius,[47] and being a cultural reset of this generation's songwriting:

> "We get to appreciate RM's music because he opened the doors to his true self. He lets us see a piece of him every once in a while. [...] He reaches out to our human struggles and personal emotions and speaks to us, sharing that he experiences the same worries and concerns; we are all the same."[48]

These are just some examples of how ARMY views RM as a revolutionary, which was his explicit desire in the log posted in 2019. He is someone who is creating change through his lyrics and message; in many ways this is achieved by just being himself. But of course, such a revolutionary title is only afforded due to the nature of the binaries that he exists between, across, around, and next to.[8] It is only because he is artist and idol, it is only because he is a member of BTS and the leader of an ARMY that he is able to step into the role of revolutionary. The very binaries that cause tension, complexities, and paradoxes in his life are the same ones that afford him great power and a fanbase ready to mobilise at a moment's notice. He is revolutionary because he is using his power for good, and utilising his platform to speak a message of self-love to millions around the world. He was long before his log.

This in itself does not seem to contain any contradiction or paradox, though it is apparent that such a hefty title must come with an enormous amount of pressure and complexity. Perhaps where the tension lies is that in the 2020 docuseries *Break the Silence* RM directly contradicts his earlier log: "I don't want to give people a message because that itself feels grandiose to me. 'A revolutionary.' That's not me."[49]

나 겨우 사람인가 봐
But, it turns out I'm just a mere human[28]
When it comes to a look at who RM is, it's nearly impossible to look past the inherent quality of his most authentic moments which often get

attributed to Namjoon, instead of his idol persona. What typifies these moments most of all are that they are completely and utterly human: ""Only human" sounds so appropriate for me right now",[1] he says at the end of 2020.

RM being himself and enjoying the simple things in life has long been a topic of interest throughout the fandom and beyond. It's not uncommon for him to post pictures from art galleries and parks, riding his bike around Seoul, or from the top of a mountain. These moments of mundane pleasures have become synonymous with RM and the act of doing so goes by the name of Namjooning. Entries on Urban Dictionary define Namjooning as "the act of living as Kim Namjoon. This includes taking walks through parks, admiring nature, hanging out with crabs, and having fun with friends";[50] "feeding your mind and soul by doing the things you love"[51] with the example of "he is namjooning all day on his bike around the park";[51] "to take long walks; to ride a bicycle; to go see art; to make music; to read; to make people's lives better";[52] "Planting Bonsai trees and being a soft farmer that loves tiny animals. Being thoughtful and loving",[53] and lastly; this useful list:

1. Breaking things (sunglasses, figurines, world records, young women's hearts).
2. Wearing sunglasses indoors.
3. Spitting fire.
4. Chasing, capturing, and examining small crabs.[54]

Namjooning is undoubtedly the true essence of Namjoon which seemingly sits in stark opposition to the claims of RM being a revolutionary. It is located at the other end of the spectrum to RM being an idol standing on a stage fulfilling #3 from the list above. Definitions and lists aside, perhaps the most Namjoon thing of all can be found in response to *Rolling Stone India*'s question on Namjooning: "How do you feel about ARMY adopting these little wholesome terms from you and incorporating [them] into their own lives?"[37] To which RM replied: "I'm very thankful, but also feel a sense of responsibility. I began music because I wanted to share my story and become a positive influence to many people, so I would be honored if I can continue to show my hard work and the results of my efforts."[37]

2020 for RM was a year where he reflected on how he could best help ARMY and channel them through his lyricism. The concerns he expressed when giving a look into *Louder than bombs* were inherently human; how can he help everyone when he's just one person? The feelings expressed through *00:00*, being plagued by questioning if he made a mistake or was at fault, and looking forward to a new day where the slate could be wiped clean, are indicative of the Namjoon that ARMY associate with art galleries and excitedly finding small crabs at the beach. These are not the larger-than-life musings of an idol, rather they are the mundane concerns of an artist that are universally understood; for they are human. Perhaps as Namjoon, he cannot do more than write lyrics and provide people with words of comfort and understanding.

Yet Namjoon is not singular, one-dimensional, or stagnant and just like the rest of the world, he is capable of more than he believes himself to be. What is most interesting about 2020 is that it seems through his metamorphosis RM had more time to be… Namjoon. Namjoon Namjooning. 2020 was the year that the lines between Namjoon and RM became the most blurred as being tied to Seoul without a world tour created more space for two to become one and strike a new balance.

안경을 벗어도 어둠은 안 흐릿해져
Even when I take off my glasses, the darkness doesn't get blurred[55]

In many respects, on a surface level, the antithesis of Namjoon is RM. Namjoon is someone who enjoys the simple pleasures in life and is humble and genuine. RM is the idol who stands on the world's stage commanding the attention of hundreds of thousands of people at a time. From the outside looking in, the life of an idol is one that is loud, performative, and often aggrandised — though it is far more nuanced than that.

RM: ONLY HUMAN

Namjoon enjoys a quiet life, yet the lifestyle of RM is full of responsibilities, interviews, meetings, performances, and more. Yet it is perhaps only the role and responsibilities of RM that gives space for Namjoon to... be Namjoon, to go Namjooning. And perhaps it is Namjoon going Namjooning that allows space for RM to be the persona that visits the hearts and minds of millions of people through screens and stages in perpetuity. If ARMY charges BTS' batteries, perhaps it is RM who charges the batteries of Namjoon, and vice versa. Perhaps it is the friction between the two that creates the static electricity to jumpstart a heart in the first place.

Though revolutionary is a title RM does not want, he still fulfils the role, and to some degree he acknowledges this. Such as "I'm okay with whatever you call me",[17] which shows an understanding of the complexities of the titles he is given, and; "I throw all of myself into this two-sided world",[20] which shows how he embraces the duality of his existence, and the nature of his work.

Namjoon is inherently human, which means that RM is, too. From his perspective the notion of revolutionary is arguably aggrandised and disingenuous, thus being a title he does not wish to claim as it flies in the face of his purpose as a human being. Yet he still wishes to share his music and his message with the world, but only insofar as it remains genuine and related to his own journey instead of being a fabricated call to action that asserts him as expert or leader over the top of others.

Instead, as previously mentioned, he is a participatory revolutionary. Just like he leads BTS from within the group, he leads ARMY as a co-revolutionary, an equal in the learning and growing process. Revolutionary, though such a title might suggest an imperialist overlord who is bigger, better, and stronger than everyone else — as that is what history has shown — is an inherently human term.

Although RM being both human and revolutionary seems contradictory, it is the very binary of such a duality that creates the tension for a revolution to be born; one rooted in a self-love journey. Even though RM may not wish to claim the title for himself, the proof is in the proverbial pudding; the revolution is underway and although he might not be the only one leading it — as he walks alongside BTS and ARMY — he was most definitely the one to say he wanted to change the world, first by being a revolutionary.[38]

In RM's *Map of the Soul: 7* behind he lamented over ARMY's pain and suffering saying "I can't do multiple things at the same time",[13] which then went on to inform the lyrics he wrote for *Louder than bombs*. It is that very tension of being just one person, unable to directly help everyone, that presumably would make RM break louder than a bomb itself. Perhaps what RM doesn't yet see, nor might he ever, is that simple statement, that way of being, admitting his shortcomings while showing his pure heart[13] in itself is revolutionary. Because that tension is what goes on to become a lyric which can transcend barriers to provide moments of healing for those who listen. It is because of RM that ARMY have learnt that self-love can change the world, and that if he is revolutionary, then so are they.

> "And I just like what Whanki Kim said, that maybe I can't do anything not Korean, because that's what I am. I used to work late and then stay up all night when things weren't working out, sometimes walking from Samseong to Sinsa station, thinking everything through. But now, like the saying, I realize that maybe I can't do more than what I am."[1]

Synthesis: I believe in a true heart and love

This chapter has been explored through the paradox of Namjoon and his persona RM. In 2020 we were able to see the same RM in new situations as the pandemic drastically impaired his ability to do what he does best: perform to a live audience. This has provided time and space for Namjoon to adjust who RM is and needs to be for BTS, ARMY, and the world. He has had more time to rest, more time for fun, and more time to enjoy different parts of life. Through this, we have seen a more relaxed RM who continues to lead by example and with a gentle hand.

RM: ONLY HUMAN

Amidst all the lists of binaries and multiplicities, it can be all too easy to forget that RM, Namjoon, is a human being just the same as everyone else. Perhaps the only difference is his circumstance, and how he uses his artistry and leadership to navigate a lifestyle many can only dream of. A lifestyle full of responsibilities and complexities, typified by hard work and being of service to others. The irony of this chapter and exploration is that idol RM is not just the antithesis of human Namjoon, but the synthesis. Just like how the darkness doesn't get blurred when he takes off his glasses,[54] the distinction between Namjoon and RM is perhaps in name only. RM is the culmination of Namjoon, his lyricism, his artistry, his leadership, being in BTS, being in relationship with ARMY, and many more intricate facets. RM is the means by which Namjoon can share who he is with the world, while also protecting parts of himself from public view.

If the question is 'persona, who the hell is RM in 2020?' the irony is that in a chapter riddled with promised paradoxes and contradictions, the answer is quite simple: RM in 2020 is just a human being trying his best. Though it can be easy to get weighed down with analyses of his lyrics or listening to melancholy *mono.* on repeat, it is important to remember that RM is someone not only of great depth, but someone who is laid back with an often child-like bemusement for small, silly things. Just as many times as he cries he surely is laughing and having fun with his brothers twice as much, if not more.

The trap anyone can easily fall into when exploring the work of an idol is believing that their sadness, their loneliness, or ruminations are all that they are. When in fact it's merely the work of an artist that explores these depths, which does not tell the full story of the human who is well known for breaking things, collecting figurines, and gets embarrassed when he makes a corny joke on a livestream.

Though there were moments of juxtapositions of paradoxical elements and experiences of RM throughout this chapter, they also served as syntheses, which is why this conclusion does not take up much space. When looking at someone with a larger-than-life persona, the first thought that comes to mind might be to view them as dualistic, as this chapter has often done. Dualisms are readily able to be converted to binaries, which are far easier to call paradoxes and juxtapose with one another. But this chapter has also acknowledged the multiplistic nature of RM, as each of his defining roles does not fit into two opposing columns that say: leader/lonely, artist/idol, BTS/ARMY, revolutionary/human. Rather, they are all superimposed over one another until the final words read: Kim Namjoon. For it is Namjoon who is the synthesis of RM, and RM who is the synthesis of Namjoon. They are two sides of the same coin, two batteries that charge one another and provide friction for growth and opportunities for catharsis.

RM holds within him countless emotions, experiences, and perspectives which he observes in those around him and from deep within. Just as he acts as a conduit for his generation and his innermost feelings, he is a synthesis of the world he sees. Or perhaps a different conceptualisation could be that he is the microcosm of the macrocosm of all that surrounds him. RM reminds us of what it truly means to be human, which is to enjoy life, to be creative, to seek to understand the world, to love, to be there for others. To be.

RM is a human be-ing.

> "I'm going to compose songs, write lyrics, practice and talk. I still believe [in] the value of [a] true heart. I believe in [a] true heart and love. That's the power that makes me move on. I look okay, right now. My heart is in *Ego*, I guess. It's somewhere between *The Eternal* and *Ego*. Sometimes sad, sometimes full of hope."[13]

References

[1] Kang, M. (2020). RM "I spend a lot of time thinking about where I am now". https://magazine.weverse.io/article/view?num=62&lang=en

[2] RM. (2015). Monster [Song]. On *RM*. Big Hit Entertainment; Doolset. (2018). *Monster* [Translation]. https://doolsetbangtan.wordpress.com/2018/09/11/monster/

[3] BANGTANTV. (2020). [BANGTAN BOMB] Happy new year 2020! - BTS (방탄소년단) [Video]. https://www.youtube.com/watch?v=zDP_EQYmT6U

[4] Hwang, H. (2020). *BTS RM won the 2020 art sponsor of the year awards for 'donating 100 million won to the Museum of Art'*. https://n.news.naver.com/entertain/article/609/0000374994

[5] Kim, S. (2019). *BTS leader RM: 3 things every fan should know about their favourite K-pop star*. https://www.scmp.com/magazines/style/news-trends/article/3026919/bts-leader-rm-3-things-every-fan-should-know-about

[6] beansss. (2020). *BTS's RM & j-Hope join SUGA this year as official members of the Korea Music Copyright Association*. https://www.allkpop.com/article/2020/01/btss-rm-j-hope-join-suga-this-year-as-official-members-of-the-korea-music-copyright-association

[7] Halsey. (2019). *BTS*. https://time.com/collection/100-most-influential-people-2019/5567876/bts/

[8] Eaglehawk, W. (2020). *Idol limerence: The art of loving BTS as phenomena*. Revolutionaries.

[9] BTS. (2020). Persona [Song]. On *Map of the soul: 7*. Big Hit Entertainment; Doolset. *Intro: Persona* [Translation]. https://doolsetbangtan.wordpress.com/2019/03/31/persona/

[10] Doolset. (2019). *Intro: Persona*. https://doolsetbangtan.wordpress.com/2019/03/31/persona/

[11] BANGTANTV. (2020). [2020 FESTA] BTS (방탄소년단) '방탄생파' #2020BTSFESTA [Video]. https://www.youtube.com/watch?v=t9zPnWQIiuw

12. Holmes, D. (2020). *The boundless optimism of BTS.* https://www.esquire.com/entertainment/music/a34654383/bts-members-be-album-interview-2020/
13. BTS. (2020). *Namjun's 7 behind* ☐ [Video]. https://www.vlive.tv/video/179339
14. MTS News. (2020). *BTS deliver heartfelt messages to their future selves for 'Map of the soul: 7' | MTV news* [Video]. https://www.youtube.com/watch?v=e57S-6RCDIY
15. Bell, C. (2018). *BTS' RM just dropped his solo playlist mono and it's like free therapy.* http://www.mtv.com/news/3102241/rm-mono-playlist-forever-rain-bts/
16. RM. (2018). *Always* [Song]. https://soundcloud.com/bangtan/always-by-rm; Doolset. (2018). *Always (RM)* [Translation]. https://doolsetbangtan.wordpress.com/2018/06/01/always-rm/
17. Younha & RM. (2020). Winter flower [Song]. On *Unstable mindset*. C9 Entertainment; Doolset. *Younha – winter flower (feat. RM)* [Translation]. https://doolsetbangtan.wordpress.com/2020/01/07/younha-winter-flower-feat-rm/
18. BTS. (2020). *Hello* ☐☐ [Video]. https://www.vlive.tv/video/212713
19. BangtanBang. (2021). *Proof RM is a genius* [Video]. https://www.youtube.com/watch?v=vJDw7sYCwqw
20. BTS. (2020). On [Song]. On *Map of the soul: 7*. Big Hit Entertainment; Doolset. *ON* [Translation]. https://doolsetbangtan.wordpress.com/2020/02/21/on/
21. Wikipedia. (2021). *Map of the soul: 7.* https://en.wikipedia.org/wiki/Map_of_the_Soul:_7#Track_listing
22. BTS. (2020). Louder than bombs [Song]. On *Map of the soul: 7*. Big Hit Entertainment; Doolset. *Louder than bombs* [Translation]. https://doolsetbangtan.wordpress.com/2020/02/21/louder-than-bombs/
23. RM. (2018). Forever rain [Song]. On *mono.*. Big Hit Entertainment; Doolset. *Forever rain* [Translation]. https://doolsetbangtan.wordpress.com/2018/10/22/forever-rain/

24. BTS. (2020). 00:00 (Zero o'clock) [Song]. On *Map of the soul: 7*. Big Hit Entertainment; Doolset. *00:00 (Zero o'clock)* [Translation]. https://doolsetbangtan.wordpress.com/2020/02/21/zero-oclock/
25. BANGTANTV. (2020). BTS (방탄소년단) speech at the 75th UN general assembly [Video]. https://www.youtube.com/watch?v=5aPe9Uy10n4
26. BTS. (2018). *BTS speech at the United Nations/UNICEF* [Video]. https://youtu.be/oTe4f-bBEKg
27. BTS. (2020). Black swan [Song]. On *Map of the soul: 7*. Big Hit Entertainment; Doolset. *Black swan* [Translation]. https://doolsetbangtan.wordpress.com/2020/01/17/black-swan/
28. BTS. (2020). *Life goes on* [Song]. On *BE*. Big Hit Entertainment; Doolset. *Life goes on* [Translation]. https://doolsetbangtan.wordpress.com/2020/11/20/life-goes-on/
29. Zach Sang Show. (2020). *BTS interview* [Video]. https://www.youtube.com/watch?v=Hk2_A-rh7IM
30. Bang, S. & Lenzo, Y (Executive Producers). (2020). *BTS In the soop* [TV Show]. Big Hit Entertainment.
31. BANGTANTV. (2020). BTS (방탄소년단) BE-hind story [Video]. https://youtu.be/cYX88pxQuCo
32. S. P. (2020). *BTS draws nearly 1 million viewers with online concert "BTS map of the soul ON:E"*. https://www.soompi.com/article/1431059wpp/bts-draws-nearly-1-million-viewers-with-online-concert-bts-map-of-the-soul-one
33. Mendez, M. (2020). *BTS' closing remarks at their 'Map of the soul on: e' concert are so emotional*. https://www.elitedaily.com/p/bts-closing-remarks-at-their-map-of-the-soul-on-e-concert-are-so-emotional-38343580
34. BTS. (2020). 잠시 (Telepathy) [Song]. On *BE*. Big Hit Entertainment; Doolset. 잠시 (Telepathy) [Translation]. https://doolsetbangtan.wordpress.com/2020/11/20/telepathy/
35. Daly, R. (2020). *Everything we learned from BTS' blockbuster 'BE' global press conference*. https://www.nme.com/en_au/blogs/bts-be-global-press-conference-2-2821618

36. BANGTANTV. (2020). *BTS (방탄소년단) RM's BE-hind 'full' story* [Video]. https://www.youtube.com/watch?v=1mkhdpbe4R0
37. Chakraborty, R. (2020). *BTS: The Rolling Stone interview.* https://rollingstoneindia.com/bts-the-rolling-stone-interview/
38. BANGTANTV. (2019). *180511 RM* [Video]. https://www.youtube.com/watch?v=XZkfFD08zio; modooborahae. (2020). *"They say there are 2 ways of changing the world. 1 is to be a revolutionary. 2 is to see the world more positively. I want to do both. I will do both."—Kim Namjoon, BangtanTV log. 2018.05.11* [Translation]. https://twitter.com/modooborahae/status/1218283064616542211?lang=en
39. Eaglehawk, W. (2019). *BTS are changing the world, here's how.* https://medium.com/revolutionaries/bts-are-changing-the-world-e601178e90d0
40. Revolutionaries. (2021). *About us.* https://www.revolutionaries.com.au/about-us
41. Eaglehawk, W. (2019). *Kim Namjoon: Revolutionary.* https://medium.com/revolutionaries/kim-namjoon-revolutionary-e08bc16f3725
42. Eaglehawk, W. (2020). *BTS donate another $1 million cementing them as new world leaders.* https://medium.com/revolutionaries/bts-donate-another-1-million-cementing-them-as-new-world-leaders-1198d45fe6b3
43. Eaglehawk, W. (2020). *We, like BTS, are revolutionaries.* https://medium.com/revolutionaries/we-like-bts-are-revolutionaries-15caae19b7a3
44. Low, L. (2019) *How RM of BTS is speaking self-love into the lives of young people.* https://medium.com/revolutionaries/how-rm-of-bts-is-speaking-self-love-into-the-lives-of-young-people-53c5639ad07f
45. Cat. (2020). *How Intro: Persona subscribes to an ethical standpoint.* https://medium.com/revolutionaries/how-intro-persona-subscribes-to-an-ethical-standpoint-79146608d10a

46. Low, L. (2019). *Mixtape review: "Mono" by RM*. https://medium.com/bulletproof/mixtape-review-mono-by-rm-9a8ed42d0e71
47. Low, L. (2020). *Winter flower, and other reasons why BTS' RM is a lyrical genius*. https://medium.com/bulletproof/winter-flower-and-other-reasons-why-btss-rm-is-a-lyrical-genius-2329a8d0b6bd
48. Jc. (2020). *RM, a cultural reset of this generation's songwriting*. https://medium.com/bulletproof/rm-a-cultural-reset-of-this-generations-music-writing-b645acb659a6
49. Bang, S. (Executive Producer). (2020). *Break the silence* [TV Show]. Big Hit Entertainment.
50. Bazzi, T. (2019). *Namjooning*. https://www.urbandictionary.com/define.php?term=namjooning
51. ktrn. (2019). *Namjooning*. https://www.urbandictionary.com/define.php?term=namjooning
52. minniholly. (2019). *Namjooning*. https://www.urbandictionary.com/define.php?term=namjooning
53. bulette, S. (2019). *Namjooning*. https://www.urbandictionary.com/define.php?term=namjooning
54. OfficialNamjooningExpert. (2019). *Namjooning*. https://www.urbandictionary.com/define.php?term=namjooning
55. BTS. (2020). 병 (Dis-ease) [Song]. On *BE*. Big Hit Entertainment; Doolset. 병 (Dis-ease) [Translation]. https://doolsetbangtan.wordpress.com/2020/11/20/dis-ease/

Outro

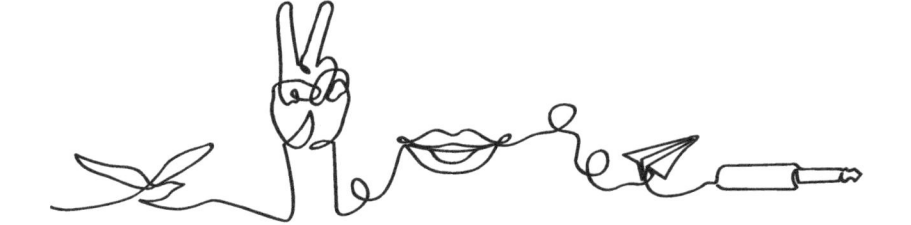

LOVE, ARMY
Wallea Eaglehawk

It feels rather fitting that this book that looks back on 2020 is going into production at the same time BTS' latest single *Butter* is to be released. Only six months after *BE* and we are already receiving new music, which presumably will be followed by a new album. The perpetual wheel of BTS' creativity and productivity turns and we are thrust into a new era once more, at which point *BE* and *Map of the Soul: 7* will become memories of 2020. Yet those iconic and groundbreaking works will not be forgotten, nor will the seven people who made them. Through working on this book and reading it many times over as it has evolved, 2020 has taken on a different shape in my mind. Now with the benefit of hindsight, celebrating BTS' wins and losses feels different. To see every moment stacked up side-by-side and to experience it in this condensed and potent form, through the eyes of strangers who I am united in spirit with as ARMY, is profound. To know that in many instances all we have done is provide an overview, or just one perspective or analysis, is overwhelming.

Looking forward to the future, so much remains uncertain. When BTS can tour again remains unclear. What they will do next always remains shrouded in mystery. Yet what 2020 has shown us all is that it will take more than a pandemic to keep BTS from ARMY. And, as the title of BTS' chapter says, we can always expect the unexpected from them; in the best possible way. It has been worthwhile reliving the journey of BTS in 2020 from each member's perspective, because it provides a timely reminder that we can carry into 2021 with us: We are not alone, we have BTS, we have each other. If one thing rings true in every chapter, it is that BTS loves ARMY, they love each other, and they are learning to love themselves each and every day, just like the rest of us. BTS will persevere, as will ARMY, as will we all; together.

Dear BTS,

We hope you enjoyed this book. If you are reading this perhaps it means we have been fortunate enough to find someone to translate it into Korean, and that this present has travelled a great distance of circumstance to find its way to you.

Please know that you are so loved by so many, and that we are eager to see all that 2021 holds for you. We will be here, cheering you on each and every step of the way.

Our spring day will come again, but until then we are kept warm by the joy that we get to share with you in moments mundane and extraordinary. Though we may feel far away, we are with you always. This book is a reminder of that which you can turn to any time to be reminded of who we know you to be.

From our heart to yours, happy eight years since debut.

Love,
ARMY

CREDITS

Bulletproof would like to thank everyone at Revolutionaries who worked on *BTS by ARMY*.

Editor
Wallea Eaglehawk

Copy editor
Mary Kinderman

Design
Paula Pomer

Production
Wallea Eaglehawk

Marketing
Federica Trogu
Wallea Eaglehawk
Catherine Truluck
Tyler Lee

Communications
Wallea Eaglehawk

CPSIA information can be obtained
at www.ICGtesting.com
Printed in the USA
BVHW071532130122
626139BV00012B/308